LATIN AMERICA IN THE POST-CHÁVEZ ERA

RELATED TITLES FROM POTOMAC BOOKS

Axis of Unity: Venezuela, Iran & the Threat to America
—Sean Goforth

The War of All the People: The Nexus of Latin American
Radicalism and Middle Eastern Terrorism
—Jon B. Perdue

Cartels at War: Mexico's Drug-Fueled Violence
and the Threat to U.S. National Security
—Paul Rexton Kan

LATIN AMERICA IN THE POST-CHÁVEZ ERA

The Security Threat to the United States

LUIS FLEISCHMAN

Foreword by MICHAEL SKOL

Potomac Books
Washington, D.C.

Library of Congress Cataloging-in-Publication Data
Fleischman, Luis, 1959–
  Latin America in the post-Chávez era : the security threat to the United States /
Luis Fleischman ; foreword by Michael Skol.—First Edition.
     p. cm
  Includes bibliographical references and index.
  ISBN 978-1-61234-601-4 (hardcover : alk. paper)
  ISBN 978-1-61234-602-1 (electronic)
  1. Latin America—Politics and government—21st century. 2. Chávez Fras,
Hugo—Political and social views. 3. Chávez Fras, Hugo—Influence. 4. Venezuela—Poli-
tics and government—1999– 5. Venezuela—Foreign relations—1999–
6. Anti-Americanism—Latin America—Latin America. I. Title.
  F1414.3.F56 2013
  987.06'42—dc23
                                                        2013001473

Printed in the United States of America on acid-free paper that meets the American
National Standards Institute Z39-48 Standard.

Potomac Books
22841 Quicksilver Drive
Dulles, Virginia 20166

First Edition

10 9 8 7 6 5 4 3 2 1

To Laura, Maia, and Julian Fleischman

CONTENTS

FOREWORD

Just when we thought Latin America was safe for democracy, one man put an end to such hopes. With the fall of the Soviet Union in 1991, Cuba moved to the brink of its own collapse, its miscarried economic and political system exposed as empty remnants of earlier discredited socialist experiments. Fidel Castro stood isolated and rejected throughout the region. The 1990s brought a remarkable, universal hemispheric consensus based on democracy, human rights, and the free market. If history had ended as the world was universally adopting Western liberal democracy and renouncing ideology altogether—as Francis Fukuyama has argued—it ended first in Latin America. But then came Hugo Chávez.

Like some kind of throwback species of shark, the coup plotter who became president of Venezuela in 1999 emerged proclaiming a "twenty-first-century socialism" that was little more than an aggressive rehash of twentieth-century socialist failures mixed with a grand serving of anti-American rhetoric. While the rest of the world had largely retreated from the antidemocratic, statist, command economy model, or had never embraced it in the first place, Chávez's Venezuela submerged merrily into those polluted waters.

The reaction in the United States and elsewhere was largely disbelief that Venezuelans could choose, and continue to choose, such a path and that Chávez could move to export what he was doing to other countries in the region. How, observers asked, could he sustain popular support for policies that, over time, revealed themselves to be even less effective than they were in other places during the previous century? How, despite the startling contrast between the country's immense oil wealth and the paltry economic and social returns of Chávez's stewardship, could he become a kind of hero to certain local and national leaders in such countries as Bolivia, Ecuador,

Nicaragua, and even Argentina? Why is opposition to Chávez's bullying ways and transnational interference so weak throughout the hemisphere? Don't the facts mean anything? Venezuelans are experiencing plummeting oil production and energy scarcities, crumbling infrastructure, and the disappearance of basic commodities from store shelves; the poor are not much better off than under the old regime despite a quintupling of oil prices; democracy is stifled and the country is becoming ever more authoritarian; and the government is involved in money laundering and drug trafficking, with corruption at levels not seen in Latin America since the colonial era. Only the presence of fifty thousand Cuban troops assures the continuation of *Chávismo*, the left-wing political ideology associated with the president. Meanwhile, Venezuelans are fleeing their country as the Cubans did from the port of Mariel in 1980. Why is the general reaction not one of anger and rejection?

Pundits, academics, journalists, and politicians have all had a hand in trying to answer some of these questions. The term "populism" has been invoked as a one-word dissertation on the meaning of Hugo Chávez and as an excuse for inaction. His oft-foretold imminent death has been hailed as the most effective solution to the challenge he represents. But the analysts who focus on one of the facets of what is happening today in Venezuela have not been able to solve the riddle. Some have indeed raised the alarm about the threat to hemispheric security that Chávez and his Bolivarian republic represent. The threat is, in fact, a very real one, but dealing with it demands a far more nuanced understanding of the situation.

In this book, Luis Fleischman presents a broad picture that is not only more accurate and more complex but also more frightening than the headline snapshots of individual pieces to the puzzle. He exposes a method to the madness and definitely provides a new way of looking at Chávez and what will happen after Chávez (and, as important, why there *is* an after-Chávez).

Accurate history and meaningful policy here have a basis for thought and action. Fleischman brings together the backstories of the multiple actors whose beliefs, interests, and actions in the aggregate tell us what Chávismo means for us and for our friends in the region. And it means a great deal. He convincingly argues that the threat is more pervasive, more durable, and more solidly based than previous and easily dismissed casual diatribes may suggest.

From Nicaragua to Ecuador, Bolivia, and Argentina; from Iran and Syria to Hezbollah, the Revolutionary Armed Forces of Colombia (Fuerzas Armadas Revolucionarias de Colombia [FARC]), and the drug cartels; from Russia and China to even Brazil, the allies, followers, beneficiaries, enablers, and tolerators of Chávez are constructing an alternate Latin America that is at best inimical to U.S. interests and, at worst and increasingly, a threat to our security and to the security and political viability of all of Latin America.

Fleischman shows how the strategic interests of each element fit into the larger pattern. Hugo Chávez may be a "clown," as some who dismiss his influence have claimed, but this clown has an entire accompanying circus working the rings, with each act pursuing its own goals but all de facto reinforcing each other. I fully share Fleischman's indignation that a movement that has moved more narcotics (increasing the level of anarchy and state failure in Central American countries), laundered more enemy (Iranian) and drug money, supported more terrorism, made common cause with more recognized enemies (such as Iran, FARC, Hezbollah, and drug cartels), and more fully undermined its own and other democracies than almost any other movement should meet with such relative disinterest on the part of so many countries, including the United States of America. If Chávez and the Bolivarian revolution do not constitute an enemy that needs to be countered, who would? As Fleischman reveals, the clear public record is already enough to have Chávez's Venezuela declared as a state supporter of terrorism, a money launderer, and a drug trafficker. Indeed, he's a clown but a dangerous one. And a refusal to recognize him as such, for fear of "provoking" the president or of being seen as out of step with much of the rest of Latin America, makes rational policymaking most difficult.

Latin America in the Post-Chávez Era also raises the right questions about what the United States should do regarding predictable scenarios in Venezuela's immediate future. And what the U.S. mandate should be in leading the rollback of the precipitous decline in the democratic practices of the Bolivarian countries and within the once democratic bastion that was the Organization of American States. It was after all the United States that led the wave of regional democratization until Chávez. If the United States does not show that it understands the difference between real and fraudulent democracy, how can we expect others to do so?

One has to also agree with Fleischman that leadership in our own hemisphere is every bit as important as leadership vis-à-vis the Middle East or Asia. Fleischman also sees an important connection between the consolidation of democracy, the rule of law, and regional security.

The last question Fleischman asks is whether Chávismo, the Bolivarian chimera, will survive the death of Chávez. His answer, backed by facts and acute analysis, is troubling. But the author also outlines what must be done to counter that challenge, now and into the future. It all begins with a reassertion of U.S. leadership. This book will help any leader find the way.

Michael Skol
former U.S. ambassador to Venezuela and
former principal deputy assistant secretary of state
for inter-American affairs

PREFACE

The first time Hugo Chávez caught my attention was in 1998, when he was elected president of Venezuela. It was only a few years after he attempted to carry out a coup d'état against the government of President Carlos Andrés Pérez. I was surprised that after the brutal violence associated with the authoritarian experiences of the 1960s and 1970s in Latin America, particularly in Chile and Argentina, the Venezuelan people elected a military man who was willing to resort to unconstitutional means to achieve power. I wondered if people's memories are so short that their despair could lead to the election of a man like Chávez.

As Chávez's Bolivarian revolution was turning increasingly authoritarian, I was astonished that it had such resonance across Latin America. I was surprised to find that certain intellectuals of the Left in the region, among them University of Essex professor Ernesto Laclau and Nobel Peace Prize laureate Adolfo Pérez Esquivel, have cheered Chávez for his populism, for effectively challenging neoliberal economic policies, or for his revolutionary socialism, and have ignored or downplayed his antidemocratic measures. Their stance made me question to what extent democracy penetrated the minds and culture of the people in a region that experienced harsh dictatorships and that only three decades ago was still begging for liberty.

In the early 2000s, I moved to Florida, where I had the opportunity to meet with Venezuelan exiles who told me about the violence and intimidation that was taking place in Venezuela and about the increasing presence of individuals from Cuba and the Middle East in the country. This violence occurred not long after the attacks of September 11, 2001, and particularly after the failed attempt to overthrow Chávez in April 2002.

My instincts immediately made a connection between the growth of radical Islamic groups—including al Qaeda, Hamas, and Hezbollah—in

the region and the potential for the radicalization of the Bolivarian revolution. Although events in Latin America seemed removed from the fanatical
wars of radical Islam, I had the feeling that the more extreme versions of
Islamist thought might have a psychological impact among the most anti-
American elements in Latin America. After all, one of al Qaeda's aims when
it struck the World Trade Center and the Pentagon (and failed to hit its
third target) was to land a blow against the United States and to show that
it is possible to defeat America. Chávez's alliances with the Revolutionary Armed Forces of Colombia (FARC), the drug cartels, and Iran and its
proxies reinforced my suspicions. I soon realized that the Bolivarian revolution was about more than merely achieving social justice for the poor.
As more pro-Chávez presidents were elected across Latin America, I clearly
saw that Venezuela had become the catalyst for a major transnational revolution, one that not only had harmed democracy but also had become a
security threat.

Despite these observations, it was difficult to conceptualize what kind
of threat Chávez represented—that is, who and what will be affected and
what the consequences would be. This book attempts to answer these questions. Nobody, including myself, possesses the whole truth; however, an
interpretation of reality cannot be dismissed for lacking "evidence beyond
reasonable doubt." One interpretation should lead to a chain of interpreta-
tions. A respectful dialogue between different views is crucial. Leaving an
issue such as this one untouched, given the high stakes, is not an option.
The 9/11 Commission Report pointed out that the intelligence community's lack of imagination and understanding of the peril prevented its analysts from developing a realistic estimate of the danger that al Qaeda posed,
despite signs that clearly required further inquiry. The commission also
noted that the U.S. government invested more resources in identifying its
enemies only after attacks were conducted on U.S. soil.

Latin America in the Post-Chávez Era is not a work based on intelligence analysis, properly speaking. My training and skills are not in that
area. Moreover, my intention is not to offer solutions to all the problems.
Instead, I warn the reader about the problems and provide a new way of
thinking about them, one that differs from those offered by the most optimistic views.

ACKNOWLEDGMENTS

I want to thank all those who helped me in different ways to complete this work. First and foremost my gratitude goes to my beloved wife and companion, Dr. Laura Kalmanowiecki-Fleischman. She read my manuscripts and made sometimes painful but always helpful comments. Her intellect, meticulousness, and serenity helped me remain focused and confident throughout the writing process.

I also want to express very special thanks to Nancy Menges, coeditor of *The Americas Report*. She read crucial chapters, provided helpful comments, and added valuable information. I also want to thank Nancy for offering me the opportunity to coedit *The Americas Report* with her and for being my intellectual partner and friend for the last nine years. I was honored when Nancy asked me to join the Menges Hemispheric Security Project and continue the work of her late husband, Dr. Constantine Menges. Dr. Menges was a former White House senior adviser and an intellectual giant from whom I had the privilege to learn and with whom I developed a warm friendship. My work at the Menges Hemispheric Security Project and *The Americas Report* helped deepen my knowledge of Latin America and my ability to look at the situation and its various nuances. Likewise, I want to thank the Center for Security Policy and its president, Frank Gaffney, as well as its chief operating officer, Christine Brim, for providing a home to *The Americas Report* and for helping sponsor wonderful conferences and other activities.

I would like to thank former assistant secretaries of state for the Western Hemisphere ambassadors Otto Reich and Roger Noriega for their helpful input. I also want to express my gratitude to former White House senior director for the Western Hemisphere Dan Fisk and former State Department director of Central American affairs and Director of the Office of Planning for Latin America ambassador Paul Trivelli for their input, for talking with me, and for allowing me to learn firsthand from them. Very special thanks go to Ambassador Michael Skol for writing the foreword. He has been an incredible source of intellectual support and encouragement to me. I also want to thank Dr. Michael Ledeen, Dr. Angel Rabasa, Dr. David Dalin, and Dr. Ray Walser for providing useful comments.

I also want to express my gratitude to my friend, the journalist Orlando Ochoa Teran. His information and analysis regarding events occurring in Venezuela were most valuable.

A very special mention goes to my great friend, the late Mark Foster, whose passing early in 2012 did not allow him to see the publication of this book. He was a mentor to me and insisted on the need for a book like this.

I also want to thank Maryann Karinch, my literary agent. She is a woman with a refined intelligence and a great sense of humor who has always believed in the value of this book and tenaciously worked for its publication.

Of course, many thanks go to Hilary Claggett, Sam Dorrance, Aryana Hendrawan, Vicki Chamlee, Kathryn Owens, Melissa Jones, Laura Briggs, Rosanne Schloss, and the entire team at Potomac Books for their belief in my work and for their strong support. Also I thank Margaret Pulles for helping spread the message of this book.

Last but not least I want to express my gratitude to my entire family, to whom this book is dedicated. They have shown me incredible love, patience, and tolerance while I was writing this book.

INTRODUCTION

In the last decade, Latin America has faced major transformations and shifts that have seriously challenged the region and the United States. During the 1980s and 1990s, the continent was moving toward democratization and was understood to be riding a third wave of inevitable and irreversible transition. However, in some countries, the first years of the twenty-first century witnessed not only a reversal of these values of democracy and freedom but also a move toward a form of state socialism. This seemingly anachronistic phenomenon began in Venezuela once Hugo Chávez was elected as president only a decade after the collapse of the Berlin Wall. Curiously enough, Venezuela is a country that had enjoyed an uninterrupted democracy since the late 1950s.

The elected governments of Bolivia, Ecuador, and Nicaragua followed Venezuela's footsteps although Nicaragua had already experienced socialism two decades earlier and under the same leader, Daniel Ortega. The revolutionary spirit and the petro-dollars of the Venezuelan-led Bolivarian revolution had also revived the Cuban model, which was believed to have ended after the collapse of the former Soviet Union. These countries combine elements of popular socialism and authoritarianism. Although they still manage to observe an element of formal democracy by holding elections, they rule in a nondemocratic manner, intimidating opposition, censoring the press, and applying other antidemocratic measures. Venezuela's Chávez is probably the most radical ruler as his government controls the country's oil production, which has been the main source of national wealth and foundation of the Venezuelan economy and social fabric. Having a single crop–based economy has also enabled the government to add some totalitarian aspects to its government.

As we will see in the book, the regimes of Bolivia, Ecuador, Nicaragua, and Venezuela so far are evolving somewhat differently from one another, and their degree of authoritarian rule varies; however, the overall pattern presents an unprecedented revolutionary wave in the region.

The Cuban revolution, which emerged in 1959, unleashed political movements and guerrilla groups throughout Latin America. However, they failed to gain significant political power. Under Chávez's leadership, the Bolivarian revolution has acquired real power and a chain of excitement in large parts of Latin America where pro-Chávez leaders have risen to power through elections. Likewise, the Bolivarian revolution achieved ideological unity and developed a foreign policy that is characterized by the rejection of American hegemony in the region and American power in general. The Bolivarian revolution rejects countries that are friends of the United States, such as Colombia, and has established ties with countries that are openly hostile to it, such as Cuba and Iran.

Under the leadership of Chávez, Bolivarian countries reached out to Iran and strengthened their relations and cooperation with it. In the case of Venezuela, such cooperation might be military and perhaps even nuclear. Likewise, the Bolivarian revolution with Venezuela at its head has strengthened its links to the Revolutionary Armed Forces of Colombia (FARC), a peasant-based, Marxist guerrilla movement that has fought against the Colombian government since the early 1960s. Similarly, the governments that support the Bolivarian revolution have deepened their links to drug cartels and view the regional war on drugs as part of a U.S. strategy to consolidate its hegemony in the region.

Despite the anxiety that such developments used to elicit, events in Latin America have often been pushed to the margins of the debate, particularly in the U.S. foreign policy establishment. Part of the reason is understandable, as the post-9/11 environment has propelled U.S. foreign policy toward a heavier focus and involvement in South-Central Asia and the Middle East. Yet, such relative passivity is still surprising given the proximity of the region. U.S. foreign policy continues to be conducted following patterns set up in the 1990s without any major revisions. U.S. policy focused on issues related to economic prosperity in the region, general cooperation at various levels, and anti-drug policies. All of these issues are certainly important aspects of a good U.S. strategy in the continent, but the United States has not considered any new policy to address the region's new geopolitical challenges. Congress and its committees and subcommittees on foreign affairs have had numerous hearings regarding the situation in Latin America, and some members of Congress have expressed genuine interest in the issue. Policy-wise, however, these testimonies and presentations have not led to major policy shifts. One exception has been the passing of the Countering Iran in the Western Hemisphere Act of 2012, a bill that requires coordination with the governments of Mexico and Canada to prevent Iranian operatives from entering the United States and counters efforts by governments, entities, and individuals in the region to assist Iran in evading U.S. and international sanctions.[1]

The same passivity applies to countries in the region and particularly to the Organization of American States (OAS). The OAS has remained passive as Venezuela and its Bolivarian allies have violated aspects of democracy. OAS members have avoided any discussion that criticizes these countries' actions, despite the fact that members have all signed the organization's democratic charter, which compels them to denounce and punish countries in the region that violate democracy or human rights.

In the nonpolitical sphere, articles, white papers, and books on these events have taken shape. Publications and online posts about this subject matter also continue to flow in the blogs and think tanks, and academic publications have also addressed it. Some of the writings have analyzed the situation from a socioeconomic point of view while others focus on the security aspects. As I will refer to this literature throughout the book, mentioning a few examples here is useful.

The British journalist and political analyst Michael Reid provides important, useful economic and political analysis and information on Latin America.[2] Reid views the continent as a battlefield between populist autocracies, led by Hugo Chávez and his allies, and democratic reformism, led by such countries as Brazil, Chile, and Mexico. Furthermore, he argues that these populist autocracies are the result of increasing nationalism and an economic philosophy that stresses the truth of dependency theory, which claims that the economic development of certain countries comes at the expense of the underdevelopment of other countries. Thus, the Bolivarian revolution is understood as a nationalist reaction to Washington-promoted liberal economic policies and globalization. Whereas Reid has a point, he fails to see the Chávez regime as more than an authoritarian regime born out of an economic logic.

Along these lines of social and economic analysis, Chávez has often been defined as populist or neo-populist, in an attempt to compare his regime with populist-authoritarian regimes of the 1930s and '40s in Latin America. Others see Chávez in the same light as former Peruvian president

Alberto Fujimori or former Brazilian president Fernando Collor de Melo. They are all viewed as outsiders who do not come from within the existing parties and establishment. Thus, those leaders fall in the same category.[3] These comparisons have not focused on the actions of the Bolivarian revolution, the type of regime these leaders build, or the domestic and foreign policies they conduct. They simply focus on one or a few characteristics of the regime, compare it with another previous historical experience, and reach conclusions accordingly. The Bolivarian regimes have also been called illiberal democracies, alluding to the fact that they are elected governments but rule in a nondemocratic fashion.[4] All of these arguments have some truth, but they all seem insufficient to explain the regimes' increasing revolutionary behavior at home and their aggressive behavior abroad.

However, Chávez's movement is more than that simple definition. It is not merely a classical populist regime or a government that reacts to injustice or that is dissatisfied with a set of policies. The Bolivarian regime is deeply revolutionary and is an attempt to refound the state. Similarly, its domestic revolutionary project is connected to a regional revolutionary project.

On the security side, Douglas Schoen and Michael Rowan wrote an important work that points out all of Chávez's connections with Iran, his support of Hezbollah, and his links to FARC, drug cartels, and others.[5] Their book, *The Threat Closer to Home: Hugo Chávez and the War against America*, denounces important aspects of the dangers involved in these relations. More important, the main point of their thesis is that Chávez and his allies represent a serious danger to the United States. Schoen and Rowan's book, with its important information, makes a major contribution to the literature; however, the authors do not provide a systematic explanation as to how Venezuela's alliances might endanger the region and the United States. Mostly they detail how Chávez and his allies connect to enemies of the United States, but they do not produce a systematic account and analysis regarding the logic of such behavior and what potential consequences and scenarios we could face in the future.

In general, those authors who have concentrated on the security aspects of the problem have focused mostly on bringing to light new facts and information about the increasing ties between Venezuela and its allies: FARC, Iran, drug cartels, and others. They indeed have provided a wealth of invaluable information, but most of the information and analyses have been given in pieces. Some focused on Iran's presence and possible interests in Latin America. Others have emphasized the threats that terrorists from the Middle East can pose on U.S. borders.

The military scholar Max Manwaring has come closer than others to explaining the uniqueness of the Bolivarian revolution and its regional implications. He analyzes Venezuelan policy while taking into account a wide number of factors. According to Manwaring, Hugo Chávez is conducting an asymmetric war to destroy U.S. hegemony in the region and to impose his idea of twenty-first-century socialism throughout the continent. Asymmetric warfare is an instrument of the weak to defeat the strong and includes various dimensions. According to Manwaring, "Chávez's concept of asymmetric war conflict involves the organized application of coercive military or nonmilitary, lethal or non-lethal, direct or indirect, or a mix of various unconventional or irregular methods."[6] Thus, Manwaring points out that Chávez's warfare involves social programs, loud and intimidating propaganda, and a centralization of power. Likewise, he uses nonstate actors, such as criminal organizations and subversive groups—including gangs, guerrilla groups, and drug cartels—to promote continental instability that could ultimately help spread his model.

Manwaring has been able to make many connections regarding Chávez's way of thinking and has tremendously contributed to the understanding of the Bolivarian revolution and its strategic actions. Most important, he breaks with the idea that a threat can only be conventionally defined. Yet, Manwaring analyzes the problem as Chávez is carrying out a systematic war to achieve the revolution's goals. Although his premise and his methodology are enlightening and lead to a greater understanding of the current challenges in Latin America, *Latin America in the Post-Chávez Era* will go into a more comprehensive social, political, and geopolitical analysis.

This book discusses the links among a set of events that have been taking place in Latin America since the early 2000s to understand the challenges that countries of the region face. Domestic developments, particularly the rise of authoritarian regimes, are part of a general tendency in the region that transcends the domestic realm and has become an international problem with security implications. Thus, I try to explain the geopolitical challenges the region and the United States are facing. This book's primary intent is to unscramble and make sense of the facts, to project future scenarios in the region, and to present a perspective that can help illuminate the whole scope of challenges to the stability and security of the region and its implications for U.S. national security and strategic interests. The book interprets the complexity and deciphers the connection and logic between different events that have taken place in Venezuela and Latin America in the last decade. In projecting future scenarios, it hopefully will provide helpful tools and concepts to makers of foreign policy in the United States and Latin America.

▌THE STRUCTURE AND LOGIC OF THIS BOOK

In chapter 1, I first discuss the roots of the Bolivarian revolution in Venezuela and in the countries that adopted it. What were the social and political conditions that enabled a situation where revolutionary forces emerged calling for the refounding of the state? The most common answer to this question is that social inequality, poverty, and market-oriented, neoliberal economic polices caused this shake-up. Whereas I do not diminish the importance of the socioeconomic dimension, I argue that these democracies are weak representative governments based on states whose foundations are also weak. Their democratic system is not strong enough to generate legitimacy or to build the institutions that provide a strong legal and administrative foundation. When these weak democracies collapse, they leave a power vacuum that opens the door for charismatic demagogues who appeal to the popular vote by articulating a general discontent and by blaming the old democratic regime.

Chapter 2 analyzes the Bolivarian regime in Venezuela and what kind of regime it is. I argue that the Bolivarian regime is neither a classic populist regime nor an illiberal democracy. By analyzing different aspects of the government, I argue that not only is the Bolivarian revolution in Venezuela indeed socialist and authoritarian but that it is also highly ideological, revolutionary, expansionist, anticapitalistic, antidemocratic, and anti-American. In addition, despite maintaining a formal democracy, the regime contains totalitarian factions that subjugate elements of civil society and the state to the revolution and tends to expand its model abroad. Therefore, the regime cannot be judged for what it appears to be but for how it acts and what it aspires to be. The electoral component of the Bolivarian regime is one of the most deceiving aspects of the regime. In fact, the Bolivarian leader has purposely promoted authoritarianism as part of a political strategy aimed at imposing the revolution on other countries of the region. By the same token, it has also provided stability to the Bolivarian revolution in the long run by concentrating as much power as possible in the hands of a few tyrants.

Next I show how this principle begins to transform the region in chapter 3. The Venezuelan regime promotes its model abroad by using its national wealth to finance electoral campaigns of those candidates with the potential to join the Bolivarian revolution. Chávez has interfered in elections by funding political candidates with socialist-leaning ideas akin to his own ideology, succeeding in Ecuador, Bolivia, and Nicaragua. The Bolivarian leader also uses violent and subversive means and connections to groups that challenge the establishment in different countries in the region. Likewise, in focusing on how the model of the Bolivarian revolution has been applied in other countries, ultimately, the objective—to maximize Latin American unity under one revolutionary government following the principles of Bolivarianism—is revealed. I argue that Chávez's expansionism is not possible merely because his regime possesses oil. The Bolivarian revolution brings about a revolutionary effervescence that has spread in the continent with messianic speed. The Bolivarian revolution's ideological expansion is comprehensive and includes, among other things, a strong anti-U.S. component that merits focus. Indeed, this new continental setting seeks to eliminate U.S. influence in the region forever.

Chapter 4 analyzes the grassroots movements and the new social movements that have emerged in Latin America. Groups and people who have never had a political voice before have developed these movements, which have become a mobilized force in the first decade of the twenty-first century. I examine what the Bolivarian revolution means to these groups and to what degree this revolution supports or influences them. Thus, as Hugo Chávez has established direct connections with indigenous and other movements in Peru, Argentina, and Brazil, his goal is to incorporate these groups into his revolutionary hurricane.

Afterward, I analyze how the Bolivarian regime connects to FARC, to drug cartels, and to Iran and its proxies. I argue that FARC, which the Colombian government defeated, was resuscitated by the Venezuelan regime. FARC has become part of the Bolivarian revolution as an insurgent continental force and as an asymmetric force of protection for the Chávez regime. Chapter 5 explains what role these relationships play, how these elements and the Bolivarian revolution share mutual interests, and, most important, what the geopolitical and social consequences of these inter-actions are. With regard to the drug cartels, the bribery and corruption that Colombia in the 1980s and 1990s and the Mexican states that border the United States and countries in Central America currently experience show the overwhelming force of the drug cartels and their effectiveness in under-mining state authority and its institutions. This circumstance might have nefarious consequences if the phenomenon continues to expand across the continent. Along the lines of Manwaring's thought, I explore the relation-ship between the Bolivarian revolution and the drug cartels—in particular, how this state of anarchy might benefit the Bolivarian revolution by de-stroying state authority in Central America and Mexico and allowing its further expansion, and how the Bolivarian revolution can serve the cartels as well.

Chapter 6 focuses on the relationship between the Bolivarian regime and Iran. I argue that Venezuela and Iran have a multiplicity of mutual interests that cannot be reduced merely to Iran's attempt to avoid political and economic isolation. Cooperation between the two countries entails various dimensions, including ideology, the use of asymmetric warfare, nuclear cooperation, and even assistance in consolidating pro-Chávez re-pressive regimes. Most important, both have pledged to destroy American power in the region and in the world in general.

Iran's involvement comes at a particular time when certain events are taking place in Latin America. Iran has become a pariah state and isolated in the world because of its pursuit of nuclear weapons. Many interpret Iran's approach to the region as a way to break its economic isolation, which has resulted from international sanctions; however, in the context of its close link to the Bolivarian leader and the revolution, Iran's pres-ence may well play a role in aiding the transformation of Latin America. In explaining the elements involved in this complex relationship, I argue that the presence of Iran in the continent stems not simply from Iran's interest to avoid sanctions but is fully tied to the agenda of the Bolivarian revolution.

Iran constitutes one of the most repressive regimes on earth and is a major rogue state that supports terrorism and asymmetric war in several areas of the world, including Lebanon, Iraq, and Afghanistan. In addition,

Iran aspires to become a nuclear power. Its ambition raises many questions not only about what Iran is doing now in Latin America but also about what it can do in the future. How can Iran fit in the current Latin American context, particularly with the rise of the Bolivarian revolution? How does this relationship benefit both entities? How does it affect regional and U.S. national security?

Chapter 7 examines the role that China and Russia can play in aiding the Bolivarian regime and how it fits their agenda. On the one hand, China is generally perceived as an economic actor that pursues commercial expansion. The high echelons of the U.S. government often support this argument. China is not only a growing economic power; it is also a growing political power with political and strategic objectives. The Bolivarian revolution's interaction with China could have major implications for the perpetuation of the Bolivarian regimes and for other strategic aspects in the region that can affect U.S. interests.

Russia, on the other hand, has fallen below the radar since the end of the Cold War. Russia continues to be a major provider of weapons to the Venezuelan regime, some of which have already fallen in the hands of FARC, a key insurgent force of the Bolivarian revolution. China and Russia, however, have a more complex agenda in Latin America. Both could play an important role in perpetuating the already convoluted regional situation and could help the Bolivarian revolution in a number of ways. I explore China's and Russia's logic and explain in depth how these countries' interactions play out and might have an impact in the region.

Then, in chapter 8, I center on American foreign and security policy in Latin America in the post–Cold War era, particularly since the Bolivarian revolution in Venezuela emerged in 1999. I emphasize the policy of the countries of the region and their reaction to the Bolivarian revolution and the other elements involved. By far, U.S. foreign policy has been woefully inadequate. I argue that U.S. foreign policy froze in the face of this new phenomenon. U.S. policy toward Latin America has been characterized by inertia since, after the terrorist attacks of 9/11, most U.S. human and material resources and energy have been concentrated in the Middle East and Afghanistan. U.S. policy on Latin America has mostly focused on developing its good neighborhood policy—certainly a noble, good, and important goal to pursue. For instance, the U.S. government has pursued free trade agreements with some Latin American countries. The United

States has also promoted plans for economic development, development of small business, and other projects. However, U.S. policy toward the security threat in the region and its implications for the United States has been somewhat confused.

In delving into the different aspects of each chapter, I describe the consequences that alliances and developments may bring about and attempt to project how the region may look in the future. In the last chapter, I provide some perspective from which U.S. foreign policy could be inspired. Among other things I address the state of the Bolivarian revolution after Chávez's death and raise the question of whether the Bolivarian revolution will end or if it will become somewhat less intense or if it will continue its course. The answer is closer to the second and third possibilities given a series of circumstances.

I also focus on providing some orientation for the direction policy-making should take and discuss short- and long-term policies for the future that will concentrate on counterbalancing the effects of the challenges described in this book. I also explore how working with friends and allies in the region and how consolidating democracy in the region will be possible. Finally, I look at ways to restore democratic state authority to those countries that have turned into failed states. Democracy is an important instrument of domestic rule since if it is consolidated in the right direction, it could help mitigate some of the social problems that gave rise to revolutionary regimes. But, most important, I develop the argument that a consolidated democracy can play an important geopolitical role in making the difference between war and peace and between stability and instability.

WHAT TRIGGERED THE REVOLUTIONARY FORCES IN LATIN AMERICA?

For more than a decade, Latin America has been facing a significant political phenomenon. New regimes have emerged in Venezuela, Bolivia, Ecuador, and Nicaragua, and all see themselves as being revolutionary. They see themselves not as governments of continuity but as the opposite. They rise against their immediate past and try to reverse it diametrically. They criticize and deconstruct state institutions, including liberal democracy, and try to replace it with participatory democracy or a democracy that bypasses political parties and parliament in favor of a direct connection between the leader or executive power and the masses. They have repudiated the political class and reaffirmed historical heroes from the nineteenth century such as Simón Bolívar.

These new governments claim to reject capitalism and try to replace it with a "socialism of the twenty-first century." They repudiate economic globalization to support economic nationalism. They speak about regional economic and political unity and condemn U.S. influence in the continent. Ironically, there is nothing contemporary about the models they worship. Instead, they have glorified and revived the half-century-old, failed, and moribund Communist Cuban revolution and its eternal dictator, Fidel Castro.

One important characteristic of these regimes and other new social forces that have emerged is that this time they rise up not against authoritarian oppressive regimes but mostly against regimes where formal democracy exists. Thus, antidemocratic forces are rising not through coups d'état but through elections. These new political forces are surfacing at least a decade or more after a third wave of democracy had swept a great portion of the continent, particularly in South and Central America.

This chapter covers the emergence of these radical regimes and the social and political causes that breed them. Why and how have these regimes

1

materialized? What are the economic, social, and political conditions that prevailed in the countries where radical regimes took power?

▌THE COLLAPSE OF THE POLITICAL SYSTEM

Although democracy began to spread throughout Latin America in the early 1980s, democratic consolidation has not been achieved. Indeed, military coups disappeared and constitutional liberties have been restored, but in some cases, security forces continue to act with criminal impunity. Legislators and policymakers tend to pursue their own interests or the interest of a minority rather than respond to their constituents' needs. Corruption and patronage have remained widespread, and in many areas, mostly in the rural ones, the rule of law does not even exist.[1]

Democracy in Latin America today—with some notable exceptions such as Chile, Costa Rica, and Uruguay—relies on a weak system of representation, an ineffective judiciary, and a general system of government that the public views with a great deal of skepticism. The party system, unlike in more consolidated democracies, is not a system of representation of different views and interests that is engaged in a dialogue and negotiation. The parties are viewed as bodies that have their own interests like any regular economic unit or body. Elected officials are viewed as selfish individuals who use their status to advance their own interests rather than in voicing the interests of those they claim to represent. Unlike in advanced countries, elected official and societal groups do not have much interaction, so elected leaders tend to overstep their boundaries. They see themselves as having a popular mandate; consequently, they no longer seek input from their constituencies to the body politic.

The absence of such mechanisms of communication and representation has damaged the accountability of the system and has made it susceptible to corruption. Because not enough sectors of civil society have any input, the state falls prey to powerful minority groups that have connections and access to the political leadership. These groups associate themselves with the state and end up dominating the system at the expense of society at large. Social inequality prevails as a result of the failure to integrate the poorest and marginal sectors of society, and a pronounced result is that the system is vulnerable to fraud and corruption.

Electoral democracy in many countries in Latin America exists in a sea of illegality and corruption. Even capitalistic policies are not implemented properly. Clear examples are market reforms and neoliberal policies, which have become key scapegoats of the new revolutionary movements and governments. Market reform was introduced in the 1990s following the successful application of such reforms in Chile during the 1970s and 1980s. A number of Latin American leaders and Washington saw these reforms as a good blueprint for economic success, stability, and social peace. They were aimed at transferring economic functions from the state to the market by privatizing state-owned companies, by cutting unnecessary public spending and public bureaucracies, and by minimizing government intervention in the market. Advocates of such policies argued that decades-old statist economics focused more on governments' seeking employment opportunities for political purposes rather than on achieving productivity. In addition, those policies also increased the economy's dependency on the state; thus, the state became the target of special interests. In other words, in times past, connections to the state rather than market competition had been crucial to achieving economic advantage. This situation enabled close connections between economic and political elites that offered privileges to business groups, whose profits then depended on political connections, at the expense of including economic actors that could be more productive and efficient.[2] Thus, the poorest sectors of society, the labor unions, and the traditional elites that benefitted from their ties to the state opposed past attempts at market reforms.[3]

The idea behind these reforms was to create more wealth in society by enabling more economic actors to become part of the social fabric. Thus, market reform was also supposed to unleash the powers of the private sector, which reformers considered to be the basis of the first world economies.

Because of this situation, a policy of deregulation, privatization, termination of business subsidies, welfare reform, and openness to a global economy was carried out throughout the continent in the 1990s. However, the turn toward a market opening coincided with huge corruption as the cases of the impeachment of President Fernando Collor de Melo (1990–1992) in Brazil and Carlos Andrés Pérez (1989–1993) in Venezuela have shown.[4] In Argentina, the privatization process under President Carlos Saul Menem (1989–1999) was also conducted with unparalleled corruption at the levels of cabinet ministers, members of Congress, and the judiciary.[5]

Mexico, Brazil, and Chile have scored some successes as they received an enormous inflow of foreign investment and experienced economic growth. Yet, few countries enjoyed the benefits of market reform and globalization,[6] as a lack of confidence in the system's legal guarantees, which were affected by institutional weakness and corruption, seriously undermined foreign investment.

Thus the failure of neoliberal economic policies was the result of a number of complex causes, primarily weak state institutions, its legal system, corruption, and an ineffectual and unconsolidated democracy. (I will discuss these concepts in more depth in chapter 9.) Neoliberal policies therefore not only failed to deliver the productivity it promised but also brought about unemployment and aggravated the sense of inequality that has existed for a long time. Latin America developed a per capita negative growth from 1998 to 2002.[7]

Consequently, a sequence of elections in Latin America led to the emergence of moderate and radical left-wing governments. The first was the election of Hugo Chávez (1998) in Venezuela, followed by Luiz Inácio Lula da Silva in Brazil (2002), Néstor Kirchner in Argentina (2003), Tabaré Vazquez in Uruguay (2004), Evo Morales in Bolivia (2005), Rafael Correa in Ecuador (2006), and Daniel Ortega—one of the key leaders of the 1979 Sandinista Revolution and a former president of the country from 1985 to 1990—in Nicaragua (2006).

According to Latin America scholars Steven Levitsky and Kenneth Roberts, what these administrations have in common is that they all constitute a reaction to the problem of social inequality, severe poverty, and exclusion.[8] However, a movement toward the Left is not homogenous in Latin America. These governments are all considered leftist in the most abstract sense, but they are definitely not all the same. The social democracies of such countries as Brazil and Uruguay are different from the radical Left regimes of Venezuela, Ecuador, Bolivia, and Nicaragua. I don't define "Left" only based on economic policy. I call "radical Left" those regimes that have appealed to the people in the name of a revolution for social equality on the one hand while bringing an authoritarian dimension to government on the other hand.

∣ THE RISE OF THE RADICAL LEFT

The Case of Venezuela

Venezuela's road to a revolutionary regime resulted after the collapse of a forty-year democratic regime. The collapse coincided with an economic crisis in the country, which depended on a single crop product, or oil. In a way, the old regime's downfall was the result of a political system that was built on the state's ability to provide welfare and employment based on oil wealth. As this economic model broke down and was replaced with austerity measures, the whole system came under question until a charismatic figure who promised to change it all replaced it.

Since 1958, Venezuela has been governed mostly by two major parties—Acción Democrática (Democratic Action [AD]) and the Comité de Organización Política Electoral Independiente (Political Electoral Independent Organization Committee [COPEI]). They shared about 80 percent of the legislative vote and 90 percent of the presidential vote from 1973 to 1988. Their party organizations were extensive, with each small town in Venezuela having a party headquarters. Furthermore, other than the Catholic Church and private sector associations, practically all organizations of civil society—including the majority of peasant federations and the labor unions—had internal elections where candidates represented the two parties. Both parties also maintained strict discipline and would expel members if they disobeyed party decisions. Thus, labor leaders avoided organizing strikes when their party was in power.

In 1958 both parties, along with the left-leaning Unión Republicana Democrática (URD), signed the Pact of Punto Fijo. According to this pact, the political parties consulted one another whenever controversial issues arose and acted based upon consensus. Thus, the parties agreed to negotiate solutions to concrete political problems.[9] Party leaders resolutely tried to avoid conflict, which they saw as a potential threat for democracy.[10] Contrary to the modern concept of democracy, political stagnation, executive-legislative impasse, and conflict in general were not seen as part of a governing process. They viewed the expression of diverse ideas and interests as obstacles to exercising governability. As a result, the URD abandoned the Punto Fijo agreement by the 1960s and joined weak opposition coalitions against AD and COPEI. However, the URD later returned to the political arena to support one of the two parties. These two parties remained the dominant parties of the national political arena for four decades. The Venezuelan two-party system came to be based more on party notables than on a representation of interests.

The reason why the Punto Fijo Pact held up for a long time relates directly to the production of oil and the use of state resources. Oil and foreign affairs policies were made by consensus, with the armed forces rewarded with high salaries and promotions. Business associations, such as Fedecamaras, Consecomercio (Commercial Council), and Conindustria (Confederation of Industry), received subsidies, low taxes, and protectionist tariffs. Likewise, worker unions and others reaped ample rewards.

Party discipline, patronage, and the Punto Fijo Pact created a situation similar to a one-party system. These parties created a welfare system based on redistribution and patronage that oil revenue sustained in great scale. In the 1960s and '70s, both parties passed land reform, nationalization of the oil industry, expansion of public education, and job creation. Thus, they achieved democracy based on economic peace, and the population remained relatively passive as long as oil revenue could sustain the social peace.

This two-party collaboration system began to decline in the 1990s, as monopolization of power predictably led to corruption. A provision embedded in the Punto Fijo agreement that forbade prosecution of corruption protected and encouraged such practices. As oil prices went down, however, the whole system declined as well. What is worse, a loss of confidence in the parties was reflected in the loss of confidence in democracy.[11] The new rulers call this *partidocracia*, or "rule by the parties." Chávez and other radical leaders in the continent later used this term repetitively to delegitimize the old regime.

These antiestablishment sentiments intensified when a package of adjustment measures was approved. A massive three-day riot known as the Caracazo took place in February 1989. This event fatally wounded the Punto Fijo regime. Against this general atmosphere of turmoil and discontent, Hugo Chávez Frias, a mid-ranking army officer, led a coup d'état in February 1992. Although the coup failed, Chávez arose as a distinct leader. Despite the loss of almost twenty lives, most of them soldiers, he surrendered and assumed responsibility for the event (a rare admission for the Venezuelan political class). Precisely because of this effort, he began to draw public attention. In interviews following the coup d'état, he pointed out that his intention was to capture President Carlos Andrés Pérez and put him on trial for corruption. In his own words, Chávez was struggling against this "government and its corruption." This type of discourse against the two-party establishment and the adjustment measures helped him win the elections in 1998.[12]

Chávez's rise to power was facilitated also by President Pérez's impeachment in 1993 on charges of corruption and by the election of Rafael Caldera the same year. Caldera, in whose house the Punto Fijo Pact was signed, ironically became the president who would pave the way for Chávez.

Caldera openly justified the people's frustration with the Pérez government and stopped short of justifying the coup d'état attempts. Running as an independent candidate, Caldera won the support of a number of small left-wing parties. For the first time in more than thirty-five years, neither the AD nor COPEI ruled Venezuela. Furthermore, not only did Caldera criticize previous government policies, but he also granted amnesty to Chávez and those who plotted with him.[13]

Caldera's government came to an end, however, as tensions with the military over the amnesty increased and as businessmen became increasingly unhappy with the presidents' alliances with the Left. Unions traditionally connected to the parties also resented Caldera's antiestablishment stand. Society grew polarized as Caldera's government weakened. Strikes and protests, conflicts between governors and federal government officials, economic uncertainty, and confrontations between Congress and the president created chaos.[14] The decline of the traditional parties and Caldera's inability to sustain a strong basis of governability paved the way for the rise of Hugo Chávez in the 1998 election.

As long as the two major parties were able to apply redistributionist policies using high price oil revenues, they were also able to maintain their power and keep democracy alive. When an economic crisis required adjusting economic policies, popular discontent came in the form of riots. The parties lost prestige and authority and were seen as corrupt political entities that took advantage of the country's vast oil wealth while leaving serious socioeconomic problems unaddressed.

Thus, during this crisis of legitimacy of the Venezuelan state and severe internal conflict, Hugo Chávez would emerge not only as the man who could combat the corruption of the Punto Fijo politicians but also as the strong leader who would establish a new revolutionary order where he would rule in the name of the poor and for the poor. Chávez's main message went against neoliberal policies, the traditional parties and their oligarchical leadership, the liberalization of trade, and the whole economic and political establishments. During his tenure he also developed a strong anticapitalistic and anti-American rhetoric since he views the United States as responsible for allying itself with old Venezuelan oligarchies and powers.

The Case of Ecuador

Ecuador represents a case where the coming of a revolutionary regime has to do with a long history of party and leadership deception and with the state's inability to properly include new, mostly indigenous sectors that became active after decades of marginalization. In contrast to Venezuela, Ecuador was not an oil-based state economy and suffered an interruption of the constitutional order for about a decade (1969–1979). Following this period Ecuador saw political reform, mostly based on the extension of suffrage.

After 1979, however, institutions remained fragile, conflicts continued to plague executive-legislative relations, and the country's poor native communities were still excluded from the political process.

This omission led to the formation in the 1980s of the largest indigenous organization called the Confederación de Nacionalidades Indígenas del Ecuador (Confederation of Indigenous Nationalities of Ecuador [CONAIE]). This organization represented 40 percent of the Indian population, yet the political parties and leaders did not pay enough attention to its needs and goals.[15]

Parties in Ecuador became vehicles to empower a political leadership of elites, but they failed to incorporate social movements and new groups into the system. Leadership continued to use elections simply as electoral vehicles for maintaining and accumulating power. Changing one's ideology for personal gain was a common phenomenon among members of the political class. One third of those elected to Congress in 1992 had switched parties because the other party had made promises of government patronage. This lack of party attachment undermined the possibility of building mass constituencies and thus weakened the system's ability to incorporate social groups.[16]

The indigenous community was the most excluded. No organized party reached out to these people. Ecuadorian Indians were forced to organize and placed their demands largely outside the formal political system and in the form of protest and mobilization. The indigenous population mainly pressed for cultural recognition, bilingual education, and land reform demands but to no avail. These demonstrations occasionally met with repressive measures. The Maoist guerrilla organization Puka Inti (Red Sun) emerged as a result of such exclusion and repression.[17]

The Ecuador-based Institute for Social and Public Opinion Studies (Instituto de Estudios Sociales y de la Opinion Pública) conducted a poll in 1996 that indicated 64 percent of Ecuadorians preferred a dictatorship to democracy and that the armed forces and the Catholic Church were the country's most respected institutions.[18] As in Venezuela, democracy was delegitimized along with the political system. The rule of the parties, or partidocracia, undermined the people's belief in democracy as a method to channel their demands.

In the economic sphere, as in Venezuela, popular sectors objected to further economic adjustment and measures that resulted in unemployment and a decline in living standards. Neoliberal policies prompted fear of unemployment, particularly in the public sector. The rural sector was also afraid that privatization would challenge indigenous land tenure and negatively affect the environment. Both land ownership and environmental protections were crucial issues for the indigenous populations.

In 1996 Ecuadorians elected Abdalá Bucaram president. Bucaram was an outsider who capitalized on the situation of general discontent. He moved on to carry out economic adjustment measures, which included higher taxes and tariffs. These policies, in addition to increased government corruption, raised the rage of the middle classes and led to the growing power of the indigenous movement. Stoppages and strikes eventually forced Bucaram out of power.

Members of parliament, which the traditional parties still dominated, concluded that the problem in Ecuador was presidential weakness. They therefore proceeded to institute constitutional reform aimed at strengthening the executive branch's power. As a result, the new constitution disempowered parliament without solving any problems.

In 1998, Jamil Mahuad, the former mayor of Quito, was elected president. As oil prices plummeted in the international market, Ecuador's economic downfall ensued. Mahuad announced a new policy of dollarization and a freeze on people's bank deposits to control inflation. The decision was made overnight and again without much public debate.[19]

Shortly thereafter, indigenous organizations marched en masse in the streets, demanding a change in economic policy and Mahuad's resignation. The groups had the support of the military, which announced the creation of a military junta for the sake of national salvation. Mahuad resigned and the presidency was provisionally assumed by Vice President Gustavo Noboa, who ruled with the support of the parliament and the military. Traditional parties opposed a coup d'état, though. The leader of this military initiative was Lucio Gutiérrez, who ran in national elections that year and won. His platform was that of an outsider. He spoke the language of the Left in very vague terms but, most important, he established ties to the indigenous movements. These groups' support proved critical to his electoral success. Gutiérrez drew six members of his cabinet from the largest and increasingly powerful indigenous organization, the CONAIE.

But once in power after the November 2002 election, Gutiérrez adopted a new policy based on an agreement with the International Monetary Fund and thereafter proceeded to carry out economic austerity policies. This move was quite contrary to the populist redistributionist policies he had voiced during his campaign, and the indigenous movements immediately withdrew their support. Likewise, an alliance developed between Gutiérrez and the former unpopular president Bucaram, who was pardoned, exonerated from all charges of corruption, and allowed to return from his exile in Panama.[20]

As discontent grew, Gutiérrez increased political repression and replaced Supreme Court members with his friends and allies. Further street uprisings ensued, and the demonstrators called to expel the political class. Their slogan of "Que se vayan todos" (Let them all go home) echoed a chant already heard a year and half earlier in Argentina, where people participating in street demonstrations expressed their distrust for the political class and the political system. In March 2006, indigenous organizations went to the streets to block roads and protest free trade agreements and neoliberal and privatization policies. Consequently, the Ecuadorian government declared a state of emergency and later expelled the American corporation Occidental Petroleum from the country to appease protestors.[21] Congress removed Gutiérrez from office in April 2006 and installed his vice president after mass demonstrations dominated by distrustful indigenous people.

The deception prior to elections and the disappointment of those who had put their hopes in Lucio Gutiérrez were not unusual in the political culture of many countries in the continent, where electoral power is valued above civil society. Candidates make promises to civil society during the electoral campaign, and once in power leaders feel entitled to govern without honoring them. This process is what the late renowned Latin American scholar Guillermo O'Donnell called delegative democracy. This term refers to the premise that "whoever wins election to the presidency is thereby entitled to govern as he or she sees fit. . . . The President is taken to be the embodiment of the nation and the main custodian and definer of its interests."[22] Delegative democracy works as long as the population remains unaware or passive. However, with the active mobilization of civil society and particularly with that of previously marginalized groups, such as the indigenous groups, this model collapsed.

This set of circumstances led to the 2006 election of the young outsider Rafael Correa as president after he had served as finance minister for a little more than a year. Correa, who would become one of Hugo Chávez's staunchest allies, won the election with the support of the indigenous movement. In the last several years, the indigenous groups had evolved from a position of political marginality into a self-conscious and politically active movement that could no longer be ignored or underestimated. Since 2000, CONAIE has become a crucial political force in Ecuador. This organization stands for the protection of the environment, and the promotion of cooperatives, organic farms, traditional trade, and bilingual education (Spanish and the Indigenous languages). It demands that the government grant lands and titles of lands for the indigenous communities and fights transnational companies that try to affect the indigenous people's natural environment. CONAIE also supports the decentralization of political power and distribution of resources and seeks social justice and equality in society.[23] Most importantly, CONAEI seeks to build a plurinational Ecuadorian society—that would include the indigenous communities and people of African ancestry. Thus, it advocates for cultural autonomy for indigenous communities and communitarian self-determination in general.

The organization became a strong bastion of support for Rafael Correa in the presidential elections. (In later years, however, CONAEI grew disappointed with the course of Correa's policies because it felt Correa was ignoring the demands of indigenous people.) Correa's message took aim against what he judged as the degeneration of institutions and the political class. He also spoke about restoring the public interests that previous Ecuadorian leaders had abandoned. Saying Ecuador was held hostage by the economic and political elites, Correa assailed the partidocracia, which he saw as responsible for the deterioration of national and state institutions. He also attacked neoliberalism and the corporations that exploited the country and prevented its economic growth and productivity.[24] Likewise, he promised to eliminate foreign domination by closing U.S. military bases designed to oversee antidrug trafficking. During his electoral campaign Correa promised a "citizens" revolution and a new order that would bring more equality to the people for whom he would rule.

The Case of Bolivia

In Bolivia, as in Ecuador, the coming of a radical regime stemmed from the mobilization of previously excluded sectors. As in all the previous cases, it is also related to a crisis of legitimacy of the democratic regime and has an ideological component. As in Ecuador, Bolivia suffered a constitutional interruption between 1964 and 1982, and then democracy was restored.

Between 1985 and 1993 Bolivia had two governments—under the presidencies of Victor Paz Estenssoro (1985–1989) and Jaime Paz Zamora (1989–1993)—that changed the existing patterns of governance. In 1985 Paz Estenssoro introduced a stabilization plan called Nueva Política Económica (NEP). This policy was based on a mix of democracy and exclusion but succeeded in achieving stability and reducing hyperinflation.[25] His policies succeeded precisely because they were based on a pact between two major parties—the Revolutionary National Movement (Movimiento Nacionalista Revolucionario [MNR]), which Paz Estenssoro led, and the Nationalist Democratic Action (Acción Democrática Nacionalista [ADN]), a party headed by Hugo Banzer, a former president during the preceding dictatorship. According to the pact, the ADN would assume patronage for a number of state corporations. In addition, a secret addendum obliged the MNR to support Banzer in the next election. So in Bolivia, a pact similar to the Venezuelan Punto Fijo agreement was created.

As in Venezuela and Ecuador, this pact was made at the expense of public debate and civil society, and its decision-making style was not dissimilar to the policymaking style of the former dictatorship. Only a handful of entrepreneurs had access to the decision-making process, which was only possible with the selective coordination and blessing of the government. It bypassed Congress and used the military to impose curfews in times of dissidence.

Since the system was a closed system with limited access and low democratization, however, it also generated patronage and corruption. As a result of its exclusionary policy, two populist parties began to organize outside the system and courted marginal groups and other sectors of society, including some businesses.

Gonzalo Sánchez de Lozada emerged as one of the entrepreneurs of that era who had ample government access. As the main architect of the NEP, he would become the main implementer of neoliberal policies.

Sánchez de Lozada was elected president in 1993 following a few years of economic and political paralysis. His victory resulted from the reputation he won during his tenure as minister of planning. Sánchez de Lozada's plan included job creation, investment, economic stability, improved health and education, popular participation, and transparency. His government did not privatize public enterprises; rather, they became more efficient thanks to a fueling of capital and involving workers in decision making within these companies. He encouraged foreign investment but also expanded the participation of Bolivian workers in the decision-making process. In his eagerness to make the system more efficient, Sánchez de Lozada adopted some measures aimed at the relocation of workers. These measures unleashed strikes and stoppages that needed the mediation of the church. He also created employment offices to aid the unemployed, but their government funding ended up being insufficient.[26]

With regard to political reform, Sánchez de Lozada adopted some reforms and amendments to the constitution aimed at strengthening representation. This effort included an electoral reform that followed the German model, according to which 50 percent of the lower house would be elected by single-member districts and the other half would be elected by proportional representation.[27] Sánchez de Lozada also created procedures favoring the direct election of the president and all mayors, lowered the voting age to eighteen, increased powers for departmental prefects, and established an independent human rights ombudsman.

He also tried to reform the judiciary, which had a bad reputation in Bolivia. A lack of access to the judiciary is ubiquitous in a multiethnic country such as Bolivia, where many people do not speak Spanish as their first language. To address this problem, Sánchez de Lozada created a constitutional tribunal to serve as an instrument of judicial review and to handle all constitutional claims, including human rights violations.

Sánchez de Lozada's anti-coca policies became a point of contention and generated protests among peasants. The government policies were twofold: On the one hand, they established eradication programs aimed at retraining peasants and workers in the coca fields for other activities. On the other hand, the government did not hesitate to repress peasant protests.

Additional strikes involved the rural irrigation cooperatives in the city of Cochabamba after the price of water increased. Strikers demanded the cancellation of contracts on water supplies with an international company. In addition, indigenous populations in the northern part of the country protested against poverty and social exclusion.[28] Under Sánchez de Lozada, the country's economy grew steadily but not enough to deal with extensive socioeconomic challenges.

After his reelection in 2002, he announced a plan to export gas to the United States using Chilean ports. This policy enraged certain nationalistic sectors (including the indigenous population) because historically in the nineteenth-century Pacific War, Chile had deprived Bolivia an outlet to the sea. This nationalism triggered a strike in Cochabamba, with people demanding that contracts with the United States be cancelled despite their potential as a good source of national income. Strikers also demanded that hydrocarbons be nationalized. Organized by Evo Morales and the indigenous movement, these strikes and roadblocks imposed a virtual siege of the city of La Paz. Sánchez de Lozada responded with a display of force, which included tanks, helicopters, and hundreds of soldiers. Dozens of people died.[29]

A strike born out of mass protests unleashed a very powerful movement that eventually would be the president's demise and bring Morales into power. Sánchez de Lozada resigned in October 2003, and Vice President Carlos Mesa succeeded him. Despite having initial popular support, in April 2005 Mesa faced a massive strike of Indians who were protesting an increase in water taxes. He resigned in the face of these protests and his inability to stop them.

It was apparent by the mid-2000s that the institutional setting of the Bolivian state, including Congress and the executive power, was no longer able to channel the demands of large sectors of society. Not the party system but mechanisms outside the system, such as mass mobilization and protests, moved to solve conflicts.[30] Large sectors of society, particularly the hitherto ignored indigenous populations, provided the backbone of a whole new antiestablishment movement.

Evo Morales played a key role in strikes that brought down two presidents, thus his actions gave him high visibility. An ethnic Indian, he was the leader of Movement toward Socialism (Movimiento al Socialismo [MAS]), which was built on a coalition of rural social movements, including the highland peasants' unions of the *cocaleros* (coca growers); other indigenous associations; and social movements. The major force behind this large coalition is based on peasant trade unionism, and its main organization is the Confederation of Peasant Workers' Unions of Bolivia (Confederación Sindical Unica de Trabajadores Campesionos de Bolivia [CSUTBC]).[31] From the CSUTBC the Morales-led indigenous party of trade union federations emerged. As other indigenous groups later joined the MAS, a strong indigenous identity remained fundamental to these social movements. They all demanded an end to neoliberalism and a radical change in the country's legal and economic structure. Most important, in their view the subject of the revolution ceased to be the working class and needed to be replaced with "the Indians" and "the peasant."[32] While the coca growers' unions dominated the MAS leadership, with Morales at its head, the party also included many urban groups that were mestizo and not purely indigenous and unions of diverse ethnic composition, such as neighborhood associations and trade unions of teachers, truck drivers, and factory workers.

In the elections of 2005, Evo Morales won the presidency with a sound majority, having general appeal to the Indians, the poor, and disaffected voters. During the electoral campaign, Morales spoke forcefully against trade liberalization and neoliberal economic policies while pledging to pursue policies of redistribution, the nationalization of natural resources, and agrarian reform. He also directed his barbs against the traditional parties, state institutions, and corruption.[33]

The Case of Nicaragua

The way in which events led to the rise of a revolutionary leader in Nicaragua differs from the cases of Venezuela, Bolivia, and Ecuador. To a certain extent, despite being in Chávez's sphere of influence today, Daniel Ortega's rise to power is paradoxically more the result of a mechanism similar to the old Venezuelan system of the Punto Fijo Pact than to the eruptions of social protests or a major crisis of legitimacy.

After Ortega and his party, the Sandinista National Liberation Front (Frente Sandinista de Liberación Nacional [FSLN]) left power in 1990,

Ortega initiated a process of concentrating the party's power in his hands. Under Ortega's leadership, the FSLN began to build a party machine, made peace with the Catholic Church, and signed a number of pacts with former bitter enemies that prompted him even to support previously un-thinkable conservative economic policies, including neoliberalism.[34] Or-tega likewise evolved from the leader of the Sandinista revolution into a party boss, alienating many Sandinistas who began to resist him. Once the revolutionary party leader who overthrew the Anastasio Somoza dictator-ship and attempted radical social change, Ortega became a party machine operator up to the point where his authority could not be questioned.

In 2001, Ortega signed a pact with Nicaraguan ex-president and leader of the Constitutionalist Liberal Party (Partido Liberal Constitucionalista [PLC]), Arnoldo Alemán. Under this pact the two party leaders agreed to approve a series of amendments to the law that would secure their two parties' full control of the government and its branches and leave other minor parties behind. Thus, such state institutions as the courts, the con-troller general, and the electoral council became strongholds of either the FSLN or the PLC, according to their electoral weight. The pact set up the frame so that government posts could also be politicized accordingly. Consequently, half of the judiciary fell under Sandinista control and soon became the strongest and most dominant political force in the National Assembly. Although elections remained free and competitive, this pact also reduced the minimum support that a presidential candidate needed to win the elections from 40 percent of the vote to 35 percent.

The party found itself divided in the 2006 presidential campaign when PLC leader Arnoldo Alemán faced corruption accusations. A new party, the Nicaraguan Liberal Alliance (ALN) was created by dissidents of the PLC. The PLC candidate, Jose Rizo, won less than 27 percent of the vote, while the ALN candidate, Eduardo Montealegre, won about 29 percent. The di-vision of the PLC largely benefitted Ortega since he received 38 percent of the vote, which was enough for him to win the presidential elections.[35]

It is important to point out that the years following Nicaragua's transi-tion to democracy in 1990 were highly problematic. Despite some reforms, the judiciary and the legislature still struggled with corruption. Further, the country suffered from instability, poverty and famine aggravated by Hurricane Mitch (1998), party patronage, polarization, and a general loss of faith in democracy.[36] But unlike in the preceding examples, such a loss of faith did not cause a revolutionary movement in Nicaragua, for the country had already experienced such a revolution and Ortega himself had led it. This time, sixteen years later, the left-wing revolutionary Daniel Ortega's second presidency came from a typical Latin American pork barrel elitist pact between two caudillos.

| SUMMARY

The revolutionary situation in Venezuela, Ecuador, and Bolivia arose not only out of economic crises but also from a crisis of the legitimacy of a deficient democratic system. Parties were largely unresponsive to the new social forces unleashed by these societies and remained oligarchic rather than open to the constituencies of civil society. Political leaders acted with a sense of having an electoral mandate rather than including different sectors of civil society in the dialogue and the law of the policymaking process. This circumstance led automatically to the public's association of the oligarchic party rule and weak parliaments with democracy. Likewise, their governments' economic reforms, such as market reforms, and other policies were carried out against a backdrop of corruption and lawlessness.

This situation of democratic and institutional weakness enabled the new revolutionary leaders (as well as some grassroots and indigenous groups that will be discussed in chapter 4) to delegitimize democracy and market reform. Nearly two decades after democracy had emerged in countries where dictators had formerly ruled, democracy was again collapsing but this time under democratically elected leadership.

Political instability, weak and oligarchic democracies, and economic crises created a revolutionary situation that paved the way for the emergence of charismatic leaders who built authoritarian regimes on populist grounds. They filled the resulting vacuum when the democratic system failed to deepen inclusion and as a result generated mass dissent. By the same token weak democracies also opened the way for manipulating and undermining democracy as Ortega did in Nicaragua.

Several new leaders have emerged in the countries discussed here. They all carry revolutionary agendas aimed at changing the whole political and social order. One leader, however, set the pace and designed the model everyone else would follow. This man is President Hugo Chávez Frías of Venezuela, first elected in 1998.

2 | THE ORIGINS OF THE CHÁVEZ (BOLIVARIAN) REVOLUTION

Observers have labeled the regime of Hugo Chávez with terms borrowed from history or from other forms of government. They have often defined it as being populist or neo-populist. In this sense, the Chávez regime is compared with previous Latin American experiences such as the rule of Juan Perón in Argentina, because the former's regime also appeals to the poor and other excluded sectors and builds its power on redistributing national resources. It is also viewed as populist because it is based on the charismatic rule of one leader who establishes a direct connection to the masses while scorning parliament, parliamentary procedure, and the division of powers.[1]

Others have identified authoritarian features in the regime and have called the new Venezuelan regime an illiberal democracy. The term "illiberal democracy" has been used to categorize a regime that combines electoral democracy with authoritarian practices, particularly as it relates to excessive power of the president at the expense of parliament and judicial independence and to limitations on business, local government, and freedom of the press.[2]

I do not disagree with these observations, but I will add that the Chávez regime contains more than populist or authoritarian features. I argue in this chapter that the Chávez regime is a truly revolutionary project whose very nature and ideology may have far-reaching consequences for the region. The Chávez regime also has totalitarian elements without being fully totalitarian. The regime's totalitarian component is crucial because it not only aims at consolidating maximum control of the Venezuelan state and society but also seeks to expand its model beyond its national boundaries.

▌CHÁVEZ AND THE BOLIVARIAN REVOLUTION: THEORY AND IDEOLOGY

Unlike many other South and Central American countries, Venezuela is one of the few that did not experience dictatorial regimes since 1958. In 1992 Hugo Chávez, a former paratrooper who rose to the rank of lieutenant colonel, staged an abortive coup attempt against the government of President Carlos Andrés Pérez and received a jail sentence for his efforts. Six years later, he was elected president as head of the Patriotic Pole, an electoral front comprised of his own Fifth Republic Movement and various parties of the nationalist Left. Chávez won presidential elections on December 6, 1998, and again after a constitutional reform, in 2000 with the largest majority in four decades. He ran on an anticorruption and antipoverty platform while repudiating the two major parties that had dominated Venezuelan politics for four decades.

Rejection of Capitalism and Democracy

Hugo Chávez has described himself as being a revolutionary. Initially he defined his revolution as being anti-exploitative and anti-imperialist. He believes that democratic capitalist and communist classless societies have failed.

The crisis of Venezuela, as described in chapter 1, raised the need to fill a political vacuum of hegemony and legitimacy after the collapse of the Punto Fijo Pact. This predicament affected a large number of people with diverse backgrounds, including the middle class and popular sectors. They all had complex and different problems, but they all shared a sense of impending disaster. Chávez capitalized on this diverse discontent and successfully found a universal message. He managed to provide hope to a large number of people with disparate interests and needs that cannot be specifically articulated. For that reason, he claims to represent the poor, the Indians, and all those who were oppressed not only by the previous regime but also by hundreds of years of colonialism and uprooting. Further, Chávez constantly plays on the image of the dichotomy of white versus black and white versus Indian. Indeed, his big generalizations and loud messages generate emotions and feelings that seemingly eliminate the need to explain or provide specific solutions to specific problems.

Chávez also chooses to castigate the United States, which he blames for neoliberalism and many decades of exploitation of Hispanic American countries. He blames neo-liberalism, for opening up markets and eliminating state ownership of companies, thus bringing suffering of Venezuela and the Americas. Chávez attributes the neoliberal economic policies promoted by Washington to the continuation of a general agenda of "U.S. imperialism" and domination.

Chávez also challenges the traditional political institutions that governed the country, including liberal democracy. He considers the model of liberal democracy to be obsolete and exhausted. Following a more or less Marxist logic, Chávez views liberal democracy as following "a pattern of domination in the economy, in politics, a negation of the right of peoples to be masters of their own destiny."[3]

Chávez emphatically talked about the substantial rights of the indigenous people and all those groups that have been marginalized by an oppressive system (including liberal democracy) throughout the years. He strives to substitute the model of representative liberal democracy, which is based on the division of powers and a strong representative government, with a model of participatory democracy that features a local council and other social bodies tied directly to the executive power. In Chávez's view, democracy is also linked to the notion of social and economic justice above rights, freedom, or liberty. This concept is confirmed in the words of former Venezuelan foreign minister Ali Rodriguez Araque, who pointed out that "democracy and poverty are incompatible" and that as long as people suffer "calamities such as hunger and scarcity, democracy is at stake and human rights are nothing but mere fiction."[4]

However, despite all of its different slogans and clearly identifiable ideas, the Chávez regime is not all that simple to define. As we will see, Chávez is not merely a Marxist, a Guevarist, or a Castroist attempting to establish a replica of Fidel Castro's regime in Cuba. De-codifying the Chávez regime requires analyzing its theory and practice. The first steps require an understanding of the two key terms Chávez uses to define the ideology of his revolution—"Bolivarianism" and "twenty-first-century socialism."

Bolivarianism

The idolatry and veneration of Simón Bolívar, the greatest liberator of Latin America, plays such an important role in Chávez's regime that the Republic of Venezuela has been renamed the Bolivarian Republic of Venezuela.

Bolívar himself was a man of a few contradictions. On the one hand, he rejected monarchy and supported liberty. Bolívar was a Republican who believed in individual liberties and the ideals of the Enlightenment based on reason and liberty, and as so many revolutionaries of the independence period did, he drew his ideas from the American Revolution. On the other hand, owing to circumstances of the time, Bolívar supported a strong central government. In his day, the wars of independence resulted in civil conflict and anarchy. Likewise, Bolívar sensed that the former colonies had no experience with self-government. He argued that the newly independent colonies were ungovernable; therefore, he supported a central authority capable of exercising a strong and stable government.

The constitution Bolívar wrote for Bolivia in 1826 provided for a strong president with the authority to have a lifelong tenure and the right to name his successor. Thus, instability resulting from frequent elections could be avoided. This idea had influenced most Spanish American constitutions, which provided strong powers to the president in order to resolve crises and to exercise governability.[5]

Bolívar pointed out that because of excessive powers by provincial governments and a lack of centralization, the democratic and federal systems of the new states of Spanish America were inadequate. Thus, in Venezuela of the early nineteenth century, according to Bolívar, "the spirit of party assembly and popular elections led us back into slavery." Bolívar argued that these institutions did not generate the virtues needed that distinguished "our brothers in the North [the United States] . . ." In the words of Bolívar: "We [Venezuelans] are dominated by the vices contracted under the rule of Spain, a nation that has only distinguished itself in ferocity, ambition, vengeance and greed."[6]

Bolívar indeed was very critical of the early democratic institutions of Spanish America as he did not see the culture of the newborn states as suitable for the democratic and federal institutions that existed in North America. Bolivar indeed feared the masses but not strong governments. Quite contrary to Chávez, Bolívar admired the United States and its system of government. He wanted eventually to establish a full democracy but did not think the people of South America were ready yet. He thought, however, that democracy needed a transition period during which a strong government could lead the nation down the right path. In this way, order could be imposed and violence and civil war avoided.[7] Thus, it would be reasonable to assume that this part of Bolívar's thinking serves at least as an excuse for Chávez to expand the power of state authority and to scorn liberal institutions, despite the radical differences in the two men's thoughts.

However, another of Bolívar's ideas—the unification of Spanish America—became key to Chávez's ideology and practice. Bolívar's dream was to create a great (South) American nation. Chávez's foreign policy, which aims at expanding his revolution in the continent, is justified based on Bolívar's concept of Spanish America's unification. Indeed, Bolívar provides the basic rationale for Chávez's international approach, which is analyzed in chapter 3.

Twenty-First-Century Socialism

Another idea that Chávez preaches in his ideology is the socialism of the twenty-first century. Chávez did not address socialism in his preaching in the first phase of his political tenure; rather, in that earlier period, he directed his rhetorical vitriol against the oligarchy that dominated Venezuelan politics before he took the reins of power. In the first phase his purpose was mainly to legitimize a post-oligarchical era. Likewise, the Chávistas, or his followers, emphasized the concept of *pueblo* (the people) to distinguish themselves from the previous regime, which was widely seen as elitist and distant.[8]

In 2005, Chávez announced his theory of twenty-first-century socialism, which he defined as being different from the failed socialism of the Soviet Union and its satellites; instead, he aimed for a system fitting Venezuela's realities and historical experiences. The concept of twenty-first-century socialism was developed by Heinz Dieterich. He advocates for participatory democracy, as the ancient Greeks used to practice it, where a maximum number of people participate in decisions that concern them. But he claims that such a democracy cannot be achieved within the existing economic system. Dieterich proposes, therefore, to replace the current price-based market economy with an economy that values its goods based on the time invested in their production. Income should then be proportional to the amount of work and time invested in creating the product and not on the fluctuation of the market. Applying the principle of time-value instead of relying on the market would require monitoring by the state; thus, Dieterich suggests replacing the market economy with a planned economy.

Dieterich does not support the abolition of private property, however. He advocates for a system where people participate in the decisions that affect their lives personally without delegating them to congressmen or parliamentarians. Modern technology such as the World Wide Web now enables maximum participation. Therefore, Dieterich supports a sort of cyber-democracy that will secure people's maximum participation on issues that concern them.[9]

In practice, Hugo Chávez is not a true follower of twenty-first-century socialism as Dieterich envisioned it.[10] By and large Chávez keeps his concept of it ill defined, and Dieterich's ideas are considerably less important to him than commonly perceived.

By the same token, Chávez does not view the working class as the main subject of the revolution; neither does he follow the guidelines of Marxism-Leninism. For Chávez, the working class and labor unions represent a component of the coalition that the Punto Fijo arrangement sustained, and he tries to discredit and abolish that regime. Chávez therefore fights existing workers' organizations and creates new ones that are loyal to him and his regime.

Thus, I argue that Chávez's ideas of Bolivarianism and twenty-first-century socialism are simply clichés and that these slogans are deceptive and misleading when analyzing the Chávez phenomenon. To understand the complex role that ideology plays in the Chávez regime, we need to turn to the theories of Norberto Ceresole. Even though Ceresole later left Chávez's circles, he remains one of the primary influences on Chávez's political behavior.[11] An understanding of Ceresole's view will help us see how the pieces come together in Chávez's ideological puzzle.

The Influence of Norberto Ceresole

Ceresole was born in Argentina and was part of the Montoneros, a Peronist left-wing guerrilla group that was active during the 1970s. While in exile in Madrid he established connections with the Basque nationalist and separatist guerrilla movement Euskadi Ta Askatasuna (Basque Homeland and Freedom [ETA]) and later became the representative of the Iranian-backed terrorist group Hezbollah in Madrid and a militant neo-Nazi. Upon his return to Argentina, he joined a group of mid-rank army officers known as the Carapintadas (Painted Faces) who led an uprising during the constitutional government of Raúl Alfonsín (1983–1989) and demanded an end to prosecutions carried against fellow military men accused of human rights violations. Ceresole personally advised the leader of the uprising, Lt. Col. Aldo Rico. Ceresole also spent time in the Soviet Union and Iran. He praised the virtues of the Iranian theocracy and suggested that the Latin

American military cooperate closely with Moscow in order to promote revolution. Ceresole staunchly supported the idea that a popular government should be highly authoritarian and sustained by the army. He viewed the military and the use of force as effective instruments of social change.[12] These ideas became a key component of Chávez's theory and practice.

Ceresole saw Chávez's Bolivarian revolutionary model as unique and revolutionary; consequently, he wrote a political philosophy that reflects and justifies Chávez's political actions. For Ceresole, Hugo Chávez exercises power by virtue of the people having delegated authority to him. According to Ceresole this popular power epitomized in the person of Hugo Chávez "is also a mandate to transform the country and relocate Venezuela in the international system." So Chávez, contrary to the model of liberal-parliamentary democracy, represents a direct connection with the people. Although Chávez was elected by democratic means, Ceresole claimed that one should follow a model that goes beyond a democratic government. While Chávez is elected with a mandate from the people, he must establish his power because he is "the people."

Moreover, Ceresole added that this model of power should not follow a dogma, a utopian vision, or even an ideology. In fact, ideas must not play any fundamental role, for the people elected a person. This model also requires the participation of the army, which Ceresole considered to be the backbone and the main support of the government. The army is part of the people and the people are represented in the leader (caudillo). Therefore, the leader can use the army (that belongs to the people) to exercise his power.

In other words, Ceresole proposed a powerful military government aimed at supporting and strengthening the leader. The relationship between the people and the leader should serve to generate power. For power to be effective, it needs to be concentrated in the hands of the leader; distribution of power can only take place from the top down. Likewise, Ceresole believed that the leadership should distribute material resources to ensure that power is kept in the hands of the leader. In Ceresole's own words, "If what is being sought is change, it cannot be applied without (concentrated) power. The more change is needed, the more power is needed."[13]

It's no wonder then that Chávez's philosophy also draws from the model of Arab absolutism. Indeed, Chávez admitted having been influenced also by Libyan dictator Muammar Gadhafi.[14] Chávez read Gadhafi's *Green*

Book in which the late dictator rejects liberal democracy in favor of direct democracy. Thus, Gadhafi "democratizes" by establishing a direct relationship between himself and the people, who are represented through conferences and councils. These bodies were supposed to govern themselves, but in reality Gadhafi's authority tended to control them all.[15] Chávez also created a parallel structure of peoples' councils that were tied to his authority and not really based on a bottom-up democratic system.

Chávez's obsession with the Arab world also fits Ceresole's idea of increasing power through the distribution of resources. Arab dictatorships, such as Gadhafi's Libya, indeed consolidate their absolute power on the basis of the state's monopoly over oil resources. This preoccupation explains why, from the beginning of his tenure in 1999, Chávez expressed his affinity with the secular Saddam Hussein's regime in Iraq. Chávez, in fact, was the first leader to visit Hussein during the Iraqi leader's post–Gulf War isolation.[16] Likewise, he feels the same accord with the theocratic Islamic Republic of Iran, another oil-based totalitarian state with which Chávez has established even deeper relations. Arab petro-dictatorships are major producers of state-controlled oil. Even their most autocratic leaders—including those in Libya, Iraq, Saudi Arabia, and Iran—use oil revenues to exercise control over their societies by buying off important sectors of their populations. In other words, ideally, oil provides the possibility of establishing a "power-based" despotic regime with a degree of legitimacy that is lacking in countries ruled by dictatorships without such resources (for example, Cuba). As it turns out, the largest portion of Venezuela's gross national product comes from oil production, which is in the hands of the state.

Ceresole also predicted that making internal changes requires a foreign policy aimed at protecting these changes. According to him, Latin America should create a network of solidarities across the region that consists of political parties and cultural and business organizations. This system would provide legitimacy to the Venezuelan social transformation. So by expanding the Venezuelan model outward into the region, the revolution would be protected against external enemies. (The implementation of this part of Ceresole's ideology is covered in chapter 3.)

Ceresole's philosophy also focused on confrontation, stressing the need to define a war and a conflict to carry out the will of the leader and bring clarity to the regime. Ceresole spoke about Venezuela as a battlefield between rich and poor. In this scenario, Chávez would represent the Venezuelan poor. Ceresole's philosophy insists on the need to find an enemy as a necessary tool to create an authoritarian rule based on (at least initially) popular support. Thus, continuous attacks on the "oligarchy," the "white hegemony," the United States, the Catholic Church, and others seem to be consistent with Ceresole's philosophy.

Rejecting the United States, in particular, provides an ideal enemy and rallying point not only for Venezuelans but also for citizens of other Latin American countries. The latter would constitute the external group that, as Ceresole had suggested, will expand and protect Chávez's Bolivarian revolution.

▌ THE REVOLUTION'S AVERSION TO THE UNITED STATES

In April 2002, Chávez accused the United States of trying to topple his government and dominate Central and South America. Based on this premise, Chávez's anti-American rhetoric is filled with hatred; it is loud and delirious.

Anti-Americanism is definitely not new in the continent. Initially, writers of the Enlightenment such as José Enrique Rodó, José Martí, and Rubén Darío developed anti-Americanism in Latin America, directing their criticism against American materialism and "anti-spiritualism." Rodó proposed constructing a spiritual culture to counteract the wild materialism of North Americans. Particularly after the Spanish-American War (1898), Darío and Martí considered the United States as a giant and expansionist neighbor that was insensitive to the culture and traditions of Spanish America.[17]

In the 1940s, a conception began to form that gave birth to the so-called dependency theory. According to that view, which was mainly promoted by Secretary-General of the Economic Commission for Latin America Raúl Prebisch, countries of Latin America were forced to produce specific products or raw materials to fulfill the needs of the Western industrialized economic powers. In return, Latin American countries received manufactured goods; thus, they were adversely affected by their trade relationships with the industrialized countries as the price of the manufactured goods they bought was higher than the price of the raw materials they sold.[18] Therefore, in the 1940s, opposition to economic dependency on the

United States and the West led to government-sponsored industrialization to substitute for Western imports.

Andre Gunder Frank, an economic historian who had considerable influence in Latin America, radicalized this approach in a general fatalistic theory of dependency. He stated that Western development and Latin American development are part of one single global process as underdevelopment is generated by the same historical process that generated economic development. Underdeveloped countries in Latin America are therefore prone to remain colonial satellites even if they develop industries, because industry is strictly subject to foreign interests.[19] The Cuban revolution and the influence of its ideas in Latin America in the 1960s exacerbated anti-Americanism even further since it viewed the United States as an imperial power associated with the Latin American economic elites who exploited the workers and the poor. Students, academics, and even the middle class, particularly in the 1960s, found inspiration in dependency theory to explain Latin American backwardness and to justify revolution. Subsequent guerrilla movements inspired by the philosophy of the Cuban-inspired Argentinian revolutionary Ernesto "Che" Guevara adopted anti-Americanism and dependency theory religiously. Many academics in Latin America and abroad embraced dependency theory from economic and social perspectives. Thus, it makes sense that Chávez opted for using dependency theory as a truism and an instrument of propaganda. The development of globalization and the global economy was seen as yet another instance of imperial economic powers exercising influence over the third world.

Likewise, during the 1970s, the United States was perceived, not without justification, as being supportive of the repressive authoritarian military regimes of South and Central America. Chávez later capitalized on that charge and held the United States historically responsible for the unpopular and repressive character of Latin American armies and for separating the army from the people. Chávez blamed the United States for "imposing" neoliberal policies on the continent and for pursuing U.S. interests rather than supporting the well-being of the Latin American people.

The Venezuelan government in the 1990s strongly spoke against neoliberal economic policies promoted by Washington, making its opposition one of the cornerstones of its aggressive policies. Chávez, using dangerous rhetoric, made anti-Americanism an instrument of national and regional mass mobilization. He blamed the Venezuelan oligarchy and previous political elites for Venezuelan troubles but still saw the United States of America as being behind them all. Along the same lines, Chávez has continuously accused the United States of being responsible for the failed coup d'état that tried to depose him in April 2002, while also constantly ranting about American plans to kill him, though he has no actual evidence to support his charges.[20]

Anti-Americanism is more than mere resentment. This rancor becomes policy and serves as an instrument of propaganda in Chávez's hands. Anti-Americanism generates solidarities with other regions of the world that share the same antipathy toward what they understand as "imperialism" in general and the United States in particular. Moreover, the many enemies that Chávez has laid claim to is consistent with Ceresole's idea of increasing one's power by fighting an enemy. Thus, anti-Americanism becomes an ideological instrument of the revolution's external expansion. Likewise, the Bolivarian revolution aims at removing U.S. hegemony from the region. Chávez would not hesitate, as we will see, to take steps to reduce the power of the United States despite the latter being the main buyer of Venezuela's oil.

In the end, what Chávez and his movement are against matters much more than what they are for. Chávez will act in a more predictable manner against his enemies than he will do so in implementing a detailed social program or a constitution. Thus, evaluating Chávez on the social programs he presents is deceptive. Chávez indeed has intended to install a new type of regime directed from above, abolishing traditional democratic institutions and replacing it with himself as the main axis of government. He also has attempted to export this type of regime to other countries by any possible means and in order to establish continental domination.

| CHÁVEZ IN ACTION

Shortly after becoming president of Venezuela early in 1999, Chávez moved to establish the basis for his regime. He convened a National Constituent Assembly to write a new constitution. Next, the government held a special election aimed at choosing delegates for the assembly, and 93 percent of the seats went to Chávez's delegates.

Immediately afterward, the Venezuelan Supreme Court, under pressure from Chávez, enabled the constituent assembly to declare a "judicial emergency" and evaluate all existing judges. Following this action, Chávez used the constituent assembly to declare a "state of emergency" and began uprooting the old political institutions of the Venezuelan state, mostly by forbidding the elected national Congress from meeting. In December 1999 a new constitution was approved by general referendum, with a turnout of 45 percent and with the approval of 72 percent of those voting.[21]

Although the constitution itself includes many points that any liberal-democratic constitution has, like basic rights to life, property, and other freedoms, it provides the state and the executive branch with considerable more power than any liberal constitution.

The Venezuelan state is defined in article 2 of the constitution as a "democratic and social rule of law and justice that holds life, liberty, justice, equality, solidarity . . . [and] social responsibility . . . as supreme values of its legal system." This automatically provides competing elements to the preservation of rights and liberties. No other modern constitution holds the principle of solidarity or social responsibility as a supreme value.

Solidarity usually emerges in groups of civil society in a rather spontaneous way and often is organized. But solidarity is not usually promoted by the state or embedded in a constitution. If solidarity is a constitutional duty, it can only be promoted from above. This automatically confers power to state prerogatives. As we shall see later, this principle enables the creation of communal councils that, under the veil of communal solidarity and mutual help, become instruments of the state and are also promoted by the state.

The same applies to social responsibility. Here the constitution opens the way for state social policies or even state socialism, which is usually a matter of policy and public debate, not a constitutional issue.

By the same token, article 3 of the constitution generally defines as "essential goals of the state, the protection and the development of the individual and respect for its dignity, the democratic implementation of the popular will and the building of a just society."

Again, this article is highly problematic because state duties such as the "development of the individual" or "building a just society" provides a vague definition that only the state can take advantage of in a rather arbitrary form. Such a notion of "development of the individual" opens the gate to totalitarian elements in government. As we shall see later, this is precisely what Chávez does. He violates rights, even those guaranteed in the constitution, in the name of state goals such as socialism or social justice.

The constitution also extended the presidential term from five to six years and allowed the president to stand for reelection once. It eliminated the bicameral parliamentary regime by scrapping the Senate and creating the one-chamber National Assembly. By the same token, the constitution increased the power of the executive branch. The president could dissolve the National Assembly (Congress) after three votes of non-confidence by two thirds of the assembly.

According to the constitution, the state "will promote private initiative," but it will also guarantee "the creation and fair distribution of wealth and the production of goods and services aimed at meeting the needs of the population, freedom of employment, initiative, commerce and industry. However, [those freedoms] shall not prevent the state from planning, rationalize and regulate the economy and promote the development of the country." This formulation provides undefined powers to the state and opens a legal door for unchecked state prerogatives, which Chávez will later take full advantage of.

The constitution also changed the role of the military, making it an active part of the "national development" of the country, not merely a guardian national security (Articles 328–331). According to Article 236.6, the president also has the power to "promote army officers from the rank of colonel or navy captain and up or appoint them to certain functions."[22] This opened the door for greater control of the composition of the armed forces. Chávez later took full advantage of these powers by purging and promoting officers based on political loyalty.

In political and real terms, a new stage was set in Venezuela that marked the increasing power of the state and executive branch over political parties and civil society. Representative democracy weakened as the executive power began to take an active role in controlling the legislative and judicial powers.

A populist and direct connection between the president and the public was established through hours-long speeches and TV programs featuring Hugo Chávez; this TV interaction became more important than parliamentary and public debate. Chávez also talked about the need to refound Venezuela in order to impose social justice.[23] He focused on the Venezuelan oil company, Petróleos de Venezuela SA (PDVSA), which is a major source of national revenue. In spite of being a public company, the PDVSA was a role model of professionalism and management; however, the government viewed PDVSA as being tied to the old regime. Chávez replaced the PDVSA management with individuals loyal to him and his revolution.

As a result of these changes in the PDVSA, the military briefly deposed and arrested Chávez in a coup d'état on April 11, 2002. The coup occurred after two military officers led a rally of protest against the government, and the Confederation of Venezuelan Workers (Confederación de Trabajadores de Venezuela), the country's largest labor union federation, and Fedecameras—the main business association and leading opponent of Chávez—called a two-day strike. A million people marched to the headquarters of Venezuela's oil company in defense of its fired management. The organizers decided to reroute the march to the president's office building and confronted about five thousand pro-government demonstrators. Nineteen people were killed and more than a hundred wounded that day.

The new elite that took the reins of power, led by businessman Pedro Carmona, showed signs of authoritarianism as it dissolved the Venezuelan National Assembly and the Supreme Court and declared the constitution void. Meanwhile, Chávez loyalists organized countermarches and mobilized their people and succeeded to consolidate popular support against the new rulers.[24] At the same time, a countercoup was organized by two generals, Raúl Baduel and Efraín Vásquez Velasco (then the commander of the army).[25]

In the end, Chávez was restored to power primarily because the disjointed opposition did not coordinate its efforts. The new rulers lost support from the military (who initially supported Carmona, including Gen. Vasquez Velasco himself) that eventually forced Carmona's resignation and restored Chávez to power. According to author Brian Nelson, since that coup Chávez seemed "to have only embraced violence and the threat of violence as an effective political tool."[26]

Eight months later, the Chávez government faced a civil strike led by the oil industry's management. Consequently, Chávez stopped daily exports of nearly three million barrels of oil and derivatives and began to import gasoline for internal use. He combated the oil strike by firing about eighteen thousand PDVSA employees. Chávez stubbornly resisted the strike until finally the opposition decided to end it. The attempted coup d'état and the long strike did not make Chávez reconsider his position or the opposition's arguments. In fact, Chávez took a tougher stance precisely as a result of the increasing opposition.

Since January 2003, the government has halted foreign exchange sales and imposed import controls. The business sector's only choice is to buy American dollars on the black market or entirely close down. Clearly, this policy was aimed at destroying the private sector. Indeed, the economy shrank and inflation increased. Many companies and factories closed down, and many businessmen and professionals left the country. Still, elements in the private sector paradoxically became wealthier while the state became a monopoly and the most powerful buyer, thus replacing the market. As a result of increasing government control, people who benefited from their connections with government itself created the Boliburguesía, or a new class of bourgeoisie, whose emergence was not the result of economic initiative or productivity but of ties to the state.[27]

Chávez also instilled general fear in Venezuelan society. The government created groups called Bolivarian Circles that were established as neighborhood-based groups to promote values and community programs, but they in fact became paramilitary forces loyal to the government. Their activities allegedly include blackmailing merchants and businessmen, drug trafficking, kidnapping, and other activities aimed to produce a sense of chaos, which leads to instability and often violence. They are also involved in the expropriation of private property and other social projects that Chávez has promoted.[28] During the coup d'état attempt against Chávez they attacked marchers and protesters.[29] In other words, the Bolivarian Circles play a role similar to that of the "Society of December 10," an organized group of Louis Bonaparte's supporters in mid-nineteenth-century France. As Karl Marx described them:

> On the pretext of founding a benevolent society, the *lumpenproletariat* of Paris had been organized into secret sections, each section being led by Bonapartist agents, with a Bonapartist general at the head of the whole. Alongside decayed *roués* with dubious means of subsistence and of dubious origin . . . [were] for Bonaparte, the party fighting force peculiar to him . . . had to improvise a public for him, . . . insult and thrash republicans, of course, under the protection of the police.[30]

Likewise, the Bolivarian Circles also function to spread the fight for Chávez.

Following the same logic, Chávez accused the media of fomenting a coup and waging psychological warfare against the government. The government investigated the major television networks for alleged violations of broadcasting regulations while covering the anti-Chávez strike. In 2004 Chávez promoted a bill called the Law on Social Responsibility of Radio and Television that imposed stringent and detailed controls over radio and television broadcasts, greatly limiting what could be aired during normal viewing hours. The logic behind the bill was to increase control over the media. Threats to and harassment of journalists by the president's supporters ensued.

Early in 2003, a large number of Venezuelan citizens challenged Chávez and collected enough signatures to conduct a recall referendum. The referendum mechanism derives from a provision in Venezuela's 1999 constitution that states if voters can gather signatures from 20 percent of the registered voters, they may ask for a recall vote on an elected officeholder midway through his or her term. According to the law, if more people voted for the recall of Chávez than voted for him as president in the 2000 election, a fresh presidential election was supposed to follow in thirty days. The necessary signatures for the recall referendum were already collected in February 2003. Chávez rejected the idea of the referendum in spite of its constitutionality.

Chávez tried to block the referendum, manipulating and intimidating those who signed the petitions. He also threatened to use military force to defend his government. On two occasions, his government invalidated the signatures collected, and on another occasion he tried to prevent the opposition from delivering the petitions by closing the country's airports. Next, Chávez tried to change the composition of the Supreme Court and make it loyal to his rule. In May 2004, an agreement to conduct a recall referendum was reached between President Chávez and the opposition after long months of opposition activities, general strikes, and the mediation efforts of César Gaviria, the secretary of the Organization of American States (OAS), and former U.S. president Jimmy Carter.[31]

Finally, after much violence that resulted in a few deaths, the recall referendum took place in August 2004 and led to a victory for Hugo Chávez. The recall referendum that Chávez had resisted for more than a year turned into one of his most effective instruments for claiming popular legitimacy. He was transformed from being an embattled president, whose legitimacy had deteriorated meteorically, into an aggressively authoritarian one. His victory in the recall referendum was the result of a huge amount of money, with Chávez distributing close to 4 percent of the gross domestic product among the people through different means.[32] That largesse enabled his victory, which, in turn, allowed him to accelerate down the path to authoritarianism.

After the election, he moved to deepen his revolution, an action that he repeated after every election. Chávez spoke about creating a "new type of man." This new man, he said, should be a fearless man who acquires a new consciousness in the image of the revolution. According to his view, the government's task is to spread values, ethics, and Bolivarian ideology. Chávez spoke about the need for military discipline to foster obedience and the importance of using the entire educational system—elementary, middle, and high schools and universities—as a means to broaden the values of social equality.[33]

In 2005 the government approved a "reform" of the criminal code that further restricted the media. For one, slandering the president became punishable by six to thirty months in prison. Likewise, insulting state representatives other than the president would also be punished with the terms depending on the rank of the person offended. Moreover, disseminating inaccurate news and defaming a person by means of print media, radio, telephone, or e-mail with the aim of "causing panic" would also incur prison sentences.[34] This new code aimed at maintaining the supremacy of the state-controlled media over competing voices.

In economic and social terms, this new stage in Chávez's revolution promised to eliminate the ownership of large land holdings (*latifundio*) and to identify unused land and elaborate a plan to make it productive. This move basically meant to expropriate private property. A government order sorted out the expropriation and immediate occupation of vacant buildings and houses in Caracas and followed by taking over a chain of private companies. According to Chávez, "Large ownership is like robbing a car even if the property was (legitimately) purchased."[35] Chávez also told a group of Venezuelan businessmen, "To be rich is bad." Taking possession of land and nationalizing companies have become the order of the day and continue to take place in a rather arbitrary way. The government has also called Fedecameras parasitic and an instrument of colonial capitalism.[36] The furious and systematic expropriation process has included hypermarkets, oil contractors, mining, transportation companies, and a myriad others. Thus, a reasonable assumption is that the overwhelming majority of companies in the private sector will not escape expropriation.

This process was also facilitated when the weakened opposition became dispirited after losing the referendum and, overwhelmingly later that year, the municipal and local elections. Then the government proceeded to take control of the Supreme Court, appointing a dozen new judges loyal to the Bolivarian revolution.[37]

As Chávez continued to take control over resources and win elections, his absolutism began to advance quickly. Indeed, he used his control of the PDVSA and other state companies to intimidate employees into voting for him. The opposition has also been gradually displaced. In the parliamentary elections of 2005, opposition parties did not even present candidates, paradoxically allowing Chávez virtually to take over the legislative branch. After his victory in the presidential elections of 2006, the assembly passed an enabling law that provided powers to the executive branch for an eighteen-month period.

The enabling law is a measure permitted by the Venezuelan Constitution on article 236.8 that concedes powers (provided previous authorization by legislative branch) to the executive branch for a determined period of time to approve decrees. In the Venezuelan case, that was not a problem to pass given the overwhelming majority Chávez enjoyed in the National Assembly. In 2007, the Chávez-dominated National Assembly approved a constitutional reform aimed at strengthening the president's power. This reform included the right of the president to run for reelection indefinitely, the right of the state to expropriate assets without judicial approval, a constitutional status to the communal councils and other extra-parliamentary bodies created by Chávez, and the president's takeover of the central bank. The referendum on the reforms took place in December 2007 and was defeated. Chávez tried again in February 2009, only three months after other municipal elections in Venezuela struck another defeat for Chávez. This time, however, Chávez won the referendum, which eliminated term limits and allowed him to run indefinitely for reelection.

The repeated votes and referendums to which the Venezuelan population was subjected have often been misinterpreted as acts of democracy. In reality, these votes were nothing but mechanisms through which the executive power gained an absolute mandate. Each election was character-ized by the government's inappropriate use of state resources, mainly oil revenue, and consequent distribution of goods.

In addition, throughout Latin America, including in Venezuela, 40 percent of the electoral processes in which the incumbent or the incum-bent's party was victorious were flawed in comparison to 15 percent of the processes in which incumbents were defeated. Moreover, the most prob-lematic cases are those in which the president sought reelection and won. In these cases, 71 percent involved flawed or failed electoral processes.[38]

Chávez's aggressiveness toward those who oppose or criticize him has succeeded in causing panic, particularly after the 2002 failed anti-Chávez coup and the 2004 recall referendum. Fear of losing one's job, persecution, and retaliation and other types of intimidation have surely impacted the results of those elections. More than anything, the government's use of public money to provide jobs or welfare and its ability to co-opt key people have enabled Chávez to hold power.

Before the presidential elections of 2006, Professor Genaro Mosquera, director of statistical research at the prestigious Universidad Central de Venezuela, pointed out that 1.3 million registered voters did not list ad-dresses, which is a requirement for voting registration. The National Elec-toral Council (Consejo Nacional Electral [CNE]) did not provide any answer to that mystery. Mosquera also reported that a high number of people on the rolls were very old and, according to the laws of nature, should have been deceased.[39]

Likewise, Chávez resorted to the practice of disqualifying candidates for office. During the 2008 local elections, more than three hundred candi-dates were deemed ineligible for office based mostly on charges that could not be proven. Such efforts to ban candidates were carried out with the complicity of the CNE and the Supreme Court, two bodies that the execu-tive power clearly controls. In the September 2010 parliamentary elections, Chávez supporters received a lower percentage of the votes than the oppo-sition did yet redistricting policies carried out shortly before the elections enabled pro-Chávez candidates to hold more seats than they deserved based on the principle of proportional representation. None of these factors re-flects the existence of a democratic state in Venezuela. Instead, they show that Chávez has used democracy as a tool to establish authoritarian rule and to expand executive prerogatives. With this observation in mind, the type of regime that Chávez has pursued needs to be carefully considered.

Many have called Chávez a neo-populist. This term refers to a sort of resurrection of the Latin American populism of the last century as practiced by such leaders as Juan Perón in Argentina and Getúlio Vargas in Brazil.[40] Populist regimes have historically been characterized by their mobilization of marginal masses. Taking an antiestablishment, anti-oligarchic approach, a charismatic leader would claim to represent the excluded sectors and establish a direct, even authoritarian relationship with the masses. Likewise, the legislature, the judiciary, and other branches of government and civil society would be subordinated to the will of the leader and his executive authority. Furthermore, the leader would redistribute monies from the state coffers among the poor to secure support and legitimacy for the regime. Often, populist regimes would establish coalitions between different sectors of society such as the workers and national industry. A social and economic policy would be established to support national industry and redistribute resources even though the ultimate authority would remain always in the leader's hands.

The Chávez regime has also been rightly referred to as an illiberal democracy—that is, a regime that mixes authoritarianism and elections. This type of regime uses the tools of democracy to take power and then rules in authoritarian ways. Post–Cold War Russia and the Central Asian republics are cases in point. In Russia, the president is elected democratically but concentrates colossal powers in his hands while harassing the press and the opposition.[41]

Undoubtedly, the Chávez regime indeed can be defined as having elements of both populism and an illiberal democracy; however, Chávez's rule exceeds that description. I would argue that his regime also embraces elements of totalitarianism that are important to stress.

▎TOTALITARIAN ELEMENTS IN VENEZUELA

There are many definitions of totalitarianism. A typical, consolidated totalitarian regime is a system of government where, in the words of former U.S. national security adviser Zbigniew Brzezinski, "instruments of political power are wielded without restraint by centralized leadership . . . for the purpose of affecting a social revolution, including the conditioning of man on the basis of certain arbitrary ideological assumptions . . . in an atmosphere of coerced unanimity of the entire population."[42]

I would argue, however, that Venezuela is not currently in this situation, because even though Chávez has managed to take control of many spaces in society, he has not yet succeeded in enforcing such a typical regime as those found in the former Soviet Union or Nazi Germany or the present-day Islamic Republic of Iran. Indeed, elections still take place in Venezuela even though they are not fair. Further, despite his suppression of the media and dissent, the number of political prisoners is not yet massive. According to the 2010 U.S. State Department's Human Rights Report, the regime held twenty-five political prisoners.[43]

However, the government does engage in the intimidation of political opponents and human rights defenders. Likewise, it has criminalized and persecuted peaceful social protests. Human rights non-governmental organizations working in Venezuela have reported 237 deaths as a result of security force actions from October 2009 through September 2010. More than 350 people were degraded or tortured in the same time period. In addition, more than 460 public officials were involved in extrajudicial killings in 2009, but the perpetrators received light punishments or were released after they appealed their cases.[44]

Moreover, despite the existence of a formal system of democracy, the Bolivarian regime has a number of other attributes that can be identified with totalitarian tendencies and intentions.

Indoctrination

Hugo Chávez began his ideological preaching early in his tenure, but he presented it in 2007 as a road map for his revolution. Chávez has created a new socialist ethos, which constitutes a set of "new ethical principles based on social justice, equity, and solidarity." To create a new regime, a radical "'new man' who embraces a revolutionary ethical spirit must be created."[45]

Building a "new man" through education and reorientation is an important stage in developing a totalitarian society. In fact, in August 2009, the Chávez-controlled Venezuelan parliament proceeded to reform the education system and adopted a new law that makes Bolivarian doctrine the basis of education at all levels, a move that educators view as requiring them to indoctrinate students with the views of the ruling party. The law has also taken away the universities' autonomy and has transferred admissions decisions to the government. As a result, demonstrations took place in which thousands of people, including university rectors, educators, and parents, participated. The police severely suppressed them.[46] Such a transformation of the educational system is clearly a totalitarian step since the state aims at having full control of the minds of the people by removing the possibility of free, independent, intellectual development.

Suppression of Civil Society and Its Institutions

As pointed out earlier in the chapter, the Chávez regime began to weaken private property ownership years ago, and the effort continues to evolve with great intensity. Communal councils were created at the request of the government, which urged the National Assembly to pass the law in 2006. According to that law, the communal councils facilitate "participation, integration and articulation among different communitarian organizations, social groups and citizens in order to allow the people to directly manage public policies and projects aimed at addressing the needs and aspirations of the community and help them build a society based on equality and social justice."

These communal councils, under the facade of representing autonomous forms of a people's organization, ultimately tie back to the central government. Thus, they become effective means of government empowerment rather than instruments of popular strength. Likewise, the establishment of the *misiones* (missions) represents another important dimension. Organized by the Chávez government, the misiones are social programs aimed at providing free primary health care and educational, employment, and literacy programs for the poor.[48] The misiones, which are usually accompanied by Cuban experts, are carried from the top-down, with government political and economic support and serve only to increase the dependency of individuals on state power and support.

Thus, socialism in Venezuela is simply a means to achieve full state control over society. Socialism, contrary to the traditional Marxian concept, is not based on the working class as an agent of change and social revolutionary transformation. The agent of change rests with the power of the state. The target of legitimacy for a state with such absolute powers is the people but only in the vaguest and most abstract sense of the word.

The concept of "the people" does not represent anybody in particular to whom the government feels accountable. The Bolivarian state does not have an attachment or commitment to any constituency, party, social movement, set of issues, or even the working class. Instead, the Bolivarian state wants to rule in a most arbitrary manner and have its prerogatives above those of any civil group. As such, the suppression of workers' organizations and unions makes sense in Bolivarian socialism. The Chávez regime relates to the masses only because the masses empower the state.

Thus, in classic populist regimes, private property did not come under attack in the same way that it does under Chávez. Populist regimes such as Perón's rule in Argentina and Vargas's in Brazil either included the national bourgeoisie in the populist coalition or established a state of compromise between the sectors. But in the Bolivarian regime, Chávez has established the weakening of private property ownership as a goal. Private property, which belongs to the individual or a body in society that is not the state, represents the ultimate bastion of individual and societal power and freedom. Authoritarian regimes that abolished civil or political liberties but allowed private property to survive never exercised full control of their societies because what belongs to individuals represents their independent power outside the state.

With regard to labor unions, under classic populist states, they were often co-opted and their leadership manipulated and intimidated. However, despite the authoritarian nature of populist regimes, labor unions have proliferated under these regimes and have seen their membership increase. Likewise, it never really fully eliminated the unions' autonomy. In general, different sectors and groups still exercised some influence in government even though the populist state remained an authoritarian state.[49] Under Chávez, however, labor unions are viewed as bodies associated with the old regime. They are perceived as political enemies that need to be eliminated. Thus, Chávez has taken numerous measures to suppress the autonomy of the working classes and even their basic right to organize. Although Venezuela is a member state, it goes against the basic rules established by International Labor Organization on this issue.

Chávez has systematically interfered in union elections and has refused to bargain collectively with already established unions. He instead has supported only pro-government unions and has created new unions to secure their loyalty to the government above workers' interests. Chávez has impeded their elections by passing laws mandating that a state institution must certify a union election. That requirement has enabled the government to veto unions that it feared were opposed to the government. Likewise, the laws reject unions that were not certified to bargain collectively, and as a result, the state has full prerogatives over unions.

The government negotiated with unions loyal to the government while making established unions wait for certification from the Chávez-controlled CNE. Likewise, the Chávez government has required that unions present different leaders and candidates in every election, most likely in order to weaken the union leaders. Following the same logic, Chávez has promoted local workers' councils and cooperatives but without the protections that labor organizations usually have.

As pointed out earlier, the Chávez government has also violated workers' rights by firing workers en masse for political reasons, mainly in response to the oil strike that took place in 2002 and early 2003. In that instance, personnel changes included the dismissal of the PDVSA's president and the replacement of its board of directors. After the strike was over, the government fired nearly half of the oil industry workforce. Chávez also ordered private oil companies not to hire the dismissed workers.[50] Because Chávez controls the judiciary, the legal system was not able to protect workers' rights effectively in light of these violations. Indeed, the Supreme Court went along with the government policy of exerting control over the unions.

The policy of state control over unions has extended beyond the oil sector and mainly to those of medical workers who protested the presence of uncertified Cuban doctors in their hospitals. Of course, other sectors have also suffered. Chávez has constantly accused unions of conspiring against his government and of serving the interests of the United States.

Intimidation and Control of the Citizenry

Regarding individual rights, the situation is even more difficult. A good example is the government's blacklisting of people based on suspicion of their being against Chávez. After the contentious August 2004 recall referendum that challenged the continuation of Chávez's presidency, the government began its process of systematic blacklisting. President Chávez authorized National Assemblyman Luis Tascón to obtain copies of the lists of those people who had signed the petition for the recall referendum and posted them on a website. The government used these lists to fire workers and block job applications.

Furthermore, in 2005 Chávez ordered the creation of a new database called the Maisanta program. That program contained detailed information on all registered voters, totaling more than twelve million citizens. The program informed the user if the registered voter had signed the recall referendum against Chávez, abstained from voting in elections, participated in the government's missions, or signed a counter-petition for a recall referendum against opposition legislators.[51] This list enabled the government to broaden the number of people it targeted by firing them or denying them a job or reneging on their contracts.[52] The government also denied them passports and benefits.[53]

The Rule of Law Replaced by Arbitrary Law

Meanwhile, Chávez's government passed laws that make insulting the president punishable by six to thirty months in prison without bail. Likewise, comments exposing another person to public contempt or hatred are punishable by one- to three-year prison sentences and inaccurate reporting that disturbs the public peace is punishable by a two- to five-year prison term.

These laws have been used to accuse private media owners, directors, and reporters of fomenting antigovernment subversion. An example is the case of Guillermo Zuloaga, president of a private TV network called Globovisión, known for being critical of the Chávez government. Vehicles parked at his residence were confiscated, and he was later accused of stealing those vehicles. Zuloaga was charged with usury, and thereafter, Chávez announced his intention to take control of Globovisión because it is a vocal opponent. Likewise, Chávez took control of Banco Federal, a private bank that a member of the television network's board of directors also owned.[54] Other private networks, such as Venevisión, Radio Caracas Televisión (RCTV), and Televen, faced sanctions because they were accused of backing the 2002 coup.

Accusations against those who do not follow Chávez's will are common. A good example is the case of Eligio Cedeño, a banker accused of corruption in 2003, detained in 2007, and thereafter conditionally released. A court ordered a retrial and reinstated the detention order, but the appeals court for Caracas ordered Cedeño's release in October 2009 because his detention had exceeded a two-year limit. Judge Maria Lourdes Afiuni granted his conditional release pending trial. Shortly afterward, intelligence officers arrested the judge on charges of corruption, aiding an evasion of justice, abuse of authority, and conspiracy. President Chávez made a personal call to send Afiuni to prison for a period of thirty-five years. Judge Afiuni was arrested in December 2009 and in February 2010 was granted house arrest. No trial was set for her until November 2012 (and later postponed).[55] She also denounced that she was raped and had an abortion while being in prison.[56] Meanwhile, the Bolivarian Intelligence Service issued a fugitive arrest warrant against Cedeño.[57] Cedeño later fled the country.

Here is another characteristic typical of totalitarian regimes: no real distinction exists between the government's capricious, arbitrary will and the law.[58] Under Chávez, valid law does not emanate from the written law itself or from a court's interpretation of what the law is. Instead, in the Chávista state, the valid law is based on "common sense" as dictated from above and not on that of free individuals. This position, where the state has total control, is identical with totalitarian states where there is "no distinction between law and ethics," or between the law and expected behavior.

Regardless of the absurdity and unlawfulness of such behavior, the behavior resulted from the multiple messages that the state sent to the individuals. It expects a certain behavior, and one's lack of compliance can lead to punishment even if the desired behavior is not written into law. Indeed, Judge Afiuni ruled in Cedeño's case following the rules and laws of the Venezuelan normative state. She used the logic of traditional Venezuelan law, but Chávez imprisoned her because she did not apply the "common sense" of the Bolivarian revolution in making her decision. According to the Bolivarian-Chávista logic, Judge Afiuni was expected to send Cedeño to prison because that action was Chávez's implicit will. That Afiuni "should have known" his wishes is a completely totalitarian attitude.

The government also has persecuted or undermined the political opposition. In the municipal and local elections of November 2008, the opposition made some important gains, including in the state of Miranda and the city of Caracas. Chávez reacted by moving some key social services, such as health care, from the jurisdiction of Miranda to the federal government and placed mobs in Caracas's city hall, undermining the work of the newly elected mayor, Alfredo Ledezma. Likewise, Manuel Rosales, one of the major opposition leaders, was forced into exile in Peru. Moreover, parliamentary elections took place in September 2010 that resulted in a victory for opposition candidates despite Chávez's multiple attempts to win these elections via (illegal) redistricting and other means. In December 2010, a few weeks before a new legislature was to begin in January 2011 with a bigger opposition presence, a new set of laws was approved that included penalties for spreading political dissent and granted executive prerogatives to President Chávez for eighteen months.[59] That move was clearly aimed at eliminating the earned power of the opposition and at strengthening his revolution by removing parliamentary obstacles.

Such mockery of the law indicates the totalitarian will of the regime. In other words, the leader's will supersedes any constitutional right or even natural law. The judiciary has to obey the executive's will; otherwise, it will be prosecuted. The merits of the case do not matter and do not need justification. The previous examples are merely part of a pattern that is not likely to change. Chávez is stubborn and inexorable as a typical totalitarian tyrant.

Moreover, Chávez does not respect even those laws that his own party has written and inspired, including the 1999 constitution. To cite a few examples, the 1999 constitution states that "the State shall guarantee to every individual, in accordance with the progressive principle and without discrimination of any kind, not renounceable, indivisible and interdependent enjoyment and exercise of human rights. Respect for and the guaranteeing of these rights is obligatory for the organs of Public Power, in accordance with the Constitution, the human rights treaties signed and ratified by the Republic and any laws developing the same."[60] In another passage, the constitution reads, "Everyone has the right to be protected by the courts in the enjoyment and exercise of constitutional rights and guarantees, including even those inherent individual rights not expressly mentioned in this Constitution or in international instruments concerning human rights."[61]

Similarly, the constitution points out, "The State is obliged to investigate and legally punish offenses against human rights committed by its authorities. Actions to punish the offense of violating humanity rights, serious violations of human rights and war crimes shall not be subject to statute of limitation. Human rights violations and the offense of violating humanity rights shall be investigated and adjudicated by the courts of ordinary competence."[62]

However, as noted previously, Chávez has scorned his own constitution by treacherously violating it. Analyzing the 1936 constitution of the Soviet Union, the political thinker and author of *The Origins of Totalitarianism*, Hannah Arendt, made the following observation: "Yet the publication of the constitution turned out to be the beginning of the gigantic super-purge which in nearly two years liquidated the existing administration and erased all traces of normal life. . . . From then on, the constitution of 1936 played exactly the same role the Weimar constitution played under the Nazi regime: it was completely disregarded but never abolished."[63]

This quotation pertains to the Bolivarian revolution in so far as Chávez maintains the constitution to cloak his regime in legitimacy but ignores it when it suits his purposes.

Control of the Military

Totalitarian regimes tend to exercise full political control of the military. This fact needs to be distinguished from legal civilian control over the military. In the former, the regime would use the military for political-revolutionary purposes.

Shortly after being elected, Chávez pointed out that if a peaceful attempt to carry out a revolution fails, an armed revolution would be the most natural alternative.[64] Indeed, the process of increasing the executive power's authority over the military began early in Chávez's tenure, as he made important moves to take command of the military. Chávez, following Ceresole's teaching, sees the military as the backbone of his social and political revolution. Consequently, he has been trying to subordinate the army to a dictatorial-revolutionary process.[65] Chávez promotes or dismisses army officers based on their loyalty to his regime. Purges in the armed forces became very severe after the attempted coup d'état on April 11, 2002.

Viewing the military as the spine of his revolution, Chávez has used it to promote his political agenda and thus secure the principal means of coercion in his hands. His military reforms were mainly focused on three aspects: loosening restrictions on the military's involvement in political activities, expanding the military's role in social and economic activities, and removing legislative authority over military promotions.[66] The move was aimed not only at promoting his political agenda but also at obtaining the loyalty of the military to both his government and his revolution. The military appreciated its new roles in the administration and in social welfare programs, including the missions.

As members of the military were involved in policymaking, they welcomed their new roles as political actors.[67] Likewise, those who were not seen as loyal to Chávez or who were critical of the president were either retired or marginalized. Discontent among those marginalized military members was one cause of the failed coup d'état against Chávez. Another reason was that the military was ordered to fire on civilians, an order that proved unacceptable to a military that had been educated in a constitutional democracy for decades.

Those members of the military who supported the coup, however, did not have any backing in other sectors of the military. The rebellious individuals did not control enough troops, thus proving that Chávez's policy of privileging military officers with roles in society—specifically in administrative and public policy positions—broke loyalties within the military. While mainly senior officers supported the coup d'état,[68] the coup was aborted thanks to those military men who did not follow the rebels. It was rejected not only by supporters of Chávez but also by supporters of constitutionalism, particularly after the new president made what they considered to be a number of unconstitutional moves such as dissolving the National Assembly.

The attempted coup d'état against Chávez clearly demonstrated, however, that his revolution could not count on military support the way he had expected. He began to view the idea of the military's complete loyalty to him more skeptically. Of course, he had taken such measures as purges, co-optation, and others to secure the men's loyalty, but Chávez never again fully believed in it.

Chávez continues to dismiss officials whom he accuses of disloyalty. In 2007, he dismissed Gen. Raúl Baduel as minister of defense. Baduel had previously been the commander of the army and before that the main military figure who saved the Chávez presidency during the April 2002 attempted coup d'état. Baduel had turned increasingly critical of Chávez's methods, and after his dismissal, he became one of the most vocal opponents of the December 2007 referendum on Chávez's indefinite reelection. Likewise, Baduel publicly pointed out that Chávez did not enjoy wide support in the military. For his actions, General Baduel was convicted on dubious charges and sentenced to eight years in jail. In 2008, Chávez expelled eight hundred military officers, including high-ranking officers, from the army on suspicion of disloyalty. Many resented Chávez's closeness to FARC, the nepotism and preferential treatment of certain officers over others, and Chávez's micromanagement of the armed forces.[69]

More important, Chávez has established an informal reserve army of popular militias that is not subordinate to the regular armed forces but is under the president's direct command. Interestingly enough, this duplication of army forces takes place in (totalitarian) countries where the political leadership does not control the army. Where the political leadership has such authority over the army, no violent paramilitary groups are likely to emerge.[70] Chávez seems to suspect that he may have further difficulties in controlling the military despite his actions aimed at keeping their loyalty.

Indeed, in October 2009, the National Assembly approved a new law concerning the military that formalizes the army's duplication. Per this legislation, the executive branch appoints military chiefs to administer Venezuelan territory, which is subdivided into six regions whose authority basically sets aside the existing political divisions. The military officers' authority would encompass the exercise of public order, defense, and regional and economic development.[71] This law basically institutes a militarization of civic and political life. The army's new function is to help duplicate purely civilian functions. The government had two reasons for pursuing this effort: first to make the military part of the revolutionary spirit and second to help destroy the jurisdiction and authority of the old Venezuelan state while remolding the Venezuelan state.

Even more important, the same legislation establishes that the Venezuelan National Armed Forces (Fuerzas Armadas Nacionales [FAN]) would comprise the Supreme Command, the Operational Strategic Command, the regular military components, and a Bolivarian National Militia. According to the document, the militia's main function "is to complement the work of the armed forces in the defense of the nation and the military regions."[72]

Interestingly, other units of the FAN include assisting the Bolivarian militia among their responsibilities, but the militia itself depends directly on the executive branch. Its role is "to establish links with the FAN and with the Venezuelan people to guarantee the defense of the nation," to organize and train the regional militia, to coordinate and support the communal councils in order to implement public polices, and to "publicize and distribute information regarding public policies established by the communal councils." According to this new law, the Bolivarian militia will also be in charge of mobilizing people in case of a state of emergency.[73]

As such, the Bolivarian militia is aimed at creating loyalty not to the army and the laws of the state but to the political regime. What is worrisome is that this force is not a typical military force with all of the rules that the profession typically requires. Indeed, these militias are manned by "citizens who work in public or private institutions. They are trained on a voluntary basis and organized by the General Command of the Militia."[74] In other words, it is a parallel military force that can recruit from the people, whether they are Venezuelans or foreigners.[75]

This development has created discontent among the armed forces. In January 2010, Venezuelan defense minister Ramón Carrizales (who previously served as vice president) resigned from his post. It was then widely believed that his resignation was over the presence of Cuban officers in the Venezuelan armed forces even though Carrizales never confirmed this report.

Moreover, a former brigadier general who had served as an aide to Hugo Chávez and retired in 2009 expressed his resentment over the authority given to Cubans in the Venezuelan army. Likewise, he complained that Cuban advisers pursued Cuban interests and not Venezuelan national interests. He also expressed concern over the question of Venezuelan sovereignty.[76]

This last point could have serious consequences and will be addressed in later chapters. Such a situation, for instance, may lead the way to incorporating foreign elements—Cubans, Iranians, guerrilla groups like the Colombian FARC, or Islamic terrorists such as Hezbollah or others—into the Bolivarian National Militia. (See chapter 6.)

| SUMMARY

The decline of private property ownership; the violation of individual rights; the intimidation of the citizenry and the media; the elimination of organized civil society groups; the use of executive prerogatives to weaken parliamentary institutions, the judiciary, and the political opposition; the eradication of the written law and its replacement by arbitrary law; and the subordination of the military to such arbitrary political will—all are clear indications of a tendency to increase the state's complete control over society. The *process* of maximizing political control by the Chávez's government, though not finished yet, has already had consequences.

The regime does not seek to consolidate its government and bring about an authoritarian peace; instead, the regime seeks to perpetuate the state of permanent revolution because it sustains the regime. An authoritarian peace might force the regime to consolidate and prove its value based on economic and social achievement. Chávez does not want that to happen.

In this sense, those who try to judge Chávez based on rational political or economic decisions could be badly misled. It is not uncommon to hear some claim that Chávez's regime will last as long as oil prices are high. This argument is generally based on the assumption that the regime seeks success or needs legitimacy in order to continue to rule. This assertion is incorrect. His type of regime is built on naked power, intimidation, and terror and does not count on legitimacy. Paraphrasing Hannah Arendt, the Chávez regime is not merely ruthless but has supreme disregard for immediate consequences, neglects national interests, and has contempt for utilitarianism and economic gain.[77] Thus, we can explain Chávez's excessive wastefulness; his destruction of the productivity and capacity of the PDVSA, the country's main source of income; and his confrontation with the United States, the main buyer of Venezuelan oil.

3 | THE CONTINENTAL EXPANSION OF THE CHÁVEZ REVOLUTION

The Bolivarian revolution installed in Venezuela has become a model for export. Hugo Chávez is its main promoter, but in some cases, leaders in the region fascinated by the new revolution have adopted his blueprint for their own countries.

The expansion of the Bolivarian revolution abroad is a crucial goal of Chávez's because he views the revolution not as national but continental and transnational. Indeed, the Venezuelan leader spends an important part of his time abroad and has established regional and international alliances (see chapters 5–7). He has also established associations with grassroots groups, mostly violent and revolutionary. This chapter analyzes the consequences of the Bolivarian revolution in the region, in particular.

Chávez seeks to achieve two parallel goals: first, to expand his model revolution to other countries in the region and, second, to achieve regional domination under his leadership through the promotion of new authoritarian regimes. Presumably, his regional domination will be facilitated by the fact that he will only need to deal with a handful of tyrants who are not accountable to anyone.

The expansion of the Bolivarian revolution has taken place by ideological, economic, and political means. In the ideological realm, the Venezuelan leader has spread his rhetoric, which is mostly directed against market reform, neoliberal policies, capitalism, globalization, representative democracy, and, particularly, the "American empire." By the same token, he claims that his revolution is not solely for the Venezuelans but for the whole of Latin America. Therefore, he calls for the "unity of Latin American workers, students, soldiers, Indians and peasants from Mexico to Cape Horn."[1]

The Bolivarian Circles have established chapters in many countries in Latin America to spread his ideology. Chávez has also launched a television network, dubbed TeleSUR, modeled after Al Jazeera to promote his ideology. But most important, Chávez has used Venezuela's multibillion-dollar oil revenues to increase his regional influence.

Chávez's "largesse," aimed at the expansion of political influence, is massive. According to a report from 2006, the Bolivarian Republic of Venezuela provided foreign countries, mostly but not only in Latin America, with financial gifts that surpassed $16 billion.[2] Astronomical rises in oil prices, coupled with the regime's increased authoritarianism, have enabled Chávez to be generous as he has exercised full control of the country's revenues without accountability.

From 1999 to 2009 Chávez has given about $43 billion to other countries. Approximately 40 percent of this support is foreign aid for social projects, including oil subsidies for Cuba, outright cash donations to Bolivia, medical equipment to Nicaragua, heating oil subsidies to more than a million low-income households in the United States, cash to relieve the debts of Ecuador and Argentina, and massive aid to a number of non-Chávista countries, such as the Dominican Republic, Haiti, and Uruguay, as well as other nations. Some have estimated that the total value of Chávez's contributions is as large as the Marshall Plan, the U.S. program to reconstruct Europe and Japan after World War II.[3]

Chávez has also actively tried to influence the internal affairs of neighboring countries directly by supporting politically and financially those left-wing candidates he perceived as potential allies and by funneling money to a number of presidential candidates in various countries: Mexico, Bolivia, Ecuador, Peru, Nicaragua, El Salvador, Panama, and Argentina among others. Although he had some setbacks, he scored some major successes. Indeed, the Venezuelan leader has managed to attract some new leaders to adopt Venezuela's political and ideological model as a blueprint for their own countries, particularly in Bolivia, Ecuador, and Nicaragua. These countries not only are allies and beneficiaries of Hugo Chávez's but also have aspired to adopt Bolivarianism as he envisioned it. In addition, Chávez has been able to attract countries in the region that did not fully embrace Bolivarianism but nonetheless became allies or part of Chávez's sphere of influence. Furthermore, through massive economic support, he has helped revitalize the half-century-old Cuban regime after two decades of impoverishment, isolation, and decline. Cuba has been the only socialist regime in the continent for decades and remains a strong symbol of Anti-Americanism in the region.

THE CASE OF BOLIVIA

In 2005, Evo Morales won the presidential election in Bolivia with the help of a diverse coalition that included miners and peasants mostly of Indian extraction, as well as government employees, the middle class, and intellectuals. Following a weekend meeting with Chávez and Fidel Castro shortly after assuming power, Morales quickly moved to nationalize the country's oil and gas sectors. He ordered the military to occupy oil and gas fields managed by foreign companies and conditioned sales of natural gas with a prohibition to resell it to Chile. (Bolivia has historical claims over land lost to Chile, which left the former landlocked.)[4] By the same token, following the model in Venezuela, Morales moved quickly to create a constituent assembly and reduce the power of the opposition. He swiftly convened the assembly to write a new constitution in order to "re-found" the Bolivian state.[5]

Such constitutional reform faced fierce opposition from certain groups, especially from six Bolivian departments (provinces), or mostly those that form a giant prosperous eastern crescent (*media fértil luna*).[6] Their resistance resulted in provincial referendums in support of autonomy and secession from Bolivia. Afterward, Morales initiated a referendum on his presidency in an effort to show his wide popular support. He won a landslide victory; however, in the same referendum, the dissident provinces voted for autonomy and won. Turmoil ensued. Provincial leaders called for civil disobedience. Street fights between supporters of the government and those supporting provincial autonomy broke out. Provincial police attacked pro-government activists while peasants supported the government even in the dissident provinces. The international community through the OAS and the newly established regional defense institution of the Union of South American Nations (Union de Naciones Suramericanas [UNASUR]) intervened to solve the problem, mostly by supporting Morales. The president himself led a 125-mile march, walking with supporters in defense of the new constitution.[7] With Bolivia broadly divided, the new constitution moved toward approval in January 2009 with its final approval coming in February 2009.

Even though the new constitution was the result of compromises and political struggles, the final document is inspired in the design of a Bolivarian type of state. The new document views the state as the only entity responsible for overseeing natural resources and the main body responsible for taking economic initiatives. It provides the state with an increasing central planning role in the economy and investment sector. It also claims hydrocarbons as property of the Bolivian people, thus declaring null and void all contracts that violate this principle. It further establishes the right to private property but leaves open the possibility of expropriation in case a public need arises that requires it.[8]

The constitution strengthens presidential powers even though, under pressure, Morales withdrew his demand for a provision that would have enabled him to run for reelection for two consecutive periods. In a nutshell, the legislative power lost strength while the executive power gained it. The legislative body's vigor was diminished because the constitution recognized the legal autonomy of the indigenous populations, one of Morales's key constituencies. Indigenous people obtained congressional seats reserved specifically for them and gained their precolonial right to their territory and to self-rule, including the government's recognition of the indigenous systems of justice. Thus, the state is currently defined as *plurinacional*, or a state consisting of many nationalities.

Article 158 of the constitution in large part reduces the legislative power to a body that responds to and approves of executive initiatives.[9] Therefore, it makes sense to say that the assembly deliberately designed the constitution to strengthen the power of Morales and his Movement toward Socialism (MAS), whose main base of support is the indigenous population. Further, the constitution also calls for the direct election of Supreme Court justices and lowers the percentage of congressional support required to confirm government appointees.[10]

Morales's power was reaffirmed when he won a landslide victory (64 percent) in the presidential elections of December 2009, thus bolstering his effort to carry out radical transformations. In his view, his victory was a mandate to carry out his agenda. "This process of change has prevailed," he proclaimed.[11] As Latin American scholar Raúl Madrid has pointed out,

"The Morales Administration has moved to overhaul existing political institutions in order to expand and prolong the (MAS) party's hold on power."[12]

Yet, Morales's radical project encountered some limitations. During his first term, both his lack of a majority in the Senate and the opposition's control over most of the provincial or departmental governments limited his ability to implement his polices. Morales also faced some resistance in 2010 when his second mandate began. In December 2010, he issued an executive decree to cut government subsidies for gasoline and diesel. This measure raised the price of fuels about 80 percent, leading to a stoppage of the transportation sector that paralyzed the country.[13] The protestors were not the wealthy residents of the lowlands but many of those who had supported Morales. To stop the strikes, Morales was forced to annul the decree.

Furthermore, in 2011, a new round of protests erupted when indigenous groups protested the construction of a highway that would have cut through an ecological Indian reserve in the Amazon. These groups that also supported Morales in the elections brought their concern to the Inter-American Court for Human Rights and forced the government to enter a dialogue with them.[14] Morales agreed temporarily to prohibit highway construction in the area of the ecological Indian reserve of Tipnis and to resolve the multiple protests both for and against construction in the said area.[15] However, in December 2012 the Morales government, after engaging in consultation with sixty-nine indigenous communities, decided to proceed with the building of the road. The decision was based on the claim that 80 percent of the indigenous communities supported the project. Many still have denounced irregularities in the consultation protocol and significant popular discontent with the process. Some indigenous communities also threatened to take the case to international tribunals.[16] Moreover, a special commission representing the Catholic Church, the Permanent Assembly of Human Rights in Bolivia (APDHB), and the Inter-American Federation of Human Rights (FIDH), reported that out of thirty-six communities the commission visited, thirty reject the proposed road. This contradicts the government's claims that 80 percent of the indigenous communities support the project.[17]

Morales's inability to resolve internal conflicts in an authoritarian fashion was apparent. If before 2010 the opposition was mainly based in the wealthy provinces, after that year the opposition came from Morales's own constituency. The Bolivian president did not have enough support or power to impose his will. Nevertheless, the Morales government has authoritarian aspirations and is not shy about carrying out repressive actions.

Authoritarian and Repressive Patterns

The main ideologue of the Morales government is its own vice president, Alvaro García Linera. According to him, Indians in Bolivia were robbed of their lands and were used to work in the mines and on the land as servants. He advocates destroying the power of the previous rulers, including their economy and property, their political power, and their culture, and to create a new hegemony based on the empowerment of the previously marginalized. García Linera also advocates eliminating the "party, system, its representatives and the destruction of the legislative and judicial power, the electoral courts, the mass media and its owners."[18] Likewise, he downgrades the status of the Spanish language and calls for the use of violence against the mestizo, white, and middle classes. The vice president also has suggested beginning a process of reeducation in the schools in order to "teach indigenous and Andean culture and language as against the position of the Catholic and other Western religions."

In the political arena, García Linera calls "to dismantle democracy, to criminalize the opposition and to create alternative means to spread information." In the vice president's view, democracy will not be achieved through elections or representative government but will be reflected in the ability "to mobilize social movements." By the same token, he believes private property and the accumulation of capital must be abolished and that the new regime's economic foundation should rest on coca production, which will provide the Indians with new opportunities.

The Bolivian government, meanwhile, has also intimidated its political opponents.[19] The cases of arbitrary arrest and detention rest on suspected or alleged political reasons of violating the law and the constitution. For example, when Bolivian police shot and killed three alleged foreign terrorists (two Hungarians and one Irishman) after they supposedly attempted to murder the president to help in the secession of the Santa Cruz Province in 2009, Morales accused the opposition of orchestrating the attacks. Foreign embassies demanded explanations for the deaths of their citizens but have yet to receive one. Violence against individuals who criticize government officials has also occurred. For example, a woman complained that she was beaten only because her husband had accused Minister of the Presidency Juan Ramón Quintana of delivering thirty-three truckloads of contraband to Brazil. Her husband happened to be the president of the National Customs Office, and she seemed to have been punished for her husband's critical posture toward a government official. According to the woman's testimony, phone threats had preceded the incident.[20]

Likewise, the government twists the concept of community justice or indigenous justice for political purposes. "Community justice" is part of the constitutional arrangement regarding indigenous autonomy and the multinational character of the state and its laws. But the government has allowed community justice to turn into mob violence. In one case, in March 2009, approximately three hundred people invaded the home of former Bolivian vice president and member of the opposition Victor Hugo Cárdenas, an Indian, while he was not home; beat his family; and evicted his wife and two children. The attackers burglarized his house, stole his belongings, and refused to allow the police to enter the property. The government was reluctant to bring the attackers to justice. Moreover, the police did not act to protect the former vice president. Vice President García Linera later stated that Cárdenas brought the attack upon himself. The vice president's attitude clearly indicates that the Bolivian government is more inclined to act arbitrarily rather than follow the rule of law.

In another case in May 2009, the Confederation of Indigenous Peoples of Eastern Bolivia (Confederación de Pueblos Indígenas de Bolivia) applied its concept of community justice to the director of indigenous development in the Department of Beni, Marcial Fabricano, by publicly whipping him fifty times. According to the confederation, which is linked to the MAS ruling party, it had punished Fabricano for not appointing MAS leaders to high-level positions in his department.[21] The government repudiated the attack and made a commitment to investigate it, but nobody was indicted or charged. This case might indicate that the Bolivian government, like Chávez, may be willing to exercise power above the law. It also illustrates that the principles of multinationality and indigenous autonomy embedded in the constitution weaken the application of the rule of law. When the laws become compromised, executive power prevails.

Similar to Chávez, Morales also has tried to exercise control over the judiciary. A legal investigation undertaken by the Morales-controlled lower house of Congress led to impeachment hearings of several justices, who have faced suspension and possible impeachment. Indeed, Morales has viewed several Supreme Court justices as being politically identified with the opposition. Similarly, the constitutional tribunal, an independent institution that has an appellate jurisdiction, had been unable to operate for most of 2009. One of the magistrates resigned, charging that government-affiliated social groups harassed tribunal members in order to force them to resign. Apparently, the purpose of such action was to remove judicial oversight of constitutionally questionable government actions.

On the one hand, Bolivian law provides for freedom of speech and the press. On the other hand, the law also provides that persons found guilty of insulting, defaming, or slandering public officials may be jailed for one month to two years. Insults against the president, vice president, or a minister increase the sentence by half. Indeed, the Morales government has reacted harshly and with animosity to criticism and has maintained an antagonistic relationship with the media. Journalists accused of violating the constitution or citizens' rights are referred to a forty-person press tribunal, an independent body authorized to evaluate journalists and apply sanctions.[22]

Regarding labor organizations, the law allows the government to dissolve unions by administrative decree. President Morales's central government has close ties with such labor organizations as the Central Union of Bolivian Workers (Central Obrera Bolivian) and the confederation of farmworkers. Yet, in order to exercise even more control over the unions, the government has funded parallel chapters in areas where it has less influence. When disagreements were registered between the unions and the government, the MAS could then mobilize the parallel organizations.[23]

Like Chávez, Morales aspires to fuse the revolution with the military and wants the military to give strength and continuity to his regime. Morales has been generous with the military in order to keep the institution on his side. Two percent of revenues generated from taxes imposed on hydrocarbon production go to the military. Moreover, Morales gave the military a role in implementing parts of the country's social policy in an attempt to make the institution an integral part of his revolution. As Chávez did, Morales sees the need to make the armed forces part of the people. This union was symbolized on "flag day" in 2007, when the Morales government organized a parade where indigenous people and the military marched together.[24] Early in 2008, Morales issued a decree providing the armed forces with key roles in enforcing custom regulations and in confiscating contraband, including giving them the ability to arrest offenders and to seize vehicles. In addition, as in Venezuela, the armed forces are also entrusted with social programs, such as baking subsidized bread and passing out bonuses for school children and senior citizens.[25]

Morales has also persuaded the armed forces to adopt the Cuban revolutionary slogan "Motherland or death: We shall win." The military accepted the slogan despite having generated some debate within the armed forces.[26] The Bolivian president still meets regularly with top military officials, and in one of his speeches he spoke directly to them about the connection between the peasant movement and the army.

Last, as Chávez has done, Morales has maintained a hostile posture toward the United States. Bolivia expelled the Drug Enforcement Administration (DEA), declared the U.S. ambassador as persona non grata, and closed one U.S. Agency for International Development office located in Chapare, the largest coca-growing region. Bolivia expelled the DEA for the same reason that Chávez did so in Venezuela: Morales views the war against drugs as imperialist interference. In the case of Bolivia, the issue is aggravated because coca is still seen as a source of national income and is still used in indigenous people's religious ceremonies. Morales ordered U.S. ambassador Philip Goldberg to leave the country in September 2008 immediately after he had visited one of the lowland provinces in the midst of anti-government protests.[27]

Morales sees a connection between domestic misfortune and foreign influence in Bolivia. He has repeatedly stressed the need to go after those "who are responsible for our miseries." This statement, of course, is mainly aimed at the United States.[28]

THE CASE OF ECUADOR

In Ecuador, after the populist leader Rafael Correa won the presidential elections with the support of indigenous and other marginal populations, he also took dramatic steps. Having campaigned under the slogan of leading a "citizens' revolution," Correa had proposed creating a constituent assembly to rewrite Ecuador's constitution and won an overwhelming 81.7 percent of the votes in a national referendum on his proposal in April 2007. Correa, who ran for the presidency, did not present candidates for the congressional election. Thus, in Congress he drew support from other minority parties but he was for attaining congressional support as Chávez did in Venezuela. Correa expected to draw his support from a direct relation with the people via means such as the referendum and, as we shall see, through a constitutional reform that provided him with more prerogative power. It did not take long for the president to clash with Congress: his electoral court proceeded to fire fifty-seven opposition legislators. A constitutional court later ordered that they be reinstated. Correa tried to prevent these legislators from taking their seats while a federal prosecutor ordered the arrest of twenty-four of them and proceeded to prosecute them on grounds of sedition.[29] As Chávez did, Correa immediately increased his control of the courts, allegedly intimidated business people, and tried to regulate news organizations.

In September 2008, Ecuadorians voted to ratify the new constitution. The vote was overwhelmingly in favor of the constitution (almost 80 percent supported it while almost 20 percent opposed it). The victory appeared to be the result of President Rafael Correa's populist policies, which benefited the poorest sectors of society by substantially increasing public spending, mostly in an unaccountable manner.[30] This first stage of his citizens' revolution aimed at building a new order where the *partidocracia* no longer ruled. One could think of the citizens' revolution in Ecuador as a revolution against institutions.

As noted in chapter 1, Ecuador was in need of reform. The political party system had grown apart from civil society and was not seen as truly representative of society; instead, the people perceived the parties as oligarchic, independent from the will of the people, and too often tied to particular interests. In Ecuador's case, a constitutional reform could have made sense if the framework of political reform had aimed at increasing relations between constituencies and elected officials, changing the system of party rule, and ensuring that all sectors were properly represented within the system. However, Correa's newly approved constitution follows the Chávista model of limiting liberties and increasing the powers of the executive.

In effect, the Ecuadorian constitution strengthens the power of the state and grants a special role to the government that goes as far as to include responsibility for the "good life," or happiness, of the people. The Ecuadorian constitution empowers the state as the guarantor of education, health care, food, social security, and water resources for the country's inhabitants.[31] The state is also in charge of eradicating poverty and making sure that national wealth is distributed evenly among its citizens. While also ensuring the right of citizens to live in a pleasant environment and proper ecosystem, the state must guarantee equal access to radio and TV broadcasts to prevent the formation of oligopolies and monopolies over the means of communications.[32] The state also ensures that those sectors of the population that have limited resources will have access to proper communications and information technology. In addition, the state is entrusted with national planning by exercising exclusive control over those strategic sectors of the country that play a crucial role in influencing the economy (energy sectors, in particular), the society, and the environment. Therefore, those sectors must be reoriented to serve "the social interest."

This new constitution uses language that gives Ecuador an appearance of upholding democracy and extending the people's rights and citizenship. It expands the division of powers to include not only the traditional division among executive, legislative, and judicial powers but also the new branches of "electoral power" and the "transparency and social control"(TSC) branch. The TSC is a supposedly autonomous entity entrusted with the control of public agencies and institutions through the Council for Public Participation and Social Control whose responsibilities include oversight of corruption. In practice, it requires the participation of representatives from various government agencies, and the TSC eventually appoints officials, such as the attorney general, from a short list chosen by the president.[33] Thus, a conspicuous prerogative power proffered to the executive branch can easily neutralize what looks like a form of far-reaching republicanism and inclusiveness.[34]

In sum, the Ecuadorian government has assumed an increased role in planning, regulating, controlling, and exercising any prerogative the state considers being of vital "social interest."[35]

Authoritarian Patterns

President Correa has not waited to use his prerogatives but has swiftly moved against the interests of foreign corporations operating in Ecuador. The government of Ecuador and its oil company, Petroecuador, attempted to collect $327 million from the French oil company Perenco. Correa claimed that per the 2006 Law 42, the government has a right to 99 percent of oil revenues from sales above certain "reference prices," and Petroecuador began seizing crude oil produced by Perenco. An internationally recognized arbitration tribunal, however, unanimously ordered Ecuador to halt seizures of Perenco's crude oil.[36] When Ecuador ignored the arbitration, Perenco suspended production. Likewise, the government has moved against a Brazilian construction company, Odebrecht, expelling it from the country for alleged overcharges. At least ten cases are now under arbitration because of Correa's attacks on foreign companies.[37]

The highest-profile case was the long-running lawsuit against Chevron over environmental damage. Ecuador had filed a lawsuit in 1993 against Texaco, which Chevron purchased in 2001, over its toxic spills on local rivers in the Lago Agrio area. Whatever the legal merits of the case, Rafael Correa used the weight of his presidential power to influence the case in the local residents' favor. It epitomizes a major anti-imperialist crusade and a claim of historical redemption for more than five hundred years of exploitation of the indigenous people. The judge in charge of the case claimed he would rule against Chevron and that appeals to the case would be denied. Likewise, a member of Correa's party, Alianza País, was quoted as saying that lawyers from the executive branch would assist the judge in writing the final verdict.[38]

In 2011 an Ecuadorian court found Chevron responsible for environmental damage in the region, but the company still insists that such judgment was obtained by fraud and extortion and with the help of a biased and unfair Ecuadorian court. (The U.S. Supreme Court rejected Chevron's attempt to block Ecuador's attempt to collect 19 billion dollars from the company in the United States but such decision is not related to the accusations Chevron made about fraud and bias but by the procedural consideration of the U.S. Supreme Court that saw no legal ground to refuse considering blocking attempts to collect the money. The court did not reject the company's arguments against Ecuador. They only rejected the attempt to challenge the right of Ecuador to pursue American courts to bar the plaintiffs from attempting to collect the money.)[39]

The right of the state to have the ultimate word on social and environmental issues is embedded in the new Ecuadorian constitution. As the concept of "social interest" is vaguely defined, it provides the state with undefined boundaries. Thus, the political logic of the executive power is reflected in the constitutional and legal logic of the judiciary, where ideology prevails over the law. The judiciary has been susceptible to pressure and corruption, and judges have been forced to reach decisions because of political pressure.[40] President Correa's verbal and legal attacks against the media have also intensified as the relationship between the press and the government has significantly deteriorated.

As in Venezuela, Ecuadorian media outlets are subject to legal harassment. President Correa attacked the TV station TeleAmazonas, which is generally critical of the government, for not paying taxes regularly. Likewise, he targeted the newspaper *El Comercio* for not verifying its sources when reporting cases of government corruption. Correa has openly defined the press as a "grave political enemy that needs to be defeated." Human rights organizations also have registered attacks against journalists and break-ins and robberies at media outlets.[41] Early in 2012, the Ecuadorian Supreme Court upheld President Correa's lawsuit against a leading opposition newspaper after it accused him of permitting troops to fire on a hospital full of people during a September 2010 police uprising against the Correa government. The court fined and sentenced the defendants to three years in prison. However, after the Inter-American Court challenged the Ecuadorian ruling, international pressure was unleashed and forced Correa to pardon the defendants.

The incident stemmed from the Ecuadorian president's authoritarian style of decision making. Without any public debate, the president cut salaries and bonuses in certain public sectors. He also promoted corporate activities in indigenous territories while ignoring the input and resistance coming from their populations. In addition, he adopted measures of deficit reduction and even encouraged foreign investment, particularly in the area of mining. It did not take long for these policies to backfire.

In September 2010 President Correa ordered cuts in salaries and bonuses for a number of sectors and vetoed a set of social laws that Congress had carefully negotiated with representatives of the social sectors. On September 30, police officers rebelled against these cuts. When Correa confronted them, the disgruntled police threw a tear gas canister that reached the president and exploded, slightly harming him. The Ecuadorian Congress, meanwhile, remained impotent in the face of Correa's aggressiveness. He threatened to dissolve Congress if it posed any opposition. In light of these events, street protests increased, with students, public servants, retirees, and indigenous populations joining the fray. Mass protests against Correa's government were not merely reacting to his economic austerity policy. The people also responded to his implementation of a Chávez-type authoritarianism, contempt for Congress, and lack of democratic procedures, including any direct relationship between the citizenry and the popular vote.

The largest indigenous organization Confederación de Nacionalidades Indígenas del Ecuador (CONAEI)—an important bastion of support for Correa during the 2006 presidential election—has had a tense relationship with Correa over mining, environmental, and other policies since 2008. The CONAIE issued a statement complaining about "the poor political leadership of a government that brings popular discontent with its constant acts of discrimination and violations of human rights." The document added that the indigenous people "refuse to recognize this dictatorial democracy given the absence of freedom of speech, the takeover of all branches of government by the executive power and the elimination of any possibility of discussion of laws proposed by the indigenous movement and other social sectors."[42] The CONAIE statement illustrates the indigenous communities' concern with the way the Ecuadorian president has conducted the government's business.

Despite Correa's defiant attitude during the police rebellion, Chief of Staff of the Ecuadorian Army, Ernesto Gutierrez, saved his government. The chief also demanded that the president change the public sector law that generated the protest and restore some of the benefits Correa intended to cut. Consequently, Correa backed off from these authoritarian policies and consented to the general's request.[43] These events demonstrated that Correa could face the veto power of the military, a key force in Ecuador. The military owns major business holdings, including agro-businesses and civilian airlines, and has played a central role in Ecuador's politics in the last decade. It has helped oust three elected presidents by withdrawing their support during congressional upheavals and protests.[44] However, the military's veto power has not prevented Correa from continuing to concentrate as much power as possible in his own hands.

In fact, in the aftermath of Correa's landslide reelection victory in February 2013, the Ecuadorian president pledged to deepen his revolution and his executive prerogatives. Immediately after this victory Correa announced that he would move ahead with a new communications law that would redistribute radio and television frequencies and tighten regulations on the media. This is a clear attempt to consolidate control of the media.

Likewise, Correa is expected to carry out more radical changes such as redistribution of land.[45]

In terms of foreign policy, like Chávez and Morales, the Ecuadorian president has also taken a strong anti-American posture. He often blames "American imperialism" for the social problems that affect Ecuadorian society. As pledged during his presidential campaign, one of his first steps was to demand the closure of the U.S. military base in Manta. The United States had built the base in 1999 after returning the Panama Canal to Panama. The U.S. military used the Manta base to monitor drug trafficking in the area.

THE CASE OF NICARAGUA

Daniel Ortega Saavedra was the leader of the Marxist Sandinista revolution of 1979. In 2006, he was elected president of Nicaragua after a sixteen-year hiatus. Ortega was a revolutionary before Chávez made his first appearance in political life.

But since his new term began in 2007, Ortega has passed a substantial number of business-related laws that the private sector has vetted. Ortega has also attracted foreign capital, which has invested in a number of important sectors including energy and electronics.[46] Likewise, in spite of his Anti-American antipathies, he has maintained free trade agreements with the United States. Yet, Ortega has used and manipulated the democratic system to advance an authoritarian regime. The state of democracy has deteriorated while Ortega's rhetoric and geopolitical alliances follow the blueprint of his ally Hugo Chávez.

As discussed in chapter 1, in 2001 Ortega signed a deal with the opposition Constitutionalist Liberal party (PLC). Known as the Pacto Ortega-Alemán, this deal included a provision that lowered the percentage necessary to win a presidential election in the first round from 45 percent to 35 percent. Ortega won the 2006 elections with 37 percent of the vote, a little more than a third of the votes cast without having to call for a run-off election. Thus, Ortega became president of Nicaragua without having the support of a solid majority.

Since the Sandinistas took the reins of power in 2006, they have ruled harshly. They have used the popular sectors and the persistent problem of poverty in Nicaragua to adopt intolerant attitudes toward opponents of the regime, as well as to assault the division of powers and the institutions of democracy. The legislative and judicial branches continue to lose authority to the bulldozing executive commander.

In November 2008 municipal elections took place with results favoring Ortega's ruling party; however, suspicions of fraud led to a major revolt. The governing Sandinista Party was suspected of electoral fraud as a means of maintaining its stronghold on power. Polls taken prior to the election showed 80 percent of the population opposed President Ortega, but the overwhelming Sandinista victory in the municipal elections did not reflect such sentiment. Before these elections, two opposition parties were disqualified from the ballot. Likewise, the government investigated fifteen organizations, accusing them of money laundering and subversion. Prior to the municipal elections, the Nicaraguan government also had expelled international observers.[47]

After the election, the PLC rallied in nonviolent demonstrations in the streets of Nicaragua. Pro-Ortega and Sandinista agitators and gangs armed with stones, golf clubs, sticks, knives, and slingshots took over the streets of the capital, Managua, to prevent the opposition's protest against electoral fraud. Nicaragua's attorney general warned protesters and the population, as a whole, that if Commander Ortega decided to call his followers to the streets, every radio station and media outlet that dared to criticize him would be destroyed.[48] Criminal charges were filed against political opponents and those civil organizations perceived as being critical of the government. Journalists were also persecuted and TV channels pressured to cancel programs expressing either independent or opposite views from those of the Sandinista government.

The government has established and promoted Councils of Citizen Power (Consejos de poder ciudadano), with the intent to undermine parties and other institutions of representative democracy. Pro-government paramilitary groups also have a strong presence in the streets of Nicaragua.[49]

President Ortega swiftly secured party control over the judiciary, the electoral court, and the police. At the close of 2009, his control of the judiciary enabled him to secure a unanimous Supreme Court ruling that overturned the constitutional ban on a reelection bid. Sandinista justices, who met without notifying three other non-Sandinista magistrates, orchestrated the ruling. Ortega's supporters staged the judicial manipulation after their attempt to call for a constitutional reform in Congress failed due to the opposition's strong resistance.[50] The Nicaraguan Supreme Court interpreted the election provision in a cynical way. The justices claimed the provision failed to protect human rights or, in other words, "the individual right of Mr. Ortega to be reelected" and failed to uphold its proper intention—to limit the potential monarchical power of one president.[51] This Supreme Court decision enabled Ortega to run for a third term in November 2011.

Ortega won the 2011 elections in the midst of more denunciations of fraud. According to the European Union's electoral mission, the vote tally was "opaque and arbitrary." In addition, numerous complaints of irregularities were reported, and the Supreme Electoral Council rejected or disqualified poll watchers.[52]

Ortega aims to concentrate power. According to such observers as Richard Feinberg, a former adviser to President Bill Clinton, Ortega is likely to continue his pro-business economic policies as he concentrates more power in his hands.[53]

This pursuit does not preclude, however, Ortega's engaging in strong anti-American rhetoric. At every international opportunity, whether it is at the United Nations or at the Summit of the Americas, the Nicaraguan president openly criticizes the United States as a terrorist, aggressive, and exploitative country. That he still abides by the free trade agreement with the United States does not mean that his speeches contain empty rhetoric. On the one hand, Ortega is a pragmatist who does not hesitate to support free trade agreements and pacts with former political enemies, but on the other hand, he identifies with the spirit of the revolution. Hugo Chávez's millions of dollars of support for Nicaragua have revitalized Ortega's true political beliefs and dictatorial practices much in the same way as they have unfolded in Cuba.

| THE CASE OF CUBA

The 1959 Cuban revolution was a source of inspiration for Guevarista guerrillas who sought to bring about change in their respective societies across the Latin American continent. With some exceptions, such as FARC, most guerrilla and underground groups that drew their ideas from the Cuban revolution have either been defeated or integrated into the democratic system. The demise of Cuba's main source of mentorship and support, the Soviet Union, further isolated Cuba. The triumph of capitalistic liberal democracy versus the failed system of communism led to the general perception that the downfall of the Cuban regime was only a matter of time.

One could argue that Venezuela's massive aid to Cuba has promoted a revival of the Castro-led regime. Venezuela has effectively replaced the Soviet Union as Cuba's benefactor; for example, Chávez sells crude oil at preferential prices to Cuba daily. As a result of Chávez's support, Cuba's economic hardship has been somewhat alleviated.

In exchange, Cuba provides Venezuela assistance with medicine and health care, but most important, it provides the know-how to build a socialist state. As noted in chapter 2, Cuban officers have provided guidance with strategic planning and military intelligence that could enable Chávez to build a security apparatus loyal to him.[54] Their strategic advice is probably one of the most crucial elements on Chávez's road toward the consolidation of total power.[55]

Some Latin American officials have told me in private that Cuba controls and even dictates the course of the Bolivarian revolution; however, I disagree with this argument. Chávez is strong willed and possesses the resources needed to expand his revolution. He provides not only financial support but also an ideological revival and hope to a continent where capitalistic democracy has not yet managed to solve many of its social problems. The success and expansion of the Chávez-led Bolivarian Alternative for the Americas (Alianza Bolivariana para los Pueblos de Nuestra América [ALBA]) is perhaps an indication that Chávez's revolutionary leadership supercedes that found in a struggling Cuba.

INTERNATIONAL BOLIVARIAN ALLIANCES

Hugo Chávez proposed establishing the Bolivarian Alternative for the Americas (ALBA) in 2005 with the purpose of expanding the social and political principles of the Bolivarian revolution. ALBA is defined as the implementation of Simón Bolívar's dream to unite all the countries of the region to form a big nation (*Patria Grande*). ALBA is the forum that gathers all the governments and peoples of Latin America and the Caribbean who understand that such unity is necessary to face the challenges of the present and the future.[56] This unity "would bring together the strengths and capabilities of the countries that are part of it and thus produce the necessary transformation to reach the level of development needed to provide continuity to our existence as sovereign and just nations."[57]

ALBA is not fashioned as an economic regional alliance similar to the European Economic Community or the South America's Southern Common Market (Mercado Común del Sur, or Mercosur). But ALBA is also an instrument intended to promote regional political unity around the Bolivarian ideology and to bring more countries under the hegemonic power of the Bolivarian revolution. In the words of Hugo Chávez, "our integration will not be based on the economy and certainly not our weak and vulnerable economies."[58] ALBA believes in economic, ideological, cultural, social, scientific and political integration.

On the economic side, Commercial Treaty of the Peoples (Tratado de Comercio de los Pueblos [TCP]) are treaties to exchange goods and services between the countries to satisfy the needs of the people while taking advantage of the resources each country possesses. This treaty was signed to counterbalance the Free Trade Agreements, "imposed" by the United States on countries of the region, which in the words of ALBA, "have led to unemployment and marginalization of our people and to the destruction of our national economies and have benefited only the penetration of big imperialist capital."[59] By the same token, Grandnational companies (Empresas Grannacionales), as opposed to transnational companies, would give priority to the production of goods and services to satisfy human needs, while breaking with the concept of profit and accumulation of capital.

ALBA seeks first to maximize regional integration and cooperation between the different countries to protect them from the advantages of the first powers (mainly the United States). It argues that free trade can only benefit the powerful United States because of its economic and technological advantages and because the U.S. government subsidizes its farmers. Second, such integration requires not only trade within the region's own markets (economic integration) but also unity and solidarity between the peoples. Third, not only countries but also all movements and organizations in the region that oppose free trade should unite. Last, ALBA claims to protect the cultural autonomy of peasants and indigenous peoples that free trade agreements and economic exploitation can destroy.

But the key element in understanding ALBA's logic can be found in the words of President Chávez himself: "There will be not independence in Venezuela if there is no integration of South America and the Caribbean.

. . . From the Bravo River to the Patagonia there is the land of the possible dream, our America. . . . The time for our second independence has arrived."[60] (As we will see later, these words will resonate across Latin America as regional integration becomes an accepted idea among countries in the region—including those that are not a part of ALBA, those that are governed by social democracies, and those that have conservative governments.)

In addition to Venezuela, Bolivia, Ecuador, Cuba, and Nicaragua, current ALBA members include Antigua and Barbuda, Dominica, St. Vincent and the Grenadines. Saint Lucia and Suriname are considered "guest countries." The small Caribbean island countries with limited resources are glad to accept membership in ALBA in exchange for Chávez's benevolence. Along with its many treaties and initiatives, ALBA has created so-called Grand National Projects. These efforts include agricultural cooperation projects, social programs aimed at reducing illiteracy in the region, health programs, and programs to reduce malnutrition.[61]

Meanwhile, Chávez engaged in other international projects, such as PetroCaribe. Launched in 2005, the eighteen-member oil alliance of Venezuela and Caribbean nations has enabled its members to purchase oil at preferential prices and under special conditions including payments in kind (barter).[62] Like ALBA, PetroCaribe also has an ideological component as it presents itself as a solution to the problems that the Spanish conquest of indigenous lands generated. It seeks to integrate state-owned oil companies in Latin America and the Caribbean so that they may jointly invest in the exploration, use, and trade in oil and natural gas. The alliance's premise is that unifying the countries into a powerful bloc will create opportunities to develop energy production capabilities.[63]

Likewise, Chávez has been (so far unsuccessfully) promoting the construction of oil pipelines from Venezuela to Colombia, Central America, and South America.[64] As during the Soviet Union years, when pipelines served to consolidate the dependency of the Soviet republics and Central European satellites on Moscow, Chávez's idea is to facilitate the flow of oil into these countries and further their dependence on him.

Other countries have not joined ALBA or the oil alliance but have remained close to Venezuela. Argentina, for example, has displayed a remarkable affinity with Venezuela's social justice agenda and its pursuit of regional independence and defiance of the giant of the north. The last two Argentinean presidents—the late Néstor Kirchner (2003–2007) and Cristina Kirchner (2007–present), both of whom belong to the populist Peronist Party—have seemingly been captivated by the Chávez agenda. Argentina's quest for independence from the International Monetary Fund initially prompted this tacit alliance with Venezuela. Chávez provided Argentina with low-cost energy and debt relief. Cristina Kirchner is also believed to have received funds from Chávez to finance her political campaign in 2007. (The Federal Bureau of Investigation has been investigating the issue since police confiscated suspected money transfers from Chávez to Kirchner from a person who flew from Miami and landed in Argentina. That person acknowledged that money from the Venezuela's oil company PDVSA was destined to Cristina Kirchner's presidential campaign).[65]

If Kirchnerism continues to dominate Argentinean politics, Chávez can count on Argentina's support as a de facto ALBA ally.

THE CASE OF HONDURAS

In the summer of 2009, Manuel Zelaya, the president of Honduras proposed making changes to the constitution after his country became an official member of ALBA. The Honduran Supreme Court declared Zelaya's referendum on modifying the constitution unconstitutional, though, since it proposed allowing the reelection of the president. The Honduran Congress also opposed Zelaya's proposition. After the Honduran president refused to comply with the Supreme Court's orders and the wishes of Congress and moved forward with his plan, the army deposed him and sent him into exile.[66] The president of the House of Representatives Roberto Micheletti replaced Zelaya, generating a crisis in Honduras that quickly brought about international involvement as the OAS viewed Zelaya's ouster as a violation of the group's democratic charter.

From an outsider's perspective, the crux of the issue is not so much whether Zelaya's removal was legal—undoubtedly an important issue in itself—but how Chávez's oil money was able to persuade the conservative Zelaya to follow the Bolivarian blueprint. After Zelaya joined ALBA the Honduran president appeared with Chávez when the Venezuelan president celebrated his tenth anniversary in power. Shortly afterward, Zelaya proposed a referendum to consult the people on whether they wished to create a constitutional assembly that would reform the existing constitution. This proposal generated protests by members of the government, Congress, the Catholic Church, and other groups that immediately suspected that Zelaya's intention was to seek reelection and implement a system similar to the one in Venezuela.[67]

As an observer during the elections in Honduras, I had the opportunity to speak with many civilian leaders, public officials, journalists, and others. Many in Honduras believe that Zelaya's resorting to a constitutional reform referendum was a condition that Chávez requested in exchange for Honduras's being accepted into ALBA and receiving Chávez's aid. It is also plausible that Chávez had promoted the concept of constitutional reform and the indefinite reelection of Zelaya with the ultimate objective of securing a long-standing ally. Otherwise, how can one explain why President Zelaya, who was elected as a conservative representing the traditional Liberal Party, would pursue a socialist constitutional reform?

What is interesting in the case of Honduras is Chávez's ability to offer benefits to a country that badly needed it and to co-opt its leader, who by virtue of his political tradition, presumably would not yield to the Bolivarian sphere of influence. Despite that Zelaya's removal aborted such a move, one cannot underestimate Chávez's power to recruit adept leaders and their countries to his ranks.

❘ CHÁVEZ'S ATTITUDE TOWARD COLOMBIA AND OTHER COUNTRIES IN THE REGION

While co-opting Latin American countries under his sphere of influence, the Venezuelan president has not hesitated to confront those countries in the region whose policies he resented. For one, Chávez views Colombia as a staunch ally of the United States and certainly as a main enemy of his hegemonic aspirations. He has opposed Plan Colombia, the American effort aimed at dismantling the activities linked to drug trafficking in Colombia. Chávez has established a strong alliance with the FARC guerrillas and has facilitated the drug cartels' operations. Both groups have been major destabilizing forces in Colombia in past decades (and this issue is explored further in chapter 5).

On several occasions Chávez threatened Colombia and even called for the Venezuelan army to be prepared for war against the country. Chávez's rhetoric directed toward Colombia has often been inflammatory. These countries' relations further deteriorated after Colombia led a raid against a FARC camp in Ecuador early in 2008. Fixated with Colombia, the Bolivarian leader also made a massive purchase of weapons from Russia in 2005, initiating an arms race that could have dangerous consequences in a continent that has known some international conflict in the last century. (For more on this topic, see chapter 7.)

Venezuela has not had any hostilities against Mexico. Although Mexico cooperates with the United States in the war against drug trafficking, Chávez allegedly helped the campaign of Andrés López Obrador, a left-wing presidential candidate who ran in 2006 against Felipe Calderón (2006–2012) and lost.[68] Likewise, in the 2006 elections in Peru, Chávez supported Ollanta Humala, the leader of an ultra-nationalist indigenous party who lost to Alan García.[69] (Ollanta Humala was eventually elected president of Peru in 2011 with a more moderate agenda.) Furthermore, Chávez is believed to have supported riots in the Puno area that Humala had organized after a series of strikes began in the country. At that time a Peruvian newspaper reported that Humala received $600,000 monthly from Hugo Chávez to promote social unrest in the country. Moreover, legislators affiliated with Humala's Nationalist Party have been traveling to Venezuela for long periods. One of them admitted that Humala was behind the strikes.[70]

With regard to Chile, another country considered to be a close ally of the United States, Chávez has been very vocal in his demand that Chile give up territory taken from Bolivia during the nineteenth-century Pacific War and allow the latter an exit to the sea. When the Venezuelan president signed an agreement to help Bolivia build military bases and train troops, it caused great alarm in Chile in 2006.[71]

▍SUMMARY

Under the inspiration of the Venezuelan leader, the presidents of the Bolivarian countries—Bolivia, Ecuador, Nicaragua, and Cuba—aspire to exercise maximum control over their countries and have established a revolutionary regional alliance. With the exception of Cuba, they find legitimacy by appealing to the people and to the poor and by standing against economic policies (for example, neoliberalism) that they identify as exploitative and inspired by the United States. Regardless of specific differences in economic policy or their appealing to the people, they strive to maximize political control and to be accountable as little as possible to their populations. Thus, they feel if they can virtually eliminate or reduce the power of their respective congresses, there would be no room for debates or resistance to the presidents' will.

From a regional perspective, the implication is that if the leaders of these countries are less accountable to the electorate and society, the advancement of the Bolivarian regional project will occur more rapidly and be less contentious. The more countries that adopt the Bolivarian blueprint, the larger the hegemony of the Bolivarian bloc will be. By uniting with a handful of strong leaders, the instruments of the Bolivarian revolution can expand its hegemony throughout the continent without any accountability to their respective Congress, civil society, or any other institution.

Having said so, it is important to acknowledge that the survival of elections and referendums is not necessarily a sign of a healthy democracy. Because these countries hold elections, particularly in the form of referendums, many have been led to believe that they are engaging in acts of democratic governance. Instead, most referendums seek to increase executive power by capitalizing on the fleeting popularity of the president. Referendums pave the way for manipulation, which is possible because the state has control over national resources and the public redistribution of goods.

Thus, in the Honduras case, it makes sense to think that possibly Chávez persuaded Zelaya to carry out a referendum for constitutional reform. It was not enough for Zelaya to be merely an ally; more important, he had to assure the Venezuelan leader that their alliance was not temporary. This point is key in understanding why the Bolivarian leader values a strong relationship between domestic transformation and foreign policy.

It is also true that leaders in these countries are autonomous insofar as they manage policies according to what they see fits their needs. Undoubtedly Chávez's Venezuela has made the most far-reaching steps toward having total control of his country. In the cases of Ecuador, Bolivia, and Nicaragua, even if they have not reached Chávez's level of control, they definitely aspire to do so. These four countries also share another dimension, in that they work in a unified bloc and endeavor to carry out a uniform foreign policy that is particularly geared toward reducing U.S. influence in the region. As chapters 5 and 6 will discuss, in this effort, they may not hesitate to join Chávez in such radical adventures as establishing bonds or connections with Iran and FARC.

Argentina is less likely to develop a full Bolivarian blueprint, but it is openly sympathetic to ALBA and the revolution. Argentina, like most of the nonrevolutionary members of ALBA, remains within Chávez's sphere of influence.

Indeed, though small ALBA countries have not yet developed into Bolivarian states, they might do so in the future. These poor countries have weakened democracies and state institutions; therefore, they are natural targets for the Bolivarians' ambitions. Chávez can bring about their transition to Bolivarianism by means of in-cash or in-kind generosity. Central American and Caribbean countries, given the feebleness of their states and democracy, are particularly vulnerable to surrender to Bolivarian influence.

Chávez's expansionism is methodic. To strengthen his ties, he cultivates not only leaders and regimes but also reaches the grass roots.

4 | THE EMERGENCE OF INDIGENOUS AND NEW GRASSROOTS MOVEMENTS IN LATIN AMERICA

The mobilization and politicization of previously marginalized groups such as indigenous and other socially marginalized populations constitute an important phenomenon in contemporary Latin America.

Beginning in the mid-1990s, new grassroots movements began to appear in the Latin American scene. These movements have different characteristics and claims depending on the country in which they emerge. Most arise as a natural result of an expanded democracy and openness of an increasing wave of democratization in Latin America. Formerly excluded groups that had no representative voice in the system or that were living at the margins of society therefore have become more and more self-conscious and have achieved a new degree of mobilization. These groups include indigenous peoples; the unemployed; masses of unorganized, poor peasants; and others. Despite Latin American states' making constitutional reforms and attempts to recognize and expand their rights, these groups have felt deceived by a deficient party system and by aloof governments.

As I indicated in the examples of Bolivia and Ecuador, indigenous groups have played an important role in toppling their countries' governments and in supporting new presidents. In both countries they developed real veto powers. In this chapter, I cover the importance of these phenomena and show how Hugo Chávez has attempted to expand the scope of his influence among these groups.

THE EMERGENCE OF THE GRASS ROOTS

The first group to emerge was the Zapatista Army of National Liberation (Ejército Zapatista de Liberación Nacional) in Mexico, which erupted on the public scene in January 1994, the eve of the signing of the North

American Free Trade Agreement by the United States, Mexico, and Canada. The Zapatista movement (also known as the Zapatistas) is an indigenous politically marginal group that first had a revolutionary socialist agenda. The group demanded an end to social and economic inequalities and their political exclusion. The Zapatistas were fierce opponents of neoliberal policies, capitalism, and globalization, which they view as the sources of their misery. The Mexican state responded to the Zapatistas by further democratizing its system, a process that grew after the Institutional Revolutionary Party (Partido Revolucionario Institucional [PRI]) lost the 2000 election after being in power more than seventy years. The Zapatistas reached an agreement with the Mexican government that encouraged indigenous people to participate in the decision-making process and in the control of public expenditures. They also secured the state's recognition of the autonomy and self-determination of its indigenous populations. Likewise, these populations were guaranteed preferential rights in exploiting the natural resources of their land and their participation in public administration at all levels of political representation.[1]

Another group that emerged in the region is the Confederation of Indigenous Nationalities of Ecuador. Comprising ten indigenous organizations, CONAIE represents a large social movement. Indigenous groups have been an important factor in Ecuadorian politics since the 1990s. Traditionally, parties in Ecuador from both the Right and the Left have regarded indigenous communities as obstacles to modernization; thus, they have ignored or suppressed their demands.[2] CONAIE stands for the protection of the environment, the resolution of land ownership conflicts, and the promotion of cooperatives, organic farms, and traditional trade. In coordination with other indigenous organizations, CONAIE mobilized its members and successfully removed presidents Jamil Mahuad and Lucio Gutiérrez from power. CONAIE would later be instrumental in bringing the pro-Chávez Rafael Correa to power in 2006. In Ecuador, the power of CONAIE is such that any political development now depends on its support.[3]

In Bolivia, the indigenous populations and the social movements they created had similar power. The Confederation of Peasant Workers' Unions of Bolivia is the largest organization. The trade union federations of the cocaleros (coca growers) led by Evo Morales emerged from the CSUTBC. A second emergent group was the Movimiento Indígena Pachakuti (Pachakuti Indigenous Movement) led by the more radical Felipe Quispe. In the early 1990s Quispe was a leader of the Ejército Guerrillero Tupak Katari

(Tupak Katari Guerrilla Army), which failed and led to his incarceration for five years.[4] Together, Morales and Quispe formed one of the largest indigenous social movements in the region. In Bolivia, indigenous people were part of a social movement that was largely integrated into the Movement toward Socialism. Once Morales was in government clashes between Morales and Quispe also took place.

In Peru, the Movimiento Etnocacerista emerged as an indigenous movement. The etnocacerista movement is ultra nationalist and demands the rule of Indians over a vast territory. One of its key leaders was Ollanta Humala, the current president of Peru. Humala is a former military attaché who served in South Korea and previously had participated in a failed military revolt against former president Alberto Fujimori (1990–2000) in October 2000. In 2005 Humala's brother, Antauro Humala, who is considered the real leader of the etnocaceristas, led an assault on a police station in the remote area of Andahuaylas. Four police officers were killed during the siege, which was carried out mostly by ex-military men.

The etnocaceristas' leadership comprises military reservists and former soldiers who oppose foreign investment and talk about creating an alliance with Bolivia and Ecuador called the Tahuantinsuyo Axis. The object of this axis, whose name "Tahuantinsuyo" refers to the four states of the Incan Empire, is to create one territory based on the Inca nation and to establish Quechua as its official language instead of Spanish. The group aspired to establish one Indian nation that would include Peru, Bolivia, Ecuador, the northern part of Argentina, and parts of Chile as well.

As noted earlier, when Ollanta Humala ran for president in 2006, he came a close second to Alan García and had received funds from Hugo Chávez. After Ollanta Humala was elected president in 2011, he distanced himself from his brother Antauro and the ideas of etnocacerism. He ran on a different platform as he ran with a coalition of several parties called, "Gana Peru" (Peru Wins). These parties include Humala's own Nationalist Party, the community Party of Peru, the Socialist Party, the Revolutionary Socialist Party, and a few others.[5] Although there are elements of the extreme Left in this coalition of parties, Humala has followed Luiz Lula Da Silva's policies in Brazil rather than the Chávez model. Humala pledged to stay within the center-left as he also vowed social inclusion but has placed technicians who are more conservative and to the right to manage the economy.[6]

Ollanta Humala's direction has disappointed members of the etnocac-erista movement, and some have expressed their discontent with Humala's government. Partly, this animosity is based on the president's refusal to free his own brother Antauro, who is serving a lengthy prison sentence for the police station assault. Further, etnocaceristas have accused the president of moving toward the right because his government has appointed business technocrats, not revolutionary socialists, to the cabinet.[7] Etnocaceristas demand that the country return to the ideas of Antauro Humala (which means embracing the original ultra-nationalist ideas of etnocacerismo). However, the movement is not nearly as momentous as one could think, despite Peru's large indigenous population.

In addition, Humala confronted local indigenous populations' ire when he changed his position and approved without previous consulta-tion a multibillion-dollar gold mining project (Project Conga) run by a foreign company. Marchers (who were not etnocaceristas) protested the environmental impact of the project, particularly on local water resources. Although Ollanta Humala agreed to negotiate with protesters, his initial reaction was to declare a state of emergency.[8]

In Chile, the separatist Mapuche Indians have also been mobilized; however, they have played an insignificant role in national politics. The Mapuches tend to mobilize in the rural areas (what they call "rural sub-version") by unifying radicalized ethnic minorities, including the Chilean urban poor and the Mapuche indigenous populations. Thus, indigenous and poor communities reinforce their identities based on anti-system ideologies.

In Brazil and Argentina, grassroots movements have acquired signifi-cant importance. In Brazil, the Landless Workers' Movement (Movimento dos Trabalhadores Sem Terra [MST]) emerged in 1984 as the military dic-tatorship ended and democracy returned to the country. This movement emerged from regional groups of farmworkers that occupied lands in the late 1970s. Its program seeks to legalize lands those workers occupied and to expropriate lands that belong to large landowners and multinational corporations. Likewise, it seeks expansion of popular participation and it opposed globalization and neo-liberalism.[9] The group later expanded into a militant and sometimes violent movement that occupied lands and blocked roads and buildings. The MST remains an independent social movement, and during the elections its members supported the Workers'

Party (Partido dos Trabalhadores [PT]), the party that has been governing Brazil since 2003. Trade unions that emerged in Brazil as a result of increased urbanization founded the PT in 1980. Contrary to many party elites in Brazil and Latin America as a whole, the PT included grassroots organizations, such as the MST, with permanent participation in decisions at every level. During the tenure of Fernando Henrique Cardozo (1994–2002), the government imposed a tax on fallow land. The MST project received additional support among the middle classes and the Catholic Church. It combines direct action and concrete negotiations with the government. The openness of the Cardozo government encouraged the movement even more as expectations began to rise.

However, the movement does more than demand agrarian reform. It is a social movement that rejects neoliberalism, the market, and globalization, and its ideological component transcends practical demands. It has remained active and militant even after its candidate Lula won the elections and became president of the Republic of Brazil. By the same token, rural farmers organized militias to protect their lands from the MST's occupation.

After Lula became president, though, he turned away from his radical discourse. Lula included conservatives in his cabinet and refused to implement radical land reform. The movement intensified efforts and waged more occupations of lands under Lula than it did under the Cardozo government. As a result, the Landless Workers' Movement clashed numerous times with the government, and the Lula administration threatened to impose martial law.

Later the landless formed coalitions with other groups and added to its agenda the struggle against unemployment. In that sense the MST has moved from operating exclusively in the rural sector and has expanded its efforts to working in the urban setting. The movement has also opposed technological modernization and the introduction of foreign capital. Later the MST expanded its ideology beyond agrarian reform and unemployment into a broader struggle against "international financial capitalism and against transnational (foreign) companies that operate the (Brazilian) agriculture."[10]

According to MST leader Joao Stedile, the group has not merely looked to obtain concrete demands but also sought to impose "hegemony in society which goes well beyond the struggle to occupy public office."[11] In other words, the Landless Workers' Movement had worked to implement the philosophy of Italian Marxist Antonio Gramsci, who believed that before it could take over the reins of government and society, the working class must first impose its way of thinking. It must wage a cultural and not a subversive takeover.[12] Therefore, the landless movement had to establish a school of ideological formation.[13]

In Argentina, new grassroots movements emerged called the *piquetero* (picketer) movement. Born out of the social protests of the 1990s that took place across the country, the piqueteros comprise numerous independent organizations—including communist, retiree, and unemployed groups—with separate leaders. The collapse of the Argentinean economy and the neoliberal model in the 2000s provided an ideological basis for unifying these independent organizations. The working classes, as well as the unemployed, the underemployed, and other marginalized sectors of society, began systematically to mobilize and organize.[14] Their most crucial moment was their participation in the December 2001 protests that helped end both the government of President Fernando de la Rúa (1999–2001) and the neoliberal market reforms that had begun under former president Carlos Menem.

The piqueteros reject the political system, including representative democracy and the whole concept of a market economy. They demand the re-statization of privatized companies and, at the political level, direct democracy in the form of local, neighborhood-based, self-ruled, and autonomous councils. Their methods of action include violence, such as using firearms, and protests aimed at stopping the country through blockading highways and bridges and taking over police stations and government offices.[15]

As noted in the preceding description, these grassroots movements are not uniform. They differ in their characteristics, intensity, successes, and even in their strategies and modus operandi as numerous factors gave rise to these movements.

Most interesting is that the political opening associated with the democratization of the 1980s raised the expectations and self-awareness of social groups that historically had been excluded from the Latin American polity. This time these groups constitute not necessarily the traditional working class, as historically defined by classical Marxism; instead, they are mostly groups that lacked political representation or stood at the margins of society. Unemployed, shantytown residents and indigenous groups became a real social and political force that continues to present a challenge to the different governments. In some cases, as in Bolivia and Ecuador, they had remarkable accomplishments. As illustrated, they maintained their autonomy as they have confronted and seriously protested their governments when they disagreed with their policies, even removing presidents from office. In Brazil, groups such as the landless movement (MST) are now part of the party in power, and at the same time have confronted the party on a number of issues, particularly on the party's inclusion of conservative elements in the government cabinet. The popularity, strength, and pragmatism of Lula's leadership and the PT's solidity contained them within the party.

It is important to note the extent to which some of these groups have played an effective role in the political events that have affected their respective countries. Some of these movements featured components of nationalism, xenophobia, and angry social resentment. Other groups tended to support direct forms of populist participation and rejected the party system and state institutions altogether, as well as the global market economy. In the case of the indigenous groups, they demanded rights, cultural autonomy, and the protection of their environment and zoning rights. Likewise, they supported the nationalization of national resources while rejecting neoliberalism and foreign investment. Also important, during the 1990s, Latin American countries adopted constitutions that included provisions that recognize the rights of indigenous people. In most cases, those reforms were the result of public debate and organized pressure from indigenous and other grassroots populations.

In short, with the expansion of democratization in the 1980s and '90s, nation-states in Latin America have also expanded the rights of indigenous people and other groups. During the two decades since democracy was restored in most of the continent and indigenous people voiced their demands,[16] Colombia, Guatemala, and Brazil have recognized indigenous rights in their constitutions, and Colombia validated the concept of indigenous territories. In Brazil, the 1988 constitution forbids the removal of Indians from their land, and Mexico and Colombia granted cultural autonomy to their indigenous populations. The multiethnic and pluri-national character of the Bolivian state is acknowledged in the 1994 constitution, which also provides that indigenous people can exercise administrative functions, taking into account their traditions, customs, and culture. Likewise, new laws have opened a process of decentralization, the direct access to public funds by indigenous communities, and the establishment of indigenous municipal districts. The constitution also provides autonomy to indigenous populations and promotes respect for social, economic, cultural, and environmental rights. The state is also committed to supporting bilingual education.[17]

Indigenous peoples have seen progress in recognizing their various rights, but the different countries have been very slow in implementing these rights and converting the written word into practice. Although the process of formal democracy granted indigenous groups their rights, it did not solve their problem of social exclusion. Deceitful and politically manipulative leaders such as Lucio Gutiérrez, who initially enjoyed the trust of the Ecuadorian Indians, and those political parties that continued to behave as party notables further alienated these groups instead of integrating them. Even though some governments may have succeeded in providing them rights in certain cases, the self-consciousness of indigenous groups clearly strengthened and their expectations grew higher with the expansion of democracy. As their expectations grew, their disappointment with the authorities increased, as did their sense of betrayal.

This situation is similar to the French philosopher Alexis de Tocqueville's description of what preceded the French Revolution. Referring to the ancient regime before the revolution, de Tocqueville pointed out that under the monarchy, "there was far more freedom than there is today but it was curiously ill-adjusted, intermittent freedom, always restricted by class distinctions and tied up with immunities and privileges. Though it enabled Frenchmen on occasion to defy the law and to resist coercion, it never went so far as to ensure even the most natural and essential rights to all alike."[18] Precisely because the system generated high expectations, patience was lost. These unfulfilled expectations made the democratic system itself vulnerable to attacks. Or as Latin American scholar Leonardo Curzio has pointed out, the "democratic disenchanted" exist "because democracy lacked the efficacy to materialize these expectations."[19]

Hugo Chávez, meanwhile, attempts to take advantage of this discontentment and uses it to strengthen the Bolivarian revolution.

THE BOLIVARIAN REVOLUTION AND THE GRASSROOTS

To connect to the grassroots, in August 2003, Hugo Chávez founded the People's Bolivarian Congress (Congreso Bolivariano de los Pueblos [CBP]).

This forum would serve as a place where "all the popular, democratic and patriotic forces would gather to discuss ways to achieve Latin American–Caribbean integrity and unity."[20] The people, or grass roots, are the oxygen for this struggle to achieve unity. The spirit of the people is embedded in the political and social organizations and the peasant, indigenous, unemployed, student, and workers' movements.

The CBP claims that for Latin America the alternative is either to unite or to perish. Unity is a means both to fight misery, backwardness, and economic dependency and to achieve happiness. This organization believes in the populace rather than in academics, intellectuals, or politicians. It views the common people as agents of historical change that need to be mobilized "in all fronts."[21]

Even though the mission statement claims to respect the pace and circumstances of these grassroots organizations and movements, depending on developments in each country, the CBP presents itself as a means to fight common problems and at the same time to build a new thought and identity in Latin America. The organization will "build a Bolivarian doctrine of liberation and a great movement of emancipation for our America."[22] Thus, Chávez has developed a strong and active relationship with a number of grassroots organizations.

Argentina is perhaps one of the most outstanding examples as Chávez maintains a strong relationship with a number of piquetero organizations. The piqueteros, who come from the most marginal sectors of society, have become experts at spreading their anger and have the support of certain enthusiastic journalists and intellectuals who celebrate that the Left is finally in power. From the beginning, Argentinean president Nestor Kirchner, a strong Chávez sympathizer, adopted a popular antibusiness ideology and attitude, which worked well with the piqueteros. He proceeded to intimidate companies, corporations, supermarkets, and other businesses in an effort to force them to lower the price of their products. Kirchner also organized an overall boycott of Shell Oil Company, using the piqueteros to demonstrate in front of the company's headquarters and to force the company to lower gas prices. Unable to resist the government's coercive pressure, Shell complied with the "request" to lower its prices. Esso (Exxon) followed. Kirchner repeated the same assault on the supermarkets when their products' prices rose.[23]

Many piquetero groups belong to the CBP. The largest, Barrios de Pie (Standing Neighborhoods), represents the unemployed, and its leader

Jorge Ceballos held cabinet positions in the Kirchner government. Although not officially part of the CBP, the Federación de Tierra y Vivienda (Land and Housing Federation) is another organization that has strong connections to Chávez. Its leader Luis D'Elia is also tied to Kirchner. He was briefly expelled from the Kirchner government when he expressed support for Iran, but President Cristina Kirchner rehired him later as the government's main spokesperson when the government confronted the rural sector on a battle over increasing taxes on the sector.

Another piquetero organization that joined the Bolivarian organization is Quebracho, which is also a member of the Argentinean Bolivarian Circles. This group, whose official name is the Patriotic Revolutionary Movement, touts an ideology based on anti-capitalism and "anti-imperialism."[24] Quebracho is an alliance of activists in a number of lose popular organizations and other pre-existent organizations of the Left that include Peronists, Socialists, Communists, and some former Montoneros, a violent peronist guerrilla active during the 1970s. Quebracho's enemies are the International Monetary Fund, the World Bank, the United States, Japan, Israel, and Argentinean associations that represent industrialists and the rural sector.[25]

Quebracho advocates the use of revolutionary violence and is convinced that violence is more effective than any other form of struggle, especially voting, to achieve its ends. It rationalizes that elections are nothing but a fraudulent game that conspires against the people while violence in the hands of people is not violence but a means of justice and self-defense. Quebracho believes that through rebellion, victory will be achieved.[26] Indeed, the movement continuously organizes antigovernment protests on any occasion and anywhere in the country.[27] Quebracho has organized violent demonstrations and occasionally vandalized and looted businesses.[28] They also attacked the British embassy during the thirtieth anniversary commemoration of the Falklands War.[29] Quebracho works with students, the unemployed, workers, and others in an effort to start a revolution. The group's revolutionary ideals are no different than Chávez's in supporting state socialism and the integration and unity of Latin America. Quebracho without hesitation embraces Chávez, who is seen as a genuine leader of the revolutionary masses.[30]

Quebracho has also a major interest in the Middle East conflict. It is staunchly anti-Zionist and pro-Iran—it even has a direct line to the Iranian Embassy.[31] As an example, during a peaceful and legal demonstration organized by members of the Argentinean Jewish community in front of the Iranian Embassy in Buenos Aires, a Quebracho tried to prevent the protestors from arriving at the site. On that occasion members of the group also expressed their support for Iran and their repudiation of Israel. Quebracho cooperates with the Islamic Association of Argentina (AIA), which has links to Hezbollah and to the government of Iran.[32] (This will be discussed in chapter 6.)

Chávez also purposely encourages the loyalty of these groups. He provides them with ideological and financial aid. In March 2007, with the permission of then president Nestor Kirchner, key CBP members Ceballos and D'Elia organized a demonstration against President George W. Bush in Buenos Aires while Bush attended the Summit of the Americas in Argentina. Hugo Chávez was the keynote speaker of that demonstration. D'Elia, according to the U.S. Embassy in Buenos Aires, received funds from the Venezuelan government that enabled him to travel and attend a special conference on Latin America in Iran, an ally of the Bolivarian leader.[33] Again, early in 2010 D'Elia returned to Iran and met with Mohsen Rabbani, the former cultural attaché at the Iranian Embassy in Buenos Aires when the Argentine Israelite Mutual Association was bombed in 1994. He is considered the main suspect in that terrorist attack.[34] Rabbani also coordinates Iranian activities in Latin America (see chapter 6).

Likewise, the former Venezuelan ambassador in Buenos Aires Roger Capella personally supervised Venezuelan-financed welfare programs for Argentinean poor neighborhoods and has publicly criticized Argentinean policies and institutions. This action is an example of the Venezuelan government's interference in the internal affairs of another country. Chávez tried to show that he was capable of delivering the goods better than the Argentina government could.

By the same token, Chávez has established relations with the etnocacerista movement in Peru and actively supported its leader Ollanta Humala in the June 2006 Peruvian elections. In July 2007, violent massive protests took place in different regions of Peru. The protests began as the Union of Education Workers led a strike against an initiative for educational reform that required teachers to take a proficiency test. Soon followed other strikes by the unions representing construction workers, farmers, and miners. As the demonstration spread, the number of strikers increased and violence intensified.[35] In the southern region of Puno, workers stormed airports and train stations and threw eggs and tomatoes at President Alan García. Angry demonstrators held several police officers hostage. Although, these protests were considered to reflect some legitimate demands, many clearly believed Hugo Chávez was behind the escalation of the demonstrations. Ollanta Humala suddenly reappeared in public, calling for García's resignation. As noted in chapter 3, a newspaper reported that he received $600,000 monthly from Chávez to promote social unrest in the country.[36] More so, legislators affiliated with Humala's Nationalist Party had been traveling to Venezuela for long periods. One of them admitted that Humala was behind the strikes.

Furthermore, the president of the Puno region Hernán Fuentes opened an office of the Bolivarian Alternative for the Americas in Puno. Fuentes—who was elected in the 2006 elections on behalf of the Avanza País party, which was led by Ulises Humala and joined with Antauro Humala—clearly expressed his support for Hugo Chávez and his rejection of García. As Chávez has done in Venezuela, Fuentes provided Puno citizens with free medical treatment (particularly in the field of ophthalmology) financed by the Venezuelan government under a project called La Misión del Milagro (Miracle Mission). Likewise, another project called Si, Yo Puedo (Yes, I can) provides literacy to peasants.[37]

ALBA offices have proliferated in Peru's southern highlands, serving as dissemination points for Chávismo. Government officials say that these so-called antipoverty centers have sprung up across Peru to promote political agitation and may have fueled protests against the government's free-market economic policies. Many centers were linked to a radical leftist organization known as the Continental Bolivarian Committee.[38]

Puno is one area that has been radicalized as a result of its alienation from the political center. Likewise, it has seen countless clashes over land. As Fuentes himself has indicated, the people's feeling in Puno is that they live in another country, as they believe that Peru's economic growth does not apply to them.[39] This attitude is typical of certain Latin American countries, particularly those with large indigenous populations and where the state has failed to reach out and integrate those populations that live within its territory. The Peruvian government's presence in this area is nonexistent; thus, the population in Puno feels largely ignored.

In Ecuador, despite its particular history as an autonomous entity and its clashes with the Correa government, the indigenous group CONAIE has supported the Bolivarian revolution and identifies with it. Luis Macas, one of CONAIE's leaders, has had a connection to Chávez for some time and strongly supports the idea of Latin American unity and integration. Macas has also adopted the Chávez-sponsored program Operation Miracle, one of the *misiones* mentioned in chapter 2. In the program, Cuban doctors restore people's eyesight and teachers work to improve the literacy of the indigenous population in Ecuador for free. CONAIE officials and representatives from other Ecuadorian indigenous groups also have attended the meetings of the People's Bolivarian Congress.

The resolutions of CONAIE's Third Congress, adopted in January 2008, states that "Latin America has initiated a set of profound structural changes, mainly in Venezuela, Bolivia, and Nicaragua." The resolution reaffirms its support for the Cuban revolution and recognizes that Ecuador is part of this process but complains that the Correa government still excludes "those social organizations that have fought against neoliberalism."[40] (As we will see, CONAEI later develops tensions with Ecuadorian president Rafael Correa and with ALBA.)

In Brazil, the MST's website worships the figure of Hugo Chávez, praising his social achievements and his radical revolution.[41] The MST came into conflict with President Lula when he adopted a pragmatic position, including installing some conservatives in his cabinet and continuing some of his predecessors' free-market policies instead of pursuing the radical social reforms the parties expected.

The same applies to the large Brazilian trade union Central Workers' Union (Central Única de Trabajadores [CUT]), which has also attracted the most radical sectors of the working class and has appealed to tactics similar to those of the Landless Workers' Movement. Lula's PT, like the Bolivian ruling Movement for Socialism, is a grassroots-based party that rose up against the historical elitist Brazilian parties.[42] The CUT, along with the MST, expressed serious disappointment over Lula's centrism and has adopted Chávez's radical agenda. It even endorsed his most outrageous positions, such as supporting the Libyan government of Muammar Gadhafi during the rebellion that ended with the dictator's death in October 2011. CUT viewed Gadhafi's repression of the rebels as resisting against the imperial powers of the North Atlantic Treaty Organization (NATO).[43]

Another entity that is inclined to be sympathetic to Chávez is the Mexican Party of the Democratic Revolution (PRD).[44] The party's founder,

Cuauhtémoc Cárdenas, is the son of President Lázaro Cárdenas (1934–1940), who in his time founded the Institutional Revolutionary Party, which dominated Mexican politics for most of the twentieth century. A party of the Left, the PRD represents those masses of people and popular organizations that felt excluded from the declining and unresponsive PRI. Since the late 1980s, the party rapidly gained support and supported mass mobilization and obstructionism against the PRI government, which it considered to be corrupt and accused of having won elections through fraud. The PRD grew and became one of the country's largest parties thanks to the efforts of Andrés López Obrador, a master of planning and winning local elections by mobilizing new supporters, especially from the lower classes.[45] In 2000 López Obrador himself became mayor of giant Mexico City. He implemented public works programs to create jobs and projected an image of honesty, very much contrary to the widespread view of the typical Mexican politician. He became the leader of the PRD but lost the 2006 presidential elections to Felipe Calderón by a small margin. After hearing the election results, López Obrador appealed and organized mass demonstrations, claiming that the election was stolen, but to no avail. Courts declared again that the election results legitimately favored Calderón.

During the election campaign López Obrador was accused of being a Mexican Chávez, something he strongly denied. Some even accused him of having received funds directly from the Venezuelan head of state. After the 2006 election López Obrador's refusal to concede the election raised the fear that the PRD might move toward the kind of praetorian politics that currently characterize Venezuela, Bolivia, and Ecuador and that the party, which is the second-largest political force in the country, could intensify its populist overtones.[46] Meanwhile, López Obrador was defeated again in the 2012 elections finishing second place with 31.6 percent of the total vote.

▌ SUMMARY

The grassroots organizations are the direct result of a process of democratization that created expectations but failed to deliver on them. These movements emerged in formal democracies where their rights have been formally extended but have not been advanced on the ground. Most of them comprise communities that prior to the appearance of democracy were politically marginalized. Their fast-growing expectations led to the people's disenchantment and quick mobilization. From the point of view of the Bolivarian revolution, therefore, they are available, ready-made masses for the revolution.

Yet, whether the Bolivarian machine might swallow these grassroots organizations is still not clear. Many of them are focused more on a national agenda than on a continental agenda. The element of autonomy that some of these groups display might prevent their subordination to the revolution. Yet, there is widespread sympathy toward Chávez, who stands as a symbol of a new order. Nevertheless, the Bolivarian revolution understands the potential of these available masses in helping the revolution. We have seen it in the case of the Puno rebellion in Peru and in Chávez's active outreach.

As Fernando Bossi, secretary of the People's Bolivarian Congress, pointed out in 2008:

> We are supporting local struggles always trying to integrate them into a larger continental agenda in order not to keep them isolated. . . . Any struggle that takes place in any country will be supported [through the CBP] by other people in Latin America in order to give them support with ideas and experiences. . . . We do not need an organization that would hold an event once in a while in order to deliberate and issue declarations. We need a movement of conscious people in order to organize actions that would conduct us to a large, unified nation (*Patria Grande*).[47]

In fact, as the examples of the Landless Workers' Movement in Brazil, the piqueteros in Argentina, and the Puno regional movement illustrate, Chávez stands as a symbol above that of any respective national president. The Ecuadorian CONAIE was perhaps the only organization that expressed reservations about the Bolivarian leadership when it rejected the ALBA summit of June 2010 because "it excluded the legitimate representatives of the indigenous communities." Because of this and its conflict with Correa over environmental policies and indigenous rights, CONAIE refused to recognize the resolutions of that summit.[48]

Chávez has been able to generate loyalties and admiration among these grassroots organizations comparable to what revolutionary leader Che Guevara enjoyed in the 1960s. All of the groups have organized and mobilized their constituencies, and because most have revolutionary instincts, these groups could become dangerous. Some of them have already demonstrated their willingness to use violence. As we will see in chapter 6, for instance, one Venezuelan indigenous group has created an entity called Hezbollah Latin America and embraced the ideas of radical Islam.

Yet, these movements or organizations are still far from being identical. If the democracies or the parties in power succeed in either in co-opting them or integrating them in the democratic system, their revolutionary potential may fade away. However, if the democratic system or the governments of the respective countries fail to integrate or substantially satisfy these groups' demands, some might become part of the insurgent Bolivarian machine.

5 | CHÁVEZ'S DANGEROUS LIAISONS WITH GUERRILLAS AND DRUG CARTELS

Hugo Chávez, as a true and determined revolutionary, will not wait until the grassroots groups take over their countries through legitimate means. Chávez would rather rely on and appeal mainly to violent and other criminal groups, which are likely to bring more immediate results.

Two such groups that existed before the Bolivarian revolution and aspired to take the reins of power are the Revolutionary Armed Forces of Colombia (FARC) and the drug cartels. They have capabilities and skills that may benefit the Bolivarian revolution. Specifically, FARC has the ability to destabilize governments through subversive activities, while drug cartels undermine state authority by corrupting state institutions, including judges, the police, and others.

At the same time, these two groups may also benefit from the Bolivarian revolution, particularly at a time when these groups are being hunted. While the Colombian government is chasing FARC and has diminished its subversive capability, the U.S. Drug Enforcement Administration has been monitoring and fighting drug trafficking all over Latin America. Thus, drug cartels have been weakened in Colombia but remain strong in Mexico and in Central America. Bolivarian countries, meanwhile, have harbored FARC guerrillas and given them a lifeline as they escaped from the Colombian authorities. Because the Bolivarian revolution and its associated countries view the fight against drug trafficking as an American imperialist enterprise, most of the Bolivarian countries have expelled the DEA from their territories.

This chapter explains the connections between the Bolivarian countries and FARC and the drug cartels. It also explores what the consequences and implications are for the region and the United States.

▌ BOLIVARIAN ALLIANCE WITH FARC AND THE DRUG CARTELS

Military analyst Max Manwaring has pointed out that President Chávez believes that asymmetric conflict is the way in which the weak fight the strong.[1] However, this style of warfare involves not merely a direct confrontation but also a process of destruction and weakening of what one considers being the enemy or the possessions and allies of that enemy.

In the words of Manwaring:

> If the irregular attacker—terrorists, drug cartels, criminal gangs, militant religious fundamentalists, or a combination of such non-state actors—blends crime, terrorism, and war, he can extend his already significant influence. . . . Using complicity, intimidation, corruption, and indifference, the irregular attacker can quietly and subtly co-opt politicians and bureaucracies and gain political control of a given geographical or political enclave. Such corruption and distortion can potentially lead to the emergence of a network of government protection of illicit activities, and the emergence of a virtual criminal state or political entity. . . . An irregular attacker can criminally co-opt and seize control of the state.[2]

It is from this premise that the role of the drug cartels and FARC in the expansion of the Bolivarian revolution should be understood.

▌ FARC AND DRUG TRAFFICKING: HISTORICAL BACKGROUND

Guerrillas in Colombia have existed since the 1960s, when the Cuban revolution inspired a wave of such groups to sweep Latin America. They believed that only armed struggle would bring about a regime of full justice for all. La Violencia (the violence) of 1948–1958 was a period when two major parties waged a civil war. By the end of La Violencia, its fierce and unscrupulously brutal combatants took the lives of about 200,000 people. The end result was a lasting peace, but its legacy inspired the growth of modern Colombian guerrilla insurgencies, especially FARC, which was founded in 1964.

FARC is the outcome of peasant-armed resistance. Resistance groups existed during La Violencia, but in the early 1960s these self-defense organizations became ensconced in a few small towns. FARC, which developed mostly during the 1970s, was closely aligned with the pro-Soviet Communist Party until the collapse of the Soviet Union. However, the guerrilla group survived while others either collapsed or negotiated with the government for a peaceful integration into the political system.

Although FARC has some roots in the peasant population, it survived mainly because it joined the illicit crop of networks that began at the end of the 1970s.[3] During that period, the cultivation of drugs in Colombia grew substantially, to the point that it became the main supplier of marijuana and cocaine to the United States. In addition, FARC controlled extensive territory, mostly where coca was cultivated.[4] This exposure later enabled the organization to create its own drug operation. FARC has used violence and committed numerous massacres in pursuing its revolution.

In 1973, the government of Colombia attempted to eradicate FARC and other guerrilla groups, but the groups managed to survive. By 1984, the Colombian government cracked down on the drug operations that helped finance the guerrillas' operations, and it offered amnesty to guerrilla groups in exchange for their disarmament. A truce of a few years ensued.[5] In 1989, however, FARC cut its ties to formal civilian allies and returned to the underground, hoping to win a war using its significant drug-based funding.

In the 1980s, Colombia found itself in disarray, and chaos mounted as the activities of the guerrillas and the drug cartels increased. State authority came under attack. The Medellín and Cali Cartels controlled between 75 and 80 percent of the cocaine traffic. Nearly 100,000 Colombians worked for those cartels, and their revenue was estimated to have been between $2 billion and $4 billion a year.[6]

Since drug activities were clearly illegal, the cartels used fierce violence as a means to survive and maintain their business operations. They resorted to assassinating judges and politicians who confronted them and to destroying newspapers that denounced them. They blew up a flight of the Colombian national airlines, Avianca, with all the passengers on board including a presidential candidate. Most important, drug cartels resorted to bribing government and law enforcement officials, including those at the highest level of government.[7] Allegedly, the Cali cartel funneled drug money to the presidential campaign of Ernesto Samper, who served as president of Colombia from 1994 to 1998. Samper was charged with having accepted $6 million from cocaine traffickers for his 1994 presidential campaign. Several high-level politicians and cabinet ministers resigned as a result of this scandal.[8] Others, like former defense minister and Samper's campaign manager Fernando Botero, were also charged. The only body with the authority to judge the president, however, was the Colombian Congress, where the president has political allies. Samper was absolved of all charges in July 1996, after a series of violent acts that included the death of several witnesses and murder attempts against politicians.[9] It is important to point out that bribery at lower levels is also important since administrators and policemen run the daily functions of the state. Indeed, it turns out that the drug cartels were able to corrupt the military, the police, and the bureaucracy as a whole.

All of these factors together generated anarchy in the streets of Colombia. State authority grew weaker and weaker. The drug cartels and the guerrillas broke the state's capability to impose order.

In an effort to defeat the drug cartels, the Colombian government resorted to some illegal methods. It recruited criminal gangs, which would later become the foundation of the United Self-Defense Forces of Colombia (Autodefensas Unidas de Colombia [AUC]), an umbrella group of the right-wing paramilitary.[10] The former leader of the AUC, the gangster Carlos Castaño, pointed out that "the AUC exists because the armed forces have not fulfilled their duty of guaranteeing lives, property and honor."[11] He implied that the AUC existed because the Colombian state's capability to exercise authority collapsed. Unfortunately, while the AUC succeeded in killing thousands of FARC members, it also killed human rights activists, journalists, academics, and other civilians.

Civil war replaced the rule of law. Colombia, paraphrasing Thomas Hobbes, had become a society in which the state of nature had no common power to enforce rules. During the 1990s, the government attempted constitutional reforms and elections; however, democracy and order continued to deteriorate as violence continued to increase. A few guerrilla groups— for example, the 19th of April Movement (M-19)—entered into negotiations. Some of the groups even received seats in the assembly. Negotiations with the FARC and other minor guerrilla groups, such as the National Liberation Army (Ejército de Liberación Nacional), however, failed.[12]

President Andrés Pastrana (1998–2002) initiated peace talks with FARC while simultaneously establishing an alliance with the United States. The latter effort gave birth to Plan Colombia, which was launched in 2000. The United States granted Colombia close to $1 billion annually in military aid to fight drug trafficking. This support was the beginning of a reconstruction process for state authority in Colombia. The fight against

FARC continued as peace talks failed. In 2002, President Pastrana called off peace talks and renewed military activities against FARC.[13]

In 2002, Alvaro Uribe was elected president of Colombia with an overwhelming majority after he campaigned on promises of taking a strong hand against the guerrillas and the cartels. Once in power, Uribe added more than 60,000 troops and 30,000 extra police. He professionalized the military and significantly expanded its control over Colombian territory, including the municipalities and the Andes Mountains. Thus, FARC was driven away from central Colombia and forced into the jungle. Thousands of guerrillas deserted, and FARC's numbers dropped significantly.[14] Later, right-wing paramilitary groups gradually disbanded. More important, the Colombian government pursued this effort in a way that maintained a balance between upholding democratic institutions and continuing the domestic battle against the drug cartels. In October 2012 Colombian president Juan Manuel Santos initiated peace negotiations with FARC but whether these negotiations will lead to tangible results is doubtful.

BOLIVARIANISM, FARC, AND THE DRUG TRADE

In the summer of 2009, the U.S. Government Accountability Office (GAO) published a report for the Senate Foreign Relations Committee that provides evidence of the activities and cooperation between the Venezuelan government and FARC and drug cartels.[15] It revealed that the flow of cocaine transiting Venezuela toward the United States, West Africa, and Europe increased more than four times from 2004 to 2007 and continues to increase sharply.[16] Most Colombian cocaine enters Venezuela along land or river routes, but traffickers also transport cocaine across the border using small aircraft operated from clandestine airstrips and submarines.[17]

Likewise, land crossings can occur almost everywhere across the border between Colombia and Venezuela. Such a high volume of commercial activity transiting both countries makes it is very difficult to distinguish between legal and illegal transportation of goods. As traffickers move cocaine from Venezuela, they go through the Caribbean toward the Atlantic Ocean and into North America, Europe, and West Africa. Cocaine destined for the United States from Venezuela transits through Central America, Mexico, the Dominican Republic, Haiti, and other Caribbean islands. Between January and July 2008, for instance, authorities seized numerous vessels with Venezuelan flags that were carrying large amounts of cocaine.[18]

According to U.S. and Colombian authorities, "Venezuela has extended a lifeline to Colombian illegal armed groups by providing them with significant support and safe haven along the border. As a result, these groups remain viable threats to Colombian security and U.S.-Colombian counternarcotics efforts." Also, "a high level of corruption within the Venezuelan government, military, and other law enforcement and security forces contributes to the permissive environment."[19]

Moreover, the Venezuelan police and security forces' cooperation with drug trafficking also presents a major problem. In the case of Venezuela, it is clearly deliberate state policy, guided and directed by Chávez and his entourage, to weaken the Colombian state. Indeed, the GAO report states that Venezuelan officials provided material support primarily to FARC, which "helped to sustain the Colombian insurgency and threaten security gains achieved in Colombia."[20] Furthermore, a Colombian army raid in Ecuador in March 2008 seized FARC computers and discovered documents belonging to FARC leader Raúl Reyes (known as the Reyes files) that seem to indicate the Venezuelan government may have provided FARC with about $300 million and other support. That support may have included supplies of Russian- and Chinese-made automatic weapons, sniper rifles, grenade launchers, and man-portable air defense system.[21]

Chávez put the elements it protected and helped to good use. The relationship between FARC and the Chávez government began early in the president's tenure through Ramón Rodríguez Chasín, a top intelligence officer who later became minister of interior and minister of justice.

In 1999, the Venezuelan government and FARC signed a memorandum of understanding, which gave FARC an advisory role to the Venezuelan government in matters related to "ideology, strategic planning and social control." Likewise, Chávez established a series of arrangements in which Venezuelan authorities would protect FARC's presence in the country. The Venezuelan government also made a commitment to provide health care and safety for FARC's operatives and to help launder its money.[22] FARC, in turn, would respect Venezuelan law and provide intelligence and training for Venezuelan armed groups (with proper authorization). In fact, in Venezuela, the Directorate of Intelligence and Prevention Service used the FARC to carry out terrorist attacks in Venezuela on behalf of the Venezuelan state. By the same token, FARC was essentially free to use Venezuelan territory, with occasional restrictions, for its own purposes. Chávez has also tried to provide an element of legitimacy to the group and made efforts to have the organization removed from the European list of terrorist organizations.[23] Most important, FARC trained armed groups, which were created to defend the Bolivarian revolution, in urban and rural guerrilla tactics. The FARC also established contacts with a number of terrorist groups in Venezuela.[24]

The Bolivarian government became more inclined to work with FARC after the attempted 2002 coup and when Chávez realized that the Venezuelan army was not necessarily going to stand by him. Thus, FARC began to assume a key role in providing both security to the Venezuelan government and military training to paramilitary forces. Chávez developed a "contingency plan" where paramilitary forces would be used "in the event of a future conspiracy." These forces would attack and "neutralize or liquidate opposition supporters, political leaders and resources through sabotage and targeted assassinations." The contingency plan was supposed to be directed and supervised by the executive power while bypassing the army.[25] Moreover, according to the intelligence analysts who compiled and analyzed the Reyes files, "the archive makes clear that Chávez has been interested in FARC as an asymmetric capability, and it indicates a number of specific actions undertaken by the group in support of the security of Chávez's regime, ranging from the training of paramilitary organizations to collaboration with the Venezuelan Intelligence services in direct terrorist activity against opposition targets in Caracas."[26]

Protecting his regime is only one of the tasks Chávez assigned to FARC. Not only does FARC destabilize the country through violent action, kidnapping, and murder, it also serves as an insurgent force that can create subversion in Colombia or any other country in the region. Indeed, according to Rodriguez Chasín, "Chávez was driven by an interest not only in defense against the perceived possibility of U.S. aggression, but also in accelerating Venezuelan regional hegemony, and the radicalization of the continent's ideological agenda."[27]

FARC's Expansion to Bolivarian Countries

FARC has lost ground in Colombia as a result of the Colombian government's successful efforts to weaken it. With FARC weakened in the country having lost territory, supply lines, areas of coca cultivation, and cocaine-trafficking routes, its activity began to move closer to the borders. Thus, the conflict in Colombia brought about a whole set of FARC and drug trafficking–related activity into Venezuela, which became a major destination for the FARC. It served as a place where guerrillas have received protection and negotiated conditions to continue their activities. But Venezuela is not the only country offering a lifeline to FARC.

According to the testimony of a major FARC leader, the group gave Chávez's good friend and ally Ecuadorian president Rafael Correa electoral campaign funding ($400,000) for his 2006 presidential bid.[28] Investigations indicate that this money was crucial in enabling the candidate to continue the electoral campaign and ultimately in securing his election.[29] Reports also show that members of Correa's inner circle, including top military officers, had direct contact with transnational drug trafficking tied to FARC.[30]

In Colombia, the Correa government was seen as highly problematic and unwilling to deal with the drug cartels and FARC because the Ecuadorian president was a Chávez ally. This situation created great tension between Colombia and Ecuador and helped trigger a Colombian military operation against FARC in the Ecuadorian area of Angostura (a mile from the Colombia-Ecuador border) in March 2008. Indeed, the Ecuadorian commission that later investigated the Angostura events found that the armed forces of Ecuador were complicit with drug and weapons trafficking. Similarly, the military helped pass FARC-manufactured drugs through Ecuador to Mexican drug cartels, which later moved the product to the United States. The commission also reported that the Ecuadorian military and FARC had tacit agreements that led the judiciary to abstain from prosecuting criminal cases and that the military was responsible for covering up criminal actions.[31] Even the chief Ecuadorian investigator, whom Correa himself initially appointed, said that Ecuador has, in fact, become a "narco-state."[32] FARC also established connections with the Confederation of Indigenous Nationalities of Ecuador.[33]

FARC also has strong connections in Bolivia. According to Douglas Farah, an investigative journalist, "There are clear indications that the FARC has maintained a presence in Bolivia for several years, and these ties have significantly increased since the Morales-led Movement Towards Socialism (MAS) party took power." Important political and intellectual figures in MAS are connected to FARC. According to testimonies by some FARC leaders there were contacts between FARC and Morales before and after he was elected president of Bolivia. Morales was interested in forming a "Committee of Solidarity" with Colombia, which was nothing but a body to support FARC and its work. Other MAS leaders such as Antonio Peredo, a national Senator and Hugo Moldiz, one of the founders of Morales' MAS party. Moldiz was seriously considered for a senior cabinet position and has served as the leader of the "People's High Command" (EMP), the main organization in charge of organizing the riots against President Sanchez de Lozada.[34]

President Daniel Ortega of Nicaragua has been a strong supporter of FARC since the late 1970s, when the Sandinistas were fighting the government of Anastasio Somoza. In a letter dated 2003, Reyes consulted Ortega about a request for weapons that FARC had made to the Libyan government as Ortega was then responsible for carrying out Libyan policies in Latin America. FARC and Ortega seem able to maintain a constant relationship through the Nicaraguan ambassador to Cuba. According to some documents, Nicaragua promised to help the FARC insofar as it was able.[35]

The FARC has also merged ideologically with the Bolivarian revolution. This transition might be the result either of the weakening of FARC or of the guerrilla group's recognition that the Bolivarian revolution is the only viable way to achieve a radical transformation or both. Nevertheless, FARC has loosened its ideology of peasant-based Marxist revolution in order to embrace the Bolivarian revolution and to commit to its expansion, including the fight against "U.S. imperialism," neoliberalism, and globalization. Likewise, it accepts the revolution's socialism and push toward continental unity.

Hugo Chávez created a body called the Bolivarian Continental Coordinator (Coordinadora Continental Bolivariana [CCB]), which later changed its name to the Bolivarian Continental Movement (Movimiento Continental Bolivariano [MCB]). The CCB/MCB has FARC as one of its members.

The CCB was founded in 2003 as an umbrella organization to integrate different social and political revolutionary groups across Latin America. It sought to "rescue and reaffirm our historical memory and Bolivarian integration in order to create a new alternative pole against the domination of the world imperial powers." The CCB also wanted to create "a movement capable of articulating the diverse revolutionary forces and to develop a strategy in order to defeat the imperialist strategy and so emancipate Latin America (Nuestra America) forever."[36] The movement expressed militant solidarity with Bolivarian Venezuela, the Cuban revolution, and with all the progressive processes that are taking place in other countries of the region. Its principles were based on solidarity with FARC and the Chávez regime and in opposition to U.S. security and economic policies in the region.[37] Most important, upon founding the organization, the CCB leaders agreed to create a "foreign legion" and to establish cells in each Latin American country.

In its second assembly in February 2008, the CCB adopted a resolution recognizing FARC and other insurgent sectors as "belligerent forces" instead of terrorist groups. Likewise, the resolution called for a unified effort to fight paramilitary forces and to support the slogan "No American soldier in our America." The CCB sought to deepen the socialist revolution throughout the continent and to continue the counteroffensive "against imperialism and the Latin American oligarchies."[38]

Carlos Casanueva, the executive director of the CCB, explained that "the organization covers under its umbrella all those groups, movements or parties that are fighting for the well being of our peoples, liberation and continental unity with the purpose of achieving a second independence." So according to Casanueva, "The CCB does not distinguish between those groups or exclude anyone except the fascists. . . . [This principle] allows for the membership of the FARC and other movements."[39]

This statement seems to confirm that FARC, in the view of Chávez and his Bolivarian movement, is an accepted force within the Bolivarian movement. FARC's capability to produce violence could become a key component of the Bolivarian revolution's fight for expansion.

In a message delivered by video to the MCB on March 24, 2012, FARC reinforced the right to rebel as an alienable right to fight injustice. FARC invoked Simón Bolívar to justify such action and in general invoked Bolívar's name as a role model of a liberator of the oppressed people and as a supporter of continental unity. FARC repeated both its determination to fight against "imperialism," particularly against Colombia, and its support for socialism. Continental unity would provide the power to fight the transnational corporations that exploit national resources to their benefit and not to the benefit of the people.[40]

When the CCB/MCB met in December 2009 in Caracas, representatives of extreme global organizations—including such terrorist groups as the Spanish ETA (the Basque insurgency), the Communist Party of El Salvador, remnants of the Red Brigades of Italy, and other armed groups—attended the conference.[41] The declaration issued after that conference is indicative of how the group sees violence as a key component in expanding the tentacles of the revolution. The declaration views the "Continental Bolivarian Movement as a means to promote the cause of the big nation" envisioned by Simón Bolívar. "We are thought and action melded with weapons against injustice. We are the combination of a variety of forms and methods of struggle." Likewise, the "Bolivarian revolution . . . will be defended with our soul and hearts and with blood loaded with anger if necessary." Then, the declaration turns more specific: "We will defeat the regime of Alvaro Uribe in Colombia. . . . We will defeat the putschist regime in Honduras and open up the way for a constitutional reform. . . . Colonialism in Puerto Rico, the Falkland Islands and the Caribbean will face us."[42]

This declaration seems to confirm that FARC and Chávez fully understand the importance of using violence as part of the Venezuelan president's continental objectives. The CCB/MSB statement is quite consistent with Venezuela's project of revolutionary export. In other words, once violence is unleashed, the destabilization process can be applied to any country in the region.

In short, FARC has ceased to be solely a Colombian organization that cares for events in Colombia and has become part of the Bolivarian revolution. Its activities and involvement turn now to regional and transnational affairs. Indeed, FARC is involved in about thirty countries to different degrees. Some of this involvement is visible, and other efforts are more clandestine.

FARC reaches out to students and regular militants with propaganda and ideology, and sometimes it helps insurgent militias. In some cases, FARC is involved in drug trafficking and in others, money laundering. In some areas, they have sought support for their organizations, and in others, they have sought to secure sanctuary.

In Peru, for instance, FARC has reached out to the Peruvian Revolutionary Movement Túpac Amaru, providing training to a splinter group and to the Revolutionary Left Movement. FARC also recruited people in Peru and provided weapons to the Maoist guerrilla group Sendero

Luminoso (Shining Path). In El Salvador, FARC used its connections with the Frente Farabundo Martí para la Liberación Nacional (Farabundo Martí National Liberation Front), now a major political party, to purchase arms and munitions.

In Chile, FARC recruited members of the Communist Party and sent them to Colombia for guerrilla training. Likewise, FARC reached out to such groups as the Frente Patriótico Manuel Rodriguez (Manuel Rodriguez Patriotic Front), the Revolutionary Left Movement, and the Mapuche indigenous movement (which is covered briefly in chapter 4).[43]

FARC members have a large presence in Paraguay. They assisted the Ejército del Pueblo Paraguayo (People's Army of Paraguay [EPP]) in the 2004 kidnapping and murder of Cecilia Cubas, the daughter of a former president Raúl Cubas Grau (1998–1999).[44] The EPP is a relatively small Marxist group, mostly active in the northeastern part of the country. Its connections with FARC have existed for more than ten years, and EPP members allegedly have received training in Colombia, Venezuela, and Cuba. The group considers Hugo Chávez a hero.[45]

In Mexico FARC has worked with the insurgent militia Ricardo Flores Magón, and it has provided financial support to left-wing politicians. In Bolivia, FARC tried to carry out activities of indoctrination. In such countries as Argentina, Brazil, and Panama, the guerrilla group mostly is involved in contacts with drug traffickers, asylum search, money laundering, and fund-raising.[46]

This information illustrates that FARC has turned into an international organization whose purpose in other countries has widened from seeking sanctuary or a means to survive to exporting guerrilla tactics and revolutionary activity. FARC's own files report that Chávez sees the group "as a strategic ally in event of [American military] aggression . . . but at the same time . . . as strategic allies for the creation of a revolutionary bloc in the continent."[47] That FARC is now connected through the Bolivarian Coordinator Movement to the Bolivarian revolution makes the possibility of the guerrillas' involvement in international seditious activities a very real one.

Drug Cartels and the Afghanization of the Region

Cocaine producers are reportedly using modern laboratories to process and manufacture their product. Furthermore, cocaine production is likely to increase as its associated infrastructure evolves. Narco-traffickers are operating mobile labs and chemicals similar to those used in Colombia to prevent detection. Meanwhile, battles over the control of smuggling routes have erupted.

As violent drug makers have multiplied and become more sophisticated, the Brazilian government has complained about smugglers' increasing traffic of processed cocaine shipments from Bolivia to Brazil.[48] In September 2011, a U.S. federal court in Miami sentenced Gen. René Sanabria-Oropeza, a former top adviser to Bolivian president Morales on anti-drug policy, to fifteen years in prison for his involvement in a drug smuggling operation. Meanwhile, Morales, who is also the head of the coca growers' trade union, has always successfully resisted attempts at coca eradication.[49]

In Nicaragua, American diplomats have privately denounced the government for having taken bribes from drug traffickers in exchange for freeing suspects. According to these allegations, Sandinista officials took money from drug enterprises and ordered Nicaraguan judges to free drug traffickers. Reportedly, the director of the state security service, with the help of two Supreme Court judges, has overseen these corrupt operations.[50]

Mexico is currently facing similar challenges to the problems that Colombia faced in the past. Indeed, in Mexico, drug trafficking has succeeded in destroying state institutions, including the law enforcement apparatus, particularly in various states that border the United States.[51] Drug cartels have been able to co-opt, bribe, and kill hundreds of policemen, judges, and politicians at all levels. For example, the police force in Tijuana, in an area that borders California, has virtually collapsed, and the city's own mayor has participated in its demise. In the state of Tamaulipas, which borders Texas, the police are divided between those who belong to the Gulf Cartel, those who belong to the Sinaloa Cartel, and those who belong to other criminal organizations. Very often rivalries between cartels have led to assassinations of police members who died not as a result of apprehending criminals but because they were part of an inter-cartel fight.[52] Most members of the gang called Zetas are former members of the Mexican police, army, and security forces who now work as an armed force for the Gulf Cartel. This state of anarchy and public corruption in Mexico has extended to various Mexican states including Baja California, Sonora, Chihuahua, Coahuila, Nuevo Leon, and Tamaulipas.

These developments could have serious consequences for the stability of any country. It is reasonable to assume that as the drug cartels expand, they will corrupt any state and spread anarchy everywhere they reach.

Many Latin American states are weak and their institutions decadent. The law suffers from ineffectual courts. Corruption is widespread at all levels of government; thus, people do not view their government institutions as legitimate entities. Yet, the Latin American states have survived because, unlike Colombia's past experience and that currently facing Mexico and other countries, they never had to confront the challenge of such a powerful element as the drug cartels. With the drug cartels and the mega-economic machine they generate moving into other areas, the Latin American states may lose their soldiers, policemen, public officials, administrators, and others to the sinful temptation of drug largesse. As drug cartels advance, along with groups such as FARC, the danger is that the rule of non-state actors will replace that of the elected government. This situation will inevitably lead to the "Afghanization" of the continent. Today Afghanistan is not a real state because it lacks what philosopher Max Weber called a "monopoly of the legitimate use of physical force within a given territory."[53] Many Latin American countries are devolving into a similar state.

Indeed, in a memorandum to the U.S. secretary of state signed in September 2008, former president George W. Bush wrote that—besides Mexico, Colombia, and Venezuela—Brazil, the Dominican Republic, Ecuador, Bolivia, Guatemala, Haiti, Jamaica, Panama, Peru, and Paraguay are either drug producers or drug transit places. Bush designated Venezuela and Bolivia as countries "that have failed to adhere to their obligations under international counternarcotics agreements." The memorandum also denounced the growing expansion of drug trafficking in Central America and concluded that the area presents a challenge to the region's limited capability to combat both the narcotics trade and organized crime.[54]

In Guatemala, for example, wealthy capos are reported to be accomplices and promoters of the drug smuggling business north to Mexico and the United States. The capos' families run this operation because they exercise control over territory where the Guatemalan state in fact has no reach. They provide jobs and daily bread to the local population, which in turn rallies to support the capos when the authorities or the United States requests their extradition.[55]

Moreover, the state has no presence in the nearly six-hundred-mile-long border separating Guatemala and Mexico. This area is one of the most important transit zones in the smuggling of people and drugs that often reach the United States.[56] For historical reasons, the Guatemalan-Mexican border has been isolated from the central governments of both countries. It lacks any regulatory law, political stability, government effectiveness, and accountability of any type. All of these aspects have worsened with time and have steadily declined since 2002. Both governments are incapable of prosecuting criminals or those who transgress the law. Impunity prevails. Ninety percent of the crimes committed do not end in jail convictions.[57] Deficient investigations and prosecutions are the result of corruption at all levels, including the police. Similarly, the judicial system is very weak. The fact that criminals are usually armed intimidates the authorities, which are then reluctant to pursue them.

In the case of Guatemala, the problem has affected the whole country, which is now in a state of disarray. Private security firms provide security to those citizens who request it and can pay for their services. More than three hundred private security firms are either working in the country or awaiting licenses. Even more astonishing is that private security firms have sixty thousand employees on staff while the Guatemalan national police force employs close to twenty thousand and the military approximately fifteen thousand.[58]

This state of lawlessness has brought about gang activity. Tens of thousands of gangs operate in Guatemalan border areas. The Mara Salvatrucha (MS-13) gang, for instance, has found fertile ground in Guatemala and other countries in Central America. Gangs provide security to drug traffickers and intimidate the population and state authorities. Highly organized and disciplined, these gangs use extreme violence, including roughly torturing and raping their victims before murdering them. Many members acquired military training as regular soldiers in their country before joining a gang. Gangs are particularly active in Guatemala and Mexico because other countries have enacted anti-gang legislation.[59] However, gangs are still operating in those other countries and add to the problem of anarchy and the challenge of governing. Gangs have also developed expertise in the fraudulent document trade, selling counterfeited documents to various terrorist groups to enable them to change their identities.[60]

Of course, corruption among the Guatemalan police forces adds to this problem. The Guatemalan Police's former Anti-Narcotics Operations Department is reported to have stolen twice as much cocaine as it interdicted in 2002.[61] Likewise, this unit was also involved in murder in order to obtain cocaine. Thus, it is reasonable to assume that firing those tainted members of the police and hiring new ones would lead to the same result because the drug business is so tempting. The same case is repeated in the Mexican states that border the United States and all across Latin America. Furthermore, just as criminal gangs and drug lords have flourished in the corrupt state institutions of Guatemala, it likely will also become fertile ground for the flourishing terrorist activities of such groups as FARC or Hezbollah or even al Qaeda.

Peru is the second-largest producer of cocaine. Peruvian farmers have created a mega underground economy in the country. Many Peruvians depend on the cultivation, processing, and export of coca and products. In 2007, Peru's coca cultivation increased by 4 percent, and its estimated cocaine production rose by 290 tons, thus making it second only to that of Colombia.[62] Revenues from cocaine exports total some $22 billion, equivalent to 17 percent of the gross domestic product. This figure is reported to be bigger than any legitimate sector of the economy.[63] As drug trafficking grows, the Peruvian state will likely succumb to corruption.

In the Dominican Republic, former president Leonel Fernández fired seven hundred police officers and forced more than thirty military officers into retirement over their alleged involvement in the drug trade. According to anticorruption attorney Tomas Castro Monegro, "Organizations that are supposedly involved in fighting corruption and narcotrafficking are involved in it." Castro also pointed out that the police and military have been engaged in corruption for a long time. According to him, the lifestyle of these officers does not match the salaries they receive as public servants.[64]

These examples are enough to show that a combination of drug trafficking with weak, corrupt state institutions can bring about dangerous and destabilizing conditions. The "narcotization" of the continent will ultimately present a bigger challenge to the United States, in particular, than merely protecting its borders or preventing higher rates of drug addiction in its population.

Indeed, in the near future as the lawlessness or the Afghanization of the continent expands, large portions of territory likely will remain outside the realm of respective national sovereignty, and the governments' abilities to police these areas will significantly diminish. The continent will become a security threat if dangerous non-state actors settle in Central America and South America without restrictions.

But no less important are Chávez's intentions to subjugate as many countries as possible and bring them to his sphere of influence. Chávez's alliance and friendship with drug cartels can use the process of Afghanization to his ends. Harnessing the violence of guerrilla groups such as FARC and others and establishing an alliance with drug cartels may generate the conditions under which a Chávez-type Bolivarian regime could take the reins of power. Whether the alternative is lawlessness or Bolivarianism, prospects for future stability on the continent look bleak.

▌SUMMARY

The goal of the Bolivarian leadership in promoting a relationship with FARC is manifold. First, FARC is a subversive force capable of helping expand the Bolivarian revolution across the continent, as is clearly stated in the resolutions of the Bolivarian Continental Coordinator/Bolivarian Continental Movement. Logically, FARC could also wage a war of attrition against an enemy country such as Colombia or any country whose regime the Bolivarian revolution may seek to change. In that sense this idea is no different than former Libyan leader Muammar Gadhafi's notion of gathering under his wing those international terrorist groups that he viewed as capable of undermining countries and regimes. FARC could play a role in expanding the Bolivarian revolution through continental insurgency. Whereas FARC at this point is not strong enough to accomplish anything major, it definitely intends to do so. Moreover, its goal becomes more plausible as the Bolivarian revolution, whose aspiration is to expand, has welcomed the group.

Max Manwaring points out that Chávez's encouragement of such groups as FARC and drug cartels is part of his intentional asymmetric war. He writes, "President Chávez . . . understands that the process leading to state failure is the most dangerous long-term security challenge facing the global community today. The argument in general is that failing and failed state status is the breeding ground for instability, criminality, insurgency, regional conflict, and terrorism."[65]

Manwaring therefore claims that Chávez considers the actions of violent and destructive guerrilla or terrorist groups and of drug cartels as "steps that must be taken to bring about the political conditions necessary to establish the Latin American Socialism of the 21st Century." As a consequence, he continues, "failed states become dysfunctional states, rogue states, criminal states, narco-states, or new people's democracies. Therefore, one can rest assured that Chávez and his Bolivarian populist allies will be available to provide money, arms, and leadership at any given opportunity."[66]

As seen in Afghanistan, the vanishing of state authority—law and law enforcement, the military, and other state institutions—is likely to leave a power vacuum. In that case, such a power void could well be filled by a strong figure that pledges a new and better order. Thus, this turbulent situation facilitates a revolution as any vacancy could be filled by another Bolivarian regime with the active help of the Venezuelan government. With its Bolivarian and twenty-first-century socialism formula, the Venezuelan government would be in a perfect position to affect this change given its ability to fund candidates and its close relationship with drug cartels. The latter are not looking to rule by themselves; instead, they are looking for weak or friendly governments that would allow them to work without interference. A Venezuelan-supported Bolivarian regime could thus enjoy both the initial support of the people and the consent of the drug cartels. Furthermore, as oil revenue is a key tool in the Venezuelan leader's pursuit of international influence, the cartels' additional income might compensate for any oil money deficits. Thus, the drug cartels could well serve as another multibillion-dollar source of income for the Bolivarian revolution.

As the drug trade expands to more and more countries, this problem becomes worse and poses a greater security threat to the countries of the region and to the United States. Then, the possibility rises that they will have to face rogue and narco states as well as terrorist groups. Not only will the expansion of anarchy to other countries in the continent create a serious security problem as more and more countries lose control of their territory but the United States will also be vulnerable in its own borders. In this scenario, erecting a wall along the U.S. border will not solve the problem, since it will not merely be a Mexican-U.S. problem any longer.

To be sure, Hugo Chávez is not the original or main cause that has helped the drug business proliferate. But he certainly has married the Bolivarian revolution with this lethal business, and both serve each other well. This menace is exacerbated now by another actor whose presence in the area Chávez has intentionally encouraged—namely, the Islamic Republic of Iran.

6 | THE BOLIVARIAN REVOLUTION'S LINKS TO IRAN AND HEZBOLLAH

The connection between Iran and Venezuela, as well as Iran's ties with the other Bolivarian countries, has often been understood within the context of their commercial relationship. Many experts have analyzed Iran's presence in Latin America as an economic and political policy aimed simply at mitigating the Islamic Republic's international isolation. Others, however, have seen Iran's presence in Latin America and the Venezuelan-Iranian relationship as posing a real threat. I agree with both accounts, and in this chapter I conceptualize the relationship between the Bolivarian revolution and Iran as a complex and multifaceted scheme that requires close examination. It encompasses multiple interests and agendas. Their connections contain ideological elements, strategic goals, and foreign and domestic policy objectives.

First of all, viewing Iran's motivation for establishing its presence in the region as fulfilling only Iran's agenda is a mistake. The relationship between Iran and Venezuela and the Bolivarian revolution has developed because their connection also advances the interests of the Bolivarian revolution. Both the Iranian and the Bolivarian revolutions have a strong ideological component that is marked by an anti-Western and particularly anti-American character. Both revolutions identify with each other as they struggle for radical changes and see themselves as victims of an imperial conspiracy.

In the last several years, thanks to Hugo Chávez's encouragement, Iran has sought to expand its economic and political leverage in Latin America. While Iran has developed a close relationship with Venezuela and expanded its relationships with the other Bolivarian countries, Iran has also succeeded in establishing stronger economic and political bonds with non-Bolivarian countries in the continent, particularly Brazil.

However, Iran is a rogue state that has not hesitated to use terrorism (even in Latin America) to achieve its ends. Now it is also seeking nuclear weapons and, as a result, is suffering sanctions and isolation in the international community. Therefore, Iran's presence in the continent cannot be treated the same as any other country that is trying to develop partnerships in Latin America. The Iranian-backed group Hezbollah, known for its multiple terrorist attacks including in Latin America, has also been increasing its presence in the region.

Thus, the Iranians' interaction with the Bolivarian revolution raises serious questions for it could have implications beyond a mere alliance of convenience. As Chávez seeks to build a continental revolution with totalitarian elements, he also strives to remove the hegemony of the United States from this region and carry out a continental transformation to impose his vision of twenty-first-century socialism. He views these aspirations as being linked to a war against dominant groups (the oligarchy) and the American empire. Therefore, Iran's presence in the continent must be seen in the context of those Bolivarian objectives as well. The Iranians' relationship with the Bolivarian leader have evolved as a result of mutual interests and generated a dynamic that could have significant geopolitical ramifications.

HISTORICAL BACKGROUND: COOPERATION BETWEEN MIDDLE EASTERN AND LATIN AMERICAN RADICALS

Associations between Latin American and Middle Eastern radical groups and dictatorships can be traced to the late 1960s. The Soviet Union during the peak of the Cold War encouraged these relationships. The Soviets believed in using the power of subversion to undermine stability and instigate revolutions in countries that did not belong to the Soviet sphere of influence. They thought that guerrilla groups in Latin America were useful tools in destabilizing targeted countries. In the Middle East, the Palestine Liberation Organization (PLO) had a similar capacity as it confronted the State of Israel. However, that relationship in the Arab world was not limited to the PLO but also to Arab countries that already had strong relations with the Soviet Union and strong anti-Western, anti-American feelings.

Beginning in the 1970s, the Cubans provided the Iraqis with training and military expertise in counterinsurgency that the latter could use against the Kurds. In October 1973, during the Yom Kippur War between

Israel and an Egyptian-Syrian coalition, the Cubans sent five hundred tank commanders to fight alongside the Syrians.[1] During that period Cuba and the PLO developed a military relationship, and Palestinian warriors received combat training, mostly in guerrilla tactics, in Cuban camps.[2] Likewise, Fidel Castro stationed thousands of Cuban troops in Libya to protect the government and train its troops in espionage, commando operations, and insurgency control within Libya. Havana even trained Col. Muammar Gadhafi's personal escort and security services.[3]

The PLO also cooperated with the Nicaraguan rebels, the Sandinistas. In September 1970, the Sandinista leader Patrick Argüello Ryan participated in an ill-fated attempt by George Habash's group, the Popular Front for the Liberation of Palestine, to hijack an El Al airliner.[4] Likewise, the Sandinistas fought alongside the PLO against the Jordanians when King Hussein opened an offensive against the PLO in September 1970 (Black September).[5]

As the rebellion in Nicaragua against Anastasio Somoza's government gained strength in the 1970s, contacts between the PLO and Nicaraguan rebels intensified. The PLO trained top Sandinista leaders such as Pedro Arauz Palacios, Tomás Borge, and Eduardo Contreras in Lebanon. Likewise, the Sandinistas received joint Cuban-PLO training as well. The PLO also ran several camps located in Nicaragua to train guerrillas to fight in El Salvador, which was then facing a civil war.[6] The PLO provided millions of dollars and weapons to the Sandinistas, with the funds coming from Libya. It is believed that the Sandinistas scored some crucial military victories thanks to this aid.[7]

Since the early 1970s, Libyan leader Gadhafi and Nicaraguan leader Daniel Ortega had maintained a close, strong relationship. The Sandinista Movement received guerrilla training in Libya in the early days of the alliance, and Gadhafi helped Ortega financially after the latter lost the presidential elections in 1990. As noted in chapter 5, Gadhafi chose Ortega to be a liaison between Libyan and Latin American leaders, and Ortega remained loyal to the Libyan leader until Gadhafi's last day. Ortega even agreed to appoint a former Nicaraguan foreign minister to serve as Libya's representative to the United Nations after Gadhafi's ambassador resigned in 2011.[8]

Like the PLO, Gadhafi developed associations with other South American guerrilla movements. He provided financial support and established connections with such guerrilla movements as FARC, M-19, the Peruvian Revolutionary Movement Túpac Amaru, and other radical and communist parties in Latin America. Gadhafi was able to share a language with radicalizing movements in Latin America that included anti-imperialism and nationalism (rather than abstract Marxist theories).[9]

Illich Ramirez Sanchez, also known as Carlos the Jackal, provides a legendary example of a South American radical who supported the Palestinian cause and whose terrorist activities in the 1970s and '80s became the topic of numerous novels and films. The Venezuelan-born Ramirez Sanchez, who is currently serving a life sentence for the assassination of two French intelligence agents, began his terrorist career working for the Popular Front for the Liberation of Palestine (PFLP). He participated in numerous terrorist attacks aimed at Israeli institutions and facilities in Europe. While imprisoned in France, Ramirez Sanchez converted to Islam and now writes of his support for radical Islamist groups such as al Qaeda.

During the 1970s, members of the Argentinean guerrilla group the Montoneros spent long periods in southern Lebanon undergoing training. Rodolfo Walsh, a well-known journalist and organic intellectual of Montoneros, wrote an amateurish and little-nuanced pamphlet in which he described the Zionist movement as a colonialist, systematic, and ruthless scheme aimed at removing the Palestinians from their home.[10] He compared the Israelis to the Nazis and wrote that the Zionist project was an enterprise of European capitalism that was no longer interested in having Jewish competitors in Europe. Zionism was a colonialist movement supported by a colonialist and capitalistic empire like Great Britain, he contended, and Jews had no right to a land that naturally belonged to the Palestinians. But his document leaves almost no doubt that a clear identity and sympathy had been established between those who supported Arab or Palestinian nationalism and the struggle of guerrillas in Latin America.

This attitude prevailed for a long time in the minds of extreme Left leaders and their compatriots, particularly those who constituted the Foro de São Paulo (São Paulo Forum). This Latin American network has forged solidarity among socialist and communist organizations and some guerrilla groups, and includes Fidel Castro, Daniel Ortega, Hugo Chávez, and FARC. The Foro has admonished the United States for its economic boycott against Iraq and attacked American allies, notably Israel, which it accused of carrying out genocide in Palestine.[11]

However, it is the Bolivarian revolution that reinforces ties of solidarity between Latin America and the most radical and tyrannical elements in the Arab and Muslim world. With radical ideologists now holding positions of power in Latin American countries, such a history of cooperation and mutual understanding makes alliances with Middle East extremists a natural step. Some of the old actors, such as Fidel Castro and Raúl Castro in Cuba and the Sandinistas in Nicaragua, are still in place. However, the main leaders of this resuscitated alliance are Hugo Chávez, the Venezuelan leader, and Mahmoud Ahmadinejad, the president of the Islamic Republic of Iran.

❘ HUGO CHÁVEZ'S RELATIONSHIPS WITH ARAB AND ISLAMIC GROUPS

Following a tradition of close relationships between guerrilla groups in Latin America and the Arab world, Chávez's links with international terrorism and rogue Arab countries should not be surprising. Not only does Chávez support revolutionary struggles from below, but he has also expressed deep admiration for rulers who have been able to perpetuate their power by ruthless means such as Saddam Hussein, Muammar Gadhafi, and the Iranian regime.

Since Venezuela has been a long-standing Organization of Petroleum Exporting Countries (OPEC) member, Chávez knows the value of oil as a means of increasing his power both domestically and abroad. Arab and Middle Eastern tyrannies that can count on multibillion-dollar revenues that enable them to create welfare dictatorships, and at the same time wield significant international leverage, provide a useful model.

In August 2000, Chávez visited Iraq during a series of trips to OPEC countries and, as noted previously, was the first leader to visit Saddam Hussein while sanctions against him were in full effect.[12] That September, Chávez hosted an OPEC summit where he and other OPEC members together agreed to increase the price of oil.[13] The ideological affinity between Hugo Chávez and Middle East dictatorships has multiple facets. They all abhor the West and resent colonialism and foreign influence. These leaders share a colonialist legacy and see colonialism and neocolonialism as the root of all current social and economic ills facing the developing world. Likewise, they view democracy as a threat against their autocratic power. Most important, from Chávez's perspective, the Middle Eastern countries' leaders have the ability to accumulate absolute power and subjugate their populations. That Chávez called Hussein's now-defunct Iraqi government "a model" for Venezuela is illustrative.[14] It is no wonder that the Venezuelan leader, who has pursued absolute control of the population and oil-based influence abroad, finds the Middle Eastern model appealing. With the collapse of Hussein's regime and Libya's accommodation with the West in 2003, Chávez obsessively turned to Iran as a logical next choice.

CHÁVEZ, IRAN, AND LATIN AMERICA

Hugo Chávez views Iran as a partner in a common cause. Venezuela and Iran are both revolutionary countries whose current ruling parties came to power after deposing an economic and political class that was viewed as oppressive and tied to the United States. For the Iranians, they saw the former shah Reza Pahlavi as an oppressor of the masses and a supporter of an elite associated with U.S. neocolonialism. The Bolivarian revolution's current leader has a similar abhorrence for the rule of the political parties and the oligarchy and associates it with "U.S. imperialism." The memories of deposed Iranian nationalist and anti-imperialist leader Mohammed Mossadeq in 1953 and an American history of intervention in Latin America feed their feeling. "Let's save the human race, let's finish off the U.S. empire," Chávez reportedly told his Iranian counterparts in a 2006 visit to Iran.[15]

Thanks to its alliances with Chávez, Iran not only has expanded its presence in Venezuela and in countries allied with Venezuela but also broadened its economic, political, and even military or paramilitary presence throughout Latin America. This relationship thus serves both Iran and Chávez and his Bolivarian revolution. Their mutual interests generate new dynamics that, as noted earlier, could have major geopolitical implications.

IRAN'S OBJECTIVES IN LATIN AMERICA

Terrorism expert and scholar Ely Karmon has pointed out that Iran is pursuing a number of goals in Latin America. First, Iran seeks Latin American support to resist international pressure against the development of its nuclear program. Second, Iran is seeking to strike back at the United States by establishing a presence in its own hemisphere and possibly destabilizing traditional U.S.-friendly governments in order to negotiate with the United

States from a position of strength. Third, since Mahmoud Ahmadinejad is losing approbation at home, a show of popularity and strength abroad might increase the theocracy's leverage domestically.[16]

All of these factors may well be true and confirmed, but when analyzing the relationship between the revolutionary regime of the Islamic Republic and that of the Bolivarian revolution, delving into the complex dynamics is worthwhile. Iran's immediate goal is to find an exit from its increasing worldwide isolation owing to its ominous nuclear program. Thus, in 2008, it agreed to an arrangement in which the Venezuelan government created a binational Iranian-Venezuelan development bank that is, in fact, a partnership between the Banco Industrial de Venezuela and Iran's Export Development Bank. This partnership created a new entity, the Banco International de Desarrollo, and embarked on other deals, such as opening offices of Iran's commercial institutions in Venezuela. Their branches have expanded into Ecuador with the clear purpose of avoiding financial sanctions on Iran.[17]

Venezuela also sold gasoline to Iran to help the country overcome the effects of sanctions that prevent companies or entities that enhance Iran's energy sector from providing Iran with gasoline. Chávez's violation of sanctions prompted U.S. president Barack Obama (2009–present) to apply mild sanctions on Venezuela's oil giant, Petróleos de Venezuela SA.[18]

Since 2006, Venezuela, along with Syria and Cuba, has been the main supporter of Iran's right to develop a nuclear weapon. In 2007, Chávez and Ahmadinejad declared an "axis of unity" against the United States with the purpose of weakening the United States, an empire they both despise. Ahmadinejad pointed out that "Iran and the nations of Latin America are fighting for liberty and encouraging anti-colonialist revolts in other countries." In the same vein, Chávez was even more open about their goals when he declared that "cooperation among independent countries, in particular between Iran and Venezuela, will be an important factor in the defeat of imperialism and in the victory of the people."[19]

Iran's penetration into Latin America is likely to grow as more Latin American countries join the Chávez sphere of influence. For example, Iran enhanced its relationship with Bolivia in 2007 when Ahmadinejad visited the country and signed a program of cooperation for more than $1 billion. Also, two health clinics opened in Bolivia under the auspices of the Red Crescent. Bolivia also pledged to support Iran's nuclear program in the United Nations and in the international community. Likewise, Iranian state television will provide Bolivian television with Spanish-speaking programming that is likely to serve as pro-Iranian propaganda.[20] Bolivia indeed has become a prominent destination for the channel HispanTV.[21] The channel, which was launched early in 2012, broadcasts news, documentaries, movies, and Iranian films twenty-four hours a day.[22]

Latin American officials estimate that between fifty and three hundred "trainers" from Iran's Revolutionary Guards are present in Bolivia. Some also believe that Iran is mining uranium in Bolivia. In 2010 the two countries signed agreements that made Iran a partner in the mining and exploitation of lithium, a material that is a key component in the development of nuclear weapons.[23]

As an academic observer, Gustavo Fernández has pointed out that the relationship between Bolivia and Iran is not likely to be particularly convenient from an economic point of view. He writes, "The possibility of generating trade between two nations separated by such enormous distances, in the absence of a means of transportation and communications, is virtually nil."[24] However, the agreements and a subsequent memorandum of understanding signed by the two countries reflect a political affinity and an anti-imperialist pact between them. President Evo Morales stressed this point during a visit to Teheran in September 2008.[25]

Relations between Iran and Nicaragua have also been strengthened after Iran promised Nicaragua $1 billion in aid and investments to develop the latter's energy and agricultural sectors. Iran made a commitment to assist Nicaragua in the construction of a deepwater port on the country's eastern shore whose cost was estimated at $350 million. Iran also promised to help Nicaragua build a hydroelectric dam and a major hospital, though observers are unsure whether these agreements may ever be realized.[26]

From these cases, however, it is possible to conclude that Iran's relationship with Bolivia and Nicaragua is a political alliance based on an ideological affinity against what they define as "imperialism." By 2007, for instance, Daniel Ortega had already issued a statement of support for Iran's pursuit of nuclear energy for "peaceful purposes." He did so in open defiance of a United Nations Security Council resolution that demanded that Iran suspend uranium enrichment activities and the construction of a heavy water reactor.[27] Ortega's support for Iran seems to be influenced by his own decades-long anti-imperialist ideology and by his new status as a beneficiary and ally of Hugo Chávez's.

Under the influence of Hugo Chávez, the relationship between Iran and Ecuador also grew closer. The two countries opened commercial bureaus in their respective capitals and signed a contract to build a refinery and a petrochemical unit in Ecuador, as well as twenty-five bilateral commercial agreements in the field of energy. Late in 2008, Iran's Supreme National Security Council secretary visited Ecuador. Afterward, Ecuadorian president Rafael Correa issued a statement declaring Iran as a strategic partner and expressing his support for the expansion of military ties between the two countries.[28] Like Nicaragua, Ecuador also supported Iran's right to develop atomic energy.[29]

Surely, although the Bolivarian countries may fail to receive any major economic benefit from their relationship with Iran, Iran's political interactions with them are still significant. In addition, to underestimate these relationships on the basis that most of the agreements signed between Iran and these countries have not been implemented is, from a geopolitical viewpoint, a gross miscalculation.

Meanwhile, it is important to point out that Iran's incursion in Latin America has transcended the Bolivarian alliance and has expanded into countries ruled by social democracies and so called moderate Left governments. The relationships between Iran and these countries are not at the same level as Iran's with the Bolivarian countries, but these connections still further enhance Iran's political and economic status in the region.

Iran and the Moderate Left

Iran's standing among moderate left-wing governments is largely influenced by the policy of developing South-South relations, which is a sort of political coalition with Arab and African countries to strengthen the power of the Third World. Brazil has mainly promoted this policy and has achieved remarkable economic growth, which has made it self-conscious in terms of its ability to become politically influential in the regional and world arena. Under the government of Luiz Inácio Lula da Silva, Brazil was eager to show its political independence regarding foreign policy and international relations.

After Iran's June 12, 2009, presidential elections, Lula was the first Western leader to recognize hard-line Iranian president Ahmadinejad as the legitimate winner in spite of widespread indications of fraud. Then Lula went further. During the 2009 United Nations General Assembly, he defended Brazil's relationship with Iran and basically said he cannot judge

Iran's nuclear ambitions or the way the June 12 elections were handled. Following Ahmadinejad's visit to Brazil that November, President Lula tried to play an international role regarding the issue of Iran's nuclear program. In alliance with Turkey, Brazil offered Iran a deal that went contrary to the U.S. and European agenda while claiming to provide a solution to the crisis that Iran's nuclear program had generated.

The deal called for the transference of low-enriched uranium to Turkey for reprocessing without discussing the 20 percent enrichment activities that Iran began in February. Turkey, in principle, would enrich the uranium and return it to Iran ready for civilian medical use. The deal did not stipulate that Iran discontinue uranium enrichment at home.[30] Likewise, it did not address the issue of nuclear weapons proliferation or the issue of transparency in Iran's nuclear program. The deal also laid down the principle that "non-nuclear weapons states" (including Iran) could enrich uranium to produce electricity in their territory and established the right of these countries to peaceful nuclear activities.[31] In other words, the deal had nothing to do with the problem of nuclear proliferation or with Iran's nuclear program. Instead it served Iran's interests in delaying UN Security council sanctions and perhaps more severe economic sanctions expected to come from the United States and European countries. The Brazilian-Turkish joint proposal allowed Iran to continue its uranium enrichment activities, largely considered a threat to international peace, thus enabling Iran to continue its nuclear program. The proposal was emphatically rejected by the United States and European countries.

Brazil's motivation derived from its support for a multipolar world where it would play the role of a world power, independent of American influence. Brazil, under Lula, supported the principle of noninterference in other sovereign countries; consequently, it failed to support such universal ideas as democracy, human rights, and nonproliferation.[32] Brazil's policy has benefitted Iran's standing in Latin America.

Another example of Iran's involvement with moderate left-wing Latin American governments is seen in Uruguay, where President José Mujica Cordano is openly identified with Lula's policies and leadership. Under Mujica's watch, four Uruguayan legislators, including the president of the House of Representatives, visited Iran and sought to strengthen their country's bond with the Middle Eastern country.[33] The Uruguayan foreign minister conducted a follow-up visit to widen bi-lateral relations on various issues. To offset the UN-imposed sanctions on Iran, Uruguay offered to barter its rice for Iranian oil to maintain its commercial connection with Iran.[34]

In general, Iran's trade with Latin American countries tripled from the moment Ahmadinejad assumed power in 2005 to 2008. Brazil is Iran's largest trading partner in Latin America with about $1.3 billion in trade in 2008 alone. Iran also has strong commercial ties with Argentina, a country that has maintained a tense association with Iran over the bombings of the Israeli Embassy in 1992 and the Argentine Israelite Mutual Association in Buenos Aires in 1994. Nonetheless, Argentina increased its exports to Iran from $29 million in 2007 to $1.2 billion in 2008.[35] According to Iranian sources, Iran "had exported around $43.7 billion worth of non-oil goods" and "imported some $61.8 billion worth of goods" in 2011, thus reaching $105 billion in annual trade.[36]

Moderate Left governments in Latin America, while not representing such extremism as that of the Bolivarian regimes, have enabled the Iranians' influence to grow in the region. In my view, there is a reason for it that goes well beyond the economic explanation.

Until the latter part of 2012 Argentina maintained a situation of political tension with Iran as a result of Argentina's order of arrest and extradition of several high officers in the Iranian government, given their involvement in the attacks against the Israeli Embassy in 1992 and the Jewish community headquarters Asociación Mutual Israelita Argentina (AMIA) in 1994.

However, in January 2013 Argentina and Iran signed a memorandum of understanding that deals directly with the terrorist attack on the Jewish headquarters, however, it does not include the attack on the Israeli Embassy.[37]

The memorandum encourages the creation of a "Truth Commission" composed by international jurists in order to analyze the documentation that exists about the AMIA bombing. That commission would comprise five members. Two members would be selected by Iran and two would be selected by Argentina. These four members cannot be either Iranians or Argentineans and must have internationally recognized credentials. The fifth member will be appointed by an agreement between the two countries following the same standards. The commission would examine the evidence and documentation, request additional information if needed, interrogate people, and issue a report and recommendations.

Of course, this agreement is problematic from the beginning. As I am writing this line, Iran already refused to allow its Minister of Defense Ahmad Vahidi, who is one of the suspects, to be interrogated. This statement was issued despite the fact that the Argentinean government affirmed that Vahidi would indeed be interrogated.[38] Furthermore, immediately afterward, Iran accused Israel of having been responsible for the attack against the Jewish community headquarters in order to gain more influence over the Argentinean government.[39]

No one would have seriously thought that the Iranians were going to acknowledge their role in the terrorist attacks in Argentina or agree to extradite those accused by the Argentinean justice ministry of having been complicit in the attack. Entertaining those thoughts is particularly ridiculous when Vahidi is himself one of the accused. Furthermore, by virtue of his own position, Vahidi has control over Iran's regular armed forces, and, most importantly, the Revolutionary Guards, who at the same time oversee Iran's terrorist operations abroad. Another key official accused is Moshen Rabbani, a cultural attaché in Argentina during the AMIA attack who is now in charge of expanding Iran's and Hezbollah's recruitment and training of operatives in Latin America.

These factors make the success of this bilateral agreement an impossible task. The question is, what prompted the initiation of this dialogue and what did each country hope to gain? If Iran's goal were merely to increase trade, it would not need to establish a dialogue with Argentina over the AMIA case, since it is an issue that could undermine commercial relations.

Perhaps the explanation might be found in other, more ideological reasons. Argentina has established a very strong alliance with President Hugo Chávez of Venezuela, who is Iran's closest ally after Syria. The alliance between Cristina Kirchner and Hugo Chávez is not only a relationship based on the convenience associated with Chávez's oil and debt relief generosity. It is also an ideological and symbolic alliance since Kirchner views Chávez as a symbol of the Left's strength and legitimacy in the region. Argentina broadcasted live the Venezuelan National Electoral Council's announcement of the results of the October 2012 elections (that gave a victory to Hugo Chávez).

In my view, Iran has become a symbol of anti-Americanism and anti-Western resistance. This explains why the moderate Brazil has also extended a generous hand to Iran in its nuclear arrangement proposal and why another moderate Left country like Uruguay sent a Congressional delegation to Iran. The expanding status of Iran as a political symbol of the Bolivarian alliance's anti-Americanism and the legitimacy Iran has gained in the non-Bolivarian Left is a dangerous development.

It is my opinion that the governments of Brazil, Argentina, and Uruguay, more so than other Latin American countries, view the power of the Left as a victorious regional movement that transcends national experiences. The Left is defined in the abstract and there is no distinction between the social democracies of the moderate Left and the authoritarian elected governments of the Bolivarian alliance.

Although there is no question all the factors just described have enhanced Iran's economic and political status in Latin America, Iran also has major strategic goals. How these goals are fulfilled, however, is intimately related to the way in which Hugo Chávez seeks to advance his own ambitions. In supporting Iran's objectives, Chávez's relationship with Iran has enhanced his own set of goals and views.

▌IRAN'S AND VENEZUELA'S MUTUAL ASSISTANCE

Chávez has numerous reasons for bringing Iran to the region. First, it is crucial to understand that Chávez's claim to revolutionary leadership over a vast region in Latin America cannot be fulfilled with the weapon of oil alone. Oil profits heavily depend on international prices, which at the same time are a function of supply and demand. Thus, Venezuela is limited by its reliance on this single product and lacks a diverse economy. Further, Venezuela's industrial and military capability is not strong enough to enable Chávez to become the kind of transnational leader he wants to be.

Iran, meanwhile, stands as Chávez's main ally. Iran assists Chávez in achieving his goals in a number of ways: by enhancing the militarization of Venezuela, most specifically in the nuclear dimension; by waging an asymmetric war against the United States and within the continent; and by consolidating Chávez's absolute regime through destabilizing Latin American states.

The Nuclear Issue

International conflicts between countries in Latin America have been rare in the last century. The region has not seen a major international military confrontation for more than a hundred years, with a few exceptions: the Chaco War between Paraguay and Bolivia in 1932–1935, the Honduras–El Salvador conflict in 1969, tensions between Chile and Argentina in 1978, the Falklands War between England and Argentina in 1982, and the Peruvian-Ecuadorian War in 1995. Furthermore, no country in Latin America including the big ones of Brazil, Argentina, and Mexico claimed hegemony or leadership over other countries in the continent. Most relationships between Brazil and the rest of the countries have remained purely bilateral. Moreover, no one country pretended to dominate the other.

Various countries have also signed treaties prohibiting nuclear weapons in the region, such as the Latin America Nuclear Weapons Free Zone Treaty of 1963, which has been expanded several times since then. In some countries like Brazil, the prohibition of nuclear weapons is in their written constitutions. Brazil and Argentina do have nuclear programs but with nonmilitary goals in mind.

With the rise of Hugo Chávez in Venezuela, however, policies began to take a different direction. In his regional ambitions and his obsession with Colombia, Chávez began an arms race in the region. Chávez has sought to arm the National Armed Forces with weapons from Russia. (The Russian sale of weapons to Venezuela is further discussed in chapter 7.)

Following Chávez's logic, pursuing nuclear armaments makes sense for a country that insists on quickly becoming a relevant and strong revolutionary power in the region. Chávez's behavior fits the model of such rulers as Saddam Hussein in Iraq, Gadhafi in Libya, or even the mullahs in Iran. In all cases, leaders have grandiose ambitions, but at the same time they are also militarily, technologically, and industrially weak. A nuclear bomb may provide them with the quickest shortcut to becoming respected and intimidating regional and world players.

Early in 2005, Venezuela raised the possibility of starting a nuclear program in cooperation with Argentina and Brazil. Both Argentina and Brazil denied that he made such a request then. However, Chávez reiterated that he aspires to have a nuclear program and specifically called for cooperation between Latin American countries and Iran.[40]

Likewise, in March 2005, during Iranian president Mohammad Khatami's visit to Caracas, Venezuela and Iran signed an agreement of commercial and technological cooperation.[41] On that occasion, Chávez defended Iran's right to produce atomic energy and to continue research in the area of nuclear development. Chávez did so repeatedly in world forums, thus becoming Iran's main international supporter of its nuclear program.

In March 2006, the two countries established a $200 million development fund and signed bilateral deals to build homes and exploit petroleum. The Venezuelan opposition raised the possibility that the deal could involve the transfer of Venezuelan uranium to Iran.[42] This argument was made again a few years later when a Venezuelan paper reported that the Israeli Mossad provided exact locations of uranium production in Venezuela. The Venezuelan minister of mining Rodolfo Sanz confirmed this information in September 2009 and stated, "We have reserves of uranium that we are detecting with the help of Iran."[43] Hugo Chávez himself also spoke about the two countries' cooperating to build a "nuclear village" in Venezuela with Iran providing the necessary technological assistance.[44]

At that time, Manhattan district attorney Robert Morgenthau, who was in charge of a number of international money laundering investigations, raised the possibility of cooperation between both countries to help Iran develop a nuclear weapon, by putting Venezuela's financial institutions at Iran's service, by offering Iran its territory to place "illicit weapons," and even by mining uranium for Iran.[45] Former U.S. assistant secretary of state for the Western Hemisphere Roger Noriega suggested the possibility that nuclear arsenals might be built in Iran and Venezuela.[46]

It is reasonable to conclude that for a man thirsty for power and filled with revolutionary ambition, a move toward acquiring nuclear weapons is a logical next step. A nuclear weapon will provide Chávez with the respect, fear, and deterrence he needs to carry out his agenda. While some Venezuelan scientists have pointed out that Venezuela does not have the capability to develop a nuclear weapon because of a "scarcity of qualified scientific personnel,"[47] the possibility that Chávez might well acquire nuclear weapons from Iran should not be dismissed.

This prospect is particularly plausible when Venezuela has been one of Iran's main supporters. As Iran is deeply grateful to Chávez for his actions, couldn't Iran reciprocate? Once Iran develops nuclear capabilities, it may be willing to give Chávez a positive answer, particularly when such a scenario also could serve Iran's interests. If Iranian nuclear weapons are placed on Venezuelan soil, that action not only will grant Venezuela a dangerous military advantage but also will provide Iran with a deterrence capability against the United States. In that case, the United States will be exposed to a direct and hazardous threat at a time of high tension between Iran and the West.

The Asymmetric War

What is an asymmetric war? In an asymmetric war, one side uses guerrillas who are willing to sacrifice themselves to kill a stronger conventional army. Iran, for example, has promoted this kind of war via its terrorist proxies, such as Hezbollah, and its protégés in the Middle East. This doctrine was imported—at least on paper—to Venezuela, and its intellectual author is Jorge Verstrynge, a Spanish radical. He wrote a technical treatise on terrorism in which he particularly praised the Islamists' use of terrorism and suicide bombers as the most effective warfare method since it "involves fighters willing to sacrifice their lives to kill the enemy." (It also reflects Iran's basic philosophy during its 1980–1988 war with Iraq.) Chávez liked Verstrynge's ideas so much that the government distributed his book to the Venezuelan army.[48]

According to Chávez, Venezuela could use asymmetric warfare methods if the Americans invaded and could wage a war of the people on all fronts against the invading U.S. military force. In this case, Iranian or Hezbollah fighters could play an important role in defending Venezuela. Because Venezuelan or Latin American soldiers would not likely carry out the suicidal acts of terrorism that Islamic fighters indeed do, Chávez could see value in the presence of Iranian-backed groups like Hezbollah.

Such an American invasion, however, is improbable. In that case, waging an asymmetric war would require far more complex fighting than using Islamists' terrorist and suicidal strategies.

Meanwhile, as we have seen in the example of Venezuela's relationship with FARC, the Bolivarian revolution needs an entity that has expertise in asymmetric war. As mentioned in chapter 5, Max Manwaring defines asymmetric war in broader terms. An asymmetric war includes not only nonconventional warfare, such as nuclear war and terrorist guerrilla attacks, but also highly complex political-psychological tactics. Such acts are exemplified in the ways drug cartels and FARC work to destabilize a region, destroy its institutions, and create anarchical and revolutionary situations. The Iranians, along with their proxy fighters, could play such a role. Such groups have had a presence for some time in the continent. At the same time, Iran's assistance in the Bolivarian revolution's asymmetric warfare might enhance Iran's goal against its own enemies in the continent.

In October 2003, *U.S. News & World Report* stated, "Middle Eastern terrorist groups were operating support cells in Venezuela and other locations in the Andean region." According to the report among those groups were "Hamas, Hezbollah, and Islamyyia al Gammat."[49] The *Miami Herald* reported in November 2004 that the people running Onidex, the agency that issues passports and identity documents, included an ardent supporter of Saddam Hussein's and the son of the representative of the Iraqi Baath Party in Venezuela, Tarik El-Assami. Years later he became Venezuela's Minister of Interior and Justice where he served from 2008 to 2012. After that he was elected governor of Aragua. Because of El-Assami's leadership, and laws that have allowed foreigners to become Venezuelan citizens relatively easily, it is widely believed that many people from the Middle East were granted Venezuelan passports. In some cases, they were not only members of Hezbollah but also were fast-tracked through the naturalization process and given high positions in the Venezuelan government.

Ecuador also has followed in Venezuela's footsteps by enabling an easy path to citizenship. Beginning in mid-2008, the Ecuadorian government ended visa requirements to enter the country. As a result, many foreigners reportedly began flowing into Ecuador. The routes by which they enter the Americas generally include a first stop in Cuba or Venezuela, and many have Iranian passports or come from Pakistan. Since these people easily obtain naturalization, many of them then travel freely across Latin America.[50]

As mentioned in chapter 5, Hezbollah and other radical Islamic groups interact with Mexican drug cartels. The former buys weapons from Islamic terrorist organizations cooperating with drug cartels and gains access to the United States via the routes already paved by drug traffickers. Michael Braun, who served a number of years at the DEA, strongly believes that members of Iran's Revolutionary Guard Corps direct Hezbollah's criminal operations in Latin America.[51]

Hezbollah and Hamas have sold large amounts of heroin and cocaine in Europe and the Middle East that they bought from narcotics traffickers in Mexico, Colombia, Peru, Bolivia, and Brazil. In return, these Middle East terrorist groups procure and sell weapons to Mexican and Colombian narcotics traffickers. These weapons have been identified as being similar to those that Islamic groups use in supporting the Palestinian cause. Authorities have also voiced a growing concern that Hezbollah might be providing drug traffickers with technology to infiltrate the United States. Indeed, they have found narco tunnels under the U.S.-Mexican border that resemble similar Hezbollah-built tunnels used in Lebanon.[52] The existence of such tunnels prompted Congress to pass and the president to sign the Border Tunnel Prevention Act of 2012, which "extends the use of wiretapping to tunnel investigations, criminalizes the intent to tunnel, and doubles the sentences for traffickers who use tunnels to move narcotics."[53]

Early in the 2000s, the mediation of Colombian and other drug dealers and members of FARC helped establish contacts between radical Islamic groups and Mexican drug traffickers.[54] Among them are the Zetas, drug gangs that operate as private armies of the Gulf Cartel, one of the largest in Mexico. They all have access to the United States.

No better example of how these relationships serve Iran and its terrorist purposes is its October 2011 attempt to assassinate the Saudi ambassador in Washington, D.C., with the help of a Zeta member. The two Iranians involved in the plot (one of them a member of the Revolutionary Guard) had planned to pay Zeta members $1.5 million to murder the Saudi ambassador in a crowded restaurant in the U.S. capital.[55]

Unlike in Middle Eastern countries, where Iran has proxy groups at its disposal, countries in the Western Hemisphere are far from Iran's natural geographical sphere of influence. Drug cartels and other local criminal elements, however, being heavily involved in many types of criminal activities, possess logistical and strategic knowledge of their operational territory and are capable of providing a tremendous service to rogue states with terrorist intentions like Iran.

An assessment made after a joint State Department–Department of Homeland Security symposium in 2011 concluded that cooperation between "illicit networks and corruption in an enabling environment could facilitate not only the movement of drugs, arms, stolen, or pirated goods and trafficked persons, but also smuggling of terrorists, weapons of mass destruction, and other dangerous weapons and technologies that threaten global security."[56] In that sense, the presence of Middle East terrorist organizations such as Hezbollah can further aggravate anarchical situations.

Thus, it is important to point out that the Bolivarian leadership encourages the presence of Iran in the region. As Venezuela and potentially other Bolivarian states are willing to harbor members of Hezbollah or of similar groups and provide them with legal papers, they are able to move and travel freely. This is automatically a threat to the region and the United

States as these individuals could obtain visas, including ones to the United States, using Venezuelan passports.

The case of Ghazi Nasr al-Din, a former business liaison at the Venezuelan Embassy in Damascus, Syria, and Fawzi Kan'an, a Lebanon-born Venezuelan citizen and businessman, is another example of the strategic cooperation between Hezbollah and Venezuela. Ghazi Nasr al-Din is a Venezuelan diplomat who was born in Lebanon and became a citizen in 2002. Associated with the Shi'a Islamic Center in Caracas, he also served as chargé d'affaires at the Venezuelan Embassy in Damascus and as director of political affairs at the Venezuelan Embassy in Lebanon. He helped Hezbollah raise money and repeatedly met with its senior officials in Lebanon to facilitate the travel of its operatives to and from Venezuela.[57] Fawzi Kan'an was a significant provider of financial support to Hezbollah and used his business to funnel money to Lebanon and even assisted in the actual movement of operatives.[58] According to the U.S. Treasury Department, such activities may have included kidnappings and terrorist attacks.[59] In addition, Hezbollah is believed to operate at least five training camps in Venezuela with the knowledge and tacit approval of the Venezuelan government.[60]

According to former assistant secretary of state Roger Noriega, the man who oversees the Hezbollah network is Moshen Rabbani. As noted previously, Argentinean prosecutors believe Rabbani masterminded the terrorist attack against the Argentine Israelite Mutual Association when he served as cultural attaché of the Iranian Embassy in Buenos Aires. Rabbani also recruits people, many of them local Arabs and Muslims in Latin America to his cause.[61] Hezbollah's activities have reached as far as Argentina, Chile, and Brazil.

In some cases Hezbollah had been able to co-opt non-Muslim Latin American indigenous groups that have identified the Islamic Revolution in Iran with their hopes for a Marxist revolution. Such is the case with Hezbollah Latin America, comprising Wayuu Guajira Indians, the largest indigenous group in Venezuela and Colombia. According to the Hezbollah Latin America website, the group was active in Argentina, Chile, Colombia, El Salvador, and Mexico.[62] The organization's headquarters was in Venezuela, and the leader of the group, Teodoro Darnott, has been a member of Chávez's initial political party, Movimiento Quinta República (Fifth Republic Movement), from its beginnings.[63]

Darnott was initially the leader of a small Marxist faction called the Guaicaipuro Movement for National Liberation (Proyecto Movimiento Guaicaipuro por la Liberación Nacional [MGLN]), which struggled against the oppression of the poor, indigenous peasants in the Valle de Caracas region."[65]

Hezbollah Latin America's website opens with an interesting quotation by the leader of the Islamic Revolution, Ayatollah Ruhollah Khomeini. "Our struggle is the struggle against all inequalities. Our struggle is the struggle of the barefoot people against uncontrolled freedom. It is the struggle of the ideological values against the dirty world of power, money and greediness." Then it proceeds to two other quotations from Khomeini. The first states that "all the political activities are part of a religious duty" and the second points out that the "Koran is not a book of prayer but a manual to organize society and to train its leaders to rule. Islam and Islamic rules are divine and their practices guarantee prosperity in this world and salvation in the world to come. (Islam) can put an end to injustice, tyranny and corruption and help mankind to achieve perfection."

The philosophy of this "new Muslim" group says that the Venezuelan revolution cannot take place unless it takes a path toward the moral and divine. The group claims that Venezuelans worship sex, money, industry, and commerce, leading society into a "swamp of immorality and corruption." Hezbollah Latin America claims that political movements and parties cannot provide an answer to these problems because they are also part of the problem. Thus, only "a theocratic, Political-Islamic force can liberate society from this situation." Likewise, the website reads, Hezbollah Latin America "respects the Venezuelan revolutionary process, and supports its social policies as well as its anti-Zionism and anti-Americanism."

On October 23, 2006, the police found two explosive devices near the American Embassy in Caracas. One of the bombs was in a box that also contained propaganda brochures for the Iran-backed organization Hezbollah. Hezbollah Latin America claimed responsibility for the attack. The suspect caught was a student at the Bolivarian University, which was founded by Chávez.[64]

Although Darnott received a ten-year sentence for his involvement in the attempt to bomb the American embassy, the subversive potential of these elements could not only serve Iranian interests in carrying out terrorist activities but could eventually also act as a potential shock force on behalf of the Bolivarian revolution in the region.

As we have seen Darnott is an Islamist and a Bolivarian. More important, according to his own account, Darnott was recruited by Hezbollah precisely because he was a social revolutionary. Furthermore, the leadership of Hezbollah in Lebanon officially approved his nomination as the organization's representative in Venezuela. Darnott was even offered weapons from Paraguay that FARC was supposed to transfer to him. Part of the agreement between Darnott and Hezbollah was that his own group, MGLN, recruit people to Hezbollah. This shows that Hezbollah attempts to recruit people who are socially marginal and discontent and tries to connect political Islam and social-revolutionary movements.

The Bolivarian revolution, in my view, sees it in the same way. The Venezuelan government, despite the detention and subsequent sentence of Darnott and the student who attempted to bomb the American embassy, never disclosed who was behind the bombing attempts.[66] In other words, it is very possible that Darnott was sacrificed while the relationship between Venezuela and Hezbollah was kept and concealed.

As I have already pointed out in chapter 4, in Argentina, the Islamic Association of Argentina (AIA) has links to Hezbollah and to the government of Iran. AIA consists mainly of Shiite converts to Islam who cooperate closely with the Iranian Embassy. The organization celebrates the anniversary of the Islamic Revolution in Iran, condemns the UN Security Council resolution that calls for sanctions against Iran, and is violently critical of Israel and the West. The violent pro-Chávez piquetero group Quebracho also has links to AIA.

It is important to note that mobilization of local Arab communities by elements associated with radical Islam or the radical Palestinians is taking place in Latin America now more than ever before. Arab communities have lived for three generations in Latin America. However, it is only recently that these Arab communities—who were never active in the area of Middle East policies—became very active politically. For instance, demonstrations against visits of Israeli officials in Latin America mobilize thousands of people, mostly citizens of Arab nations.

In addition, Islamic websites, which include a substantial component of Israel delegitimizing, flourish in Latin America. Many of these websites have been promoted by Iran; however, it is not yet clear how influential they are on the Latin American population. The concern here is not that regular people may visit these websites but that the local population of Arab origin, who have lived peacefully for well over a century, may turn more and more radical. Since radical Muslims have tried to penetrate natural Arab or Muslim communities in other countries, it makes sense that their messages would be targeted toward Argentinean Arabs or Argentinean Muslims.

As an example, in Argentina relations between Arabs and Jews were always cordial even though it was mainly based on personal relations between individual Arabs and Jews. After the terrorist attack on the Jewish community headquarters in Buenos Aires in 1994, the organized Jewish community initiated a dialogue that was welcomed by the Argentinean chapter of Federation of Arab Groups/Societies (FEARAB). Since then dialogue has evolved between both communities, according to the leadership of the Argentinean Jewish community.[67]

However, in December 2010 FEARAB issued a communiqué condemning the organized Argentinean Jewish community (AMIA) for their opposition to Argentina's unilateral recognition of a Palestinian state. That was not a mere repudiation of AMIA's statement. The Arab group—considered to be moderate and an umbrella organization of local Arab communities—went so far as to declare that AMIA was not loyal to Argentina but to Israel. This is an accusation usually made by the most virulent anti-Semites. The statement also pointed out that the Palestinian people have lived under occupation for sixty-two years. This basically means that the group considers Israel to be an illegitimate state from its birth in 1948 and not since the Israeli take over of the West Bank and Gaza in 1967.[68]

Furthermore, on a different occasion FEARAB's general secretary denounced connections between the Buenos Aires police and the State of Israel, pointing his finger toward the spokesperson of the force—who happened to be Jewish—accusing him of being a spokesperson for the Israel Defense Force.[69] The Arab leader did not present any evidence to support such an accusation.

In Chile it has been reported that since the second intifada broke out in 2000 Chilean Arabs and Muslims have become more militant, particularly in college campuses. Chilean Jewish leaders have pointed out that relations between Jews and Arabs are totally set by the Arab-Israeli conflict.

A Shiite sheikh stated on Chilean TV that the State of Israel should cease to exist.[70] But this radicalism is not only connected with the Arab-Israeli conflict. I would even say that this conflict is a good instrument in the hands of radicalism.

The radicalization is general. As an example, a mosque located in the Tri-border area between Brazil, Argentina, and Paraguay has been identified as a chapter of Hezbollah. The cleric is a Shiite man named Hamid Nasrallah who is a family member of Hassan Nasrallah, the leader of Hezbollah in Lebanon.[71]

The tri-border area has a large Arab population and is also known for being a place where money is laundered to, funds are raised, and money transfers are made to terrorist organizations. These attempts by radicals to hijack local communities is a development that needs to be taken very seriously. As we have shown through the example of Darnott, radical Islam and the radical Left can find common ground. This is the alliance between Bolivarian Venezuela and the Islamic Republic of Iran.

The Bolivarian revolution has become associated with Iran and Hezbollah in the same way that it has with FARC. Thus, one can assume that Hezbollah might eventually turn into another paramilitary branch of the revolution. Of course, the presence of local sympathizers or the rise of radicalism makes this risk even higher. Therefore, the presence of Hezbollah operatives in Venezuela—particularly the training of Venezuelans in Hezbollah-supervised camps—both promotes the organization's agenda and helps Chávez achieve his own purposes.

The Repressive Apparatus

In 2005, the Venezuelan airline Conviasa began flying regular direct flights between Tehran and Caracas, as well as between Damascus and Caracas. *La Stampa*, an Italian newspaper, pointed out that these flights among those cities provide a way for Venezuela to help Iran ship materials for manufacturing missiles to Syria, fulfilling a military cooperation agreement that Syria and Iran signed in 2006. According to *La Stampa*, the materials are eventually destined for the Revolutionary Guard Corps, the main force protecting the Iranian regime. In exchange for delivering those military materials, Iran provided Venezuela with members of their Revolutionary Guard Corps and its elite unit, Al Quds, to strengthen Venezuela's secret services and police.[72]

A few years later, in April 2010, the Pentagon reported the presence of paramilitary Al Quds operatives in Venezuela.[73] The Quds force is aligned with terrorists in Iraq, Afghanistan, Israel, North Africa, and Latin America, and its members provide terrorists with weapons, funding, and training. The presence of the Revolutionary Guard Corps—the foundation upon which the Iranian Islamic totalitarian regime has been built—is very telling. Iran's, and Hezbollah's, involvement in Latin America thus raises another issue that needs to be taken into consideration—that is, the role that Iran could play in helping a regime, such as in Venezuela and in other Latin American countries that follow the Bolivarian model, consolidate absolute power.

As discussed, President Chávez has initiated a process of duplicating traditional Venezuelan institutions, such as the judiciary, the security apparatus, and the military. He is creating a "dual state." In this situation, the normative state, which is supposed to regulate societal functions through a system of clear laws and courts, gradually collapses to a prerogative state that uses discretionary-arbitrary power.[74] Many totalitarian regimes and harsh dictatorships, including those of Hitler, Joseph Stalin, and Saddam Hussein, have practiced this process of gradual, or in some cases abrupt, duplication with the objective of annulling the legal institutions in favor of concentrating powers in the hands of the leader or, in the best-case scenario, the party.

As noted in chapter 2, in keeping with Chávez's view of the armed forces as being the backbone of his social and political revolution, he has also attempted to monopolize and subordinate the military to his will. His administration purged military officers for treason and gave key military posts to officers loyal to the Bolivarian revolution. Further, from the beginning, Chávez created pro-government paramilitary forces outside the formal law enforcement apparatus to generate fear and intimidation among the population. Also, he established a new militia that is able to include non-Venezuelans. It is realistic to assume that this sort of foreign legion force could play a similar role to that of the Revolutionary Guard in Iraq, Bashar al-Assad's forces in Syria, and other armies aimed at generating loyalty to the regime and provide a possible alternative force in case he encounters any future sedition. President Chávez's militias may well include foreign nationals of Middle Eastern extraction, as well as Cubans, FARC guerrilla fighters, and others, since Chávez is gradually duplicating the regular army, which he does not trust.

The Cuban regime, indeed, could help Chávez consolidate a regime based on absolute power, but Iran's Revolutionary Guard Corps would be able to reinforce such a consolidation. The latter's Quds force could build an even more ruthless state than the Cubans for such groups manage the art of violence better than any military man could. Thus, that the Revolutionary Guard has allegedly been seen aboard Conviasa's direct flights to Caracas makes perfect sociological and political sense.

Should the repressive power and revolutionary zeal of Cuba fade in a post-Castro era, the highly sophisticated and repressive apparatus of Iran and its Revolutionary Guard Corps could provide a living model. In this case, the Middle Eastern individuals obtaining Venezuelan passports likely could be Hezbollah-type mercenaries who would join the duplicated security apparatus Chávez is building to counterbalance the Venezuelan army. This process could be advanced if Chávez or his followers, after his death, try to avoid transferring power.

Even more ominous, this case is likely to be reproduced in other countries that now are satellites of the Chávez regime. For instance, Venezuelan army officials have a presence in Bolivia, and it is reasonable to assume, as investigative journalist Douglas Farah does, that they are teaching the doctrine of asymmetric war to the Bolivian army.[75] In fact, as a part of Chávez's project of expanding his revolution in the continent, he has also promoted such doctrines among allies.[76] The extent of his success is not clear yet. If he is successful, it will involve not merely establishing alliances with Iran but also fostering a real direct influence of Iran on these countries' political and security apparatuses. In other words, a widespread Iranian-style repression in the continent could turn into a generalized threat to consolidate autocratic regimes. As Iran develops closer relationships with these countries, the destruction of democracy and the consolidation of all-controlling regimes may move faster and faster.

┃ SUMMARY

Iran's presence in Latin America is manifold. It seeks political clout in Latin America as well as relief from its economic isolation, but the real challenges Iran presents come from its being a major rogue state and its complex interaction with the Bolivarian revolution. Thus, its presence in Latin America needs to be evaluated not only in terms of its own agenda but also in terms of the Bolivarian revolution's agenda or, more specifically, that of

Venezuelan president Hugo Chávez. At the same time, both revolutions have objectives that overlap.

First, Iran seeks to develop a nuclear weapon. Venezuela and its Bolivarian allies have not only provided international political support for Iran in its endeavor but also, in the case of Venezuela, are likely to make use of a nuclear Iran. Venezuela and Iran could bring nuclear weapons to Venezuela or to one of its allies with major consequences for U.S. national security and regional security. It is important to remember that Iran does not have a sound conventional army. Instead of a developing a strong air force or armored force, most of Iran's military investments have not been directed toward its missile and nonconventional (particularly nuclear) forces and its networks of global terrorism.[77] As the Iranians attempt to build a nuclear weapon, they have increased their military capacity through surrogates, mostly by building positions of strength along the borders of its adversaries. Now, the power of Iran and its ominous behavior are indeed reaching backyard. Meanwhile, Chávez may aspire to obtain a nuclear weapon, knowing that it will make him a player in the region, but Venezuela can only become a nuclear power with the aid of Iran. If nuclear weapons are posted on Venezuelan territory or if ready-made nuclear weapons are handed to the Venezuelan government, both the region and the United States will face a major existential crisis.

Next, the Iranians have another expertise the Bolivarian revolution might adopt—namely, asymmetric warfare. The Iranians have supplied arms to the Taliban in Afghanistan and have been heavily involved in trying to influence events in Iraq. They supported radical anti-American Shi'ite cleric Moqtada al-Sadr, helping to escalate the Shi'a-Sunni cleavage in Iraq.[78] Iran could well use these skills overseas to commit sabotage or terrorist attacks. Its attempt to use a Mexican gang member to assassinate the Saudi ambassador in Washington illustrates its reach.

The Iranians have experience in everything the Bolivarian revolution needs. Iran is a violent force capable of generating chaos and subversion. Thus, the increasing presence of the Iranian-backed Hezbollah in Latin America might not only be limited to attacks against Israeli, Jewish, or U.S. institutions. Members of this terrorist group can serve as asymmetric fighters against any army or government the Bolivarian revolution considers an enemy. More important, Hezbollah certainly could help the Chávez regime and such groups as FARC in their efforts to destabilize countries

that are considered enemies or targets of the Iranian revolution like Colombia. Thus, the Iranians can undermine the rule of law and the balance
of power throughout the continent. The destabilizing power of FARC, for
instance, becomes even worse if a Hezbollah-Iranian component is added
to the equation. The greater the presence of these terrorist groups in the
region, the more the West needs to take into account their potential impact, particularly if they unite with other forces, such as the drug cartels
and FARC, and if they recruit militants from local Muslim communities.
Furthermore, reports on Venezuelans training in Hezbollah camps in Lebanon, as well as the presence of Hezbollah-run camps in Venezuela, are
alarming phenomena.

In exploring how Iran could play an important role in the Chávez
revolution by undermining the authority, bureaucracies, and security systems of Latin American states, we also need to consider how Iran's helping
Chávez foment anarchy in the area and turning it into another Afghanistan
would create a nightmare for the United States in its own backyard. Thus,
Iran's presence cannot be judged in conventional terms as Gen. Douglas
Fraser, former commander of U.S. Southern Command, did when he said
that "there is no indication that the Iranian presence in Latin America
constitutes a threat" to the United States.[79] Neither can we agree with Stephen Johnson, former assistant secretary of defense for the Western Hemisphere, and the Congressional Research Service of the U.S. Congress when
they maintain that Hezbollah's interests in the region are limited to illicit
fund-raising ventures to support the group's activities in Lebanon.[80] We
also should not view Iran's penetration in the continent merely as a means
to circumvent trade sanctions and its international isolation.

Instead, Iran's presence in Latin America must be viewed in light of
Iran's own revolution and its history of waging asymmetric war. This point
is most important because being at a disadvantage from a conventional
point of view, the Bolivarian revolution also must rely on asymmetric
methods. Furthermore, both Chávez and Ahmadinejad wish to subjugate
and diminish the power of the United States. They can do so by exposing
the area and the United States to a nuclear threat, by promoting other revolutions and consolidating anti-American regimes, by making U.S. borders
vulnerable to terrorism, by subverting the continent's power structures,
and by further encouraging drug trafficking, which will inevitably lead to
the destruction of state authority and to chaos in the Americas' backyard.

In addition, Iran's experience in maintaining an extremely repressive regime is likely to help the Bolivarian revolution survive. Chávez is looking to perpetuate power in Venezuela and the rest of the Bolivarian countries. As stated, if change occurs in Cuba after the rule of the Castro brothers ends, Iran's repressive tactics could play an even more important role in consolidating dictatorships in the Bolivarian countries.

Finally, given all of these facts, the rise of Iran's political and economic leverage in the area, particularly among non-Bolivarian countries, raises concerns. Although countries ruled by the moderates are not necessarily supporters of the Bolivarian revolution, they are not necessarily against the Bolivarian model either. This stance, in addition to their advocacy of South-South solidarity, has helped give Iran a footing in the area. If they view Iran as a country that deserves support and not as a perpetrator of violence, its presence will continue to grow in the continent. It is no wonder then that Iran and Hezbollah's proselytizing activities have increased in countries such as Brazil and Argentina.

To consider Iran's presence in Latin America by focusing solely on Iran's immediate economic or political interests is important but narrow. The magnitude of the Bolivarian revolution involves a plethora of components that should not be overlooked.

7 | THE ROLES OF CHINA AND RUSSIA

Very often, foreign policy analysts and political leaders view China as an economic power seeking even greater economic power. In that sense, China's increasing presence in Latin America is viewed largely as part of China's natural economic growth and its search for natural resources. Although its penetration in the area is to a great extent economic and technological, China also has a geopolitical and strategic agenda that has not been taken with the degree of seriousness it requires. Its presence in Latin America must also be understood in the framework of its interaction with the Bolivarian revolution and how the latter can benefit from its relationship with China.

Russia, meanwhile, has become the main arms supplier for Venezuela and other Bolivarian countries such as Cuba. In light of these arms' imports for the Bolivarian revolution, one must also review the deeper implications of Russia's involvement in Latin America.

In this chapter, I explore the logic of Chinese and Russian policies in the continent. Both governments have similar goals but at the same time different approaches. Along these lines, the presence of both powers in Latin America and the associated implications are examined.

CHINA AND LATIN AMERICA IN PERSPECTIVE

In November 2008, China's government issued a white paper highlighting the areas in which it seeks to cooperate with Latin American countries. In it, China sets a number of goals. Some of them are common goals that nations establish when they wish to engage each other in a cordial and fruitful relationship. The paper states that China and Latin America "are at a similar stage of development and face the common task of achieving development. Both sides cherish the desire for greater mutual understanding and closer cooperation. . . . [Thus the] future growth of relationship between the two sides enjoys great potential and broad prospects. . . ."[1]

Therefore, among China's goals for Latin America, the paper outlines the following points:

- Both sides "will strengthen dialogue and communication, enhance political mutual trust, expand strategic common ground, and continue to show understanding and support on issues involving each other's core interests and major concerns."
- Both sides will "deepen cooperation and achieve win-win results. The two sides will leverage their respective strengths, tap the potential of cooperation, and seek to become each other's partner in economic cooperation and trade for mutual benefit and common development."
- Both sides will "draw on each other's strengths to boost common progress and intensify exchanges. The two sides will carry out more cultural and people-to-people exchanges, learn from each other and jointly promote development and progress of human civilization."
- The one China principle is the political basis for the establishment and development of relations between China and Latin American and Caribbean countries and regional organizations. The overwhelming majority of countries in the region are committed to the one China policy and the position of supporting China's reunification and not having official ties or contacts with Taiwan. The Chinese Government appreciates such a stance. China is ready to establish and develop state-to-state relations with all Latin American and Caribbean countries based on the one China principle."
- The Chinese Government will continue to strengthen coordination and cooperation on international issues with Latin American and Caribbean countries, and maintain regular consultation with them on major international and regional issues. The two sides will continue to support each other on such important issues as sovereignty and territorial integrity. China stands ready to work with Latin American and Caribbean countries to strengthen the role of the United Nations, make the international political and economic order more fair and equitable, promote democracy in international

relations and uphold the legitimate rights and interests of developing countries. China supports a greater role of Latin American and Caribbean countries in international affairs."

- "The Chinese Government will continue to work with its Latin American and Caribbean counterparts in the spirit of equality and mutual benefit to expand and balance two-way trade and improve the trade structure to achieve common development. At the same time, it will work with these countries to properly settle trade frictions through consultation and cooperation. China will, on the basis of mutual benefit and win-win cooperation, give positive consideration to concluding free trade agreements with Latin American and Caribbean countries or regional integration organizations."

- "The Chinese Government encourages and supports qualified Chinese companies with good reputation in investing in manufacturing, agriculture, forestry, fishing, energy, mineral resources, infrastructure, and service sector in Latin America and the Caribbean to promote the economic and social development of both sides. The Chinese Government will continue to welcome investment by Latin American and Caribbean businesses in China."

The white paper covers such issues as economic cooperation, mutual investment, trade and technological exchanges, and other types of cooperation, including military cooperation.

Establishing protocols on these topics is not unusual for a growing economy; however, I argue that China's offer to assist in all these economic and technological areas also has strategic considerations. As Edward Friedman, a scholar and expert on China, points out, "Analysts in Latin America who imagine China as a purely economic actor misunderstand the People's Republic of China, where politics is privileged."[2] China's white paper proposes military and strategic cooperation with Latin American countries. This collaboration entails a far more complex issue that can only be understood in terms of China's political agenda and its military expansion.

▌CHINA'S STRATEGIC EXPANSION

In 2006, a group of Chinese scholars associated with the Chinese government wrote a study titled *The Rise of Great Powers*, which became a twelve-part documentary that was broadcast on Chinese television. This study concluded that national power is a function of economic development tied to foreign trade. Such national power, according to these scholars, can be further enhanced with expanded naval (military) power. The authors believe that sea power is a means to an end, with the goal being to promote commerce and shipping. Naval power ensures that this trade takes place without interference or obstacles.[3]

Upon analyzing the Dutch case, the study argues that Dutch naval power developed mainly as a commercial enterprise. Because the Dutch were purely motivated by commerce, they wrongly assumed that commercial enterprises and profit seeking could sustain their power. Thus, the Dutch failure to build a real naval military power prevented it from defending itself from foreign threats. The Union of Soviet Socialist Republics, meanwhile, built its military and naval power without establishing economic strength. This oversight virtually led to the union's collapse. Therefore, the study points out, developing maritime power is necessary but insufficient to support the rise of a big power. Naval power must be tied to a larger economic project.

In the case of the United States, the Chinese are impressed with how the United States has exercised naval command in the world. The scholars observe that the United States did not achieve such dominion through wars and aggression but rather through strategy.[4]

In examining China's case, the study claims that the influence of foreign powers in the islands around China, particularly in the East and South China Sea, undermines China's strategic goals of expansion. Therefore, China's insistence in claiming those islands is vital.[5] Beijing wants to settle these territorial disputes in its favor, expand its maritime periphery, and develop alternative pathways to break out into the open ocean.[6] In this sense, the Sino-Japanese quarrel over the Senkaku/Diaoyou Islands is particularly problematic.[7]

China's claim over these islands reflects an element of aggressiveness in China's foreign policy. The islands were recognized as Japanese territory after World War II. As an oil company began energy exploration for Japan, China sent a fleet to the area and warned Japan to stop the work on the oil fields. China has also conducted military activities, including submarine exercises that frequently entered the Japanese Economic Exclusive Zone.[8] By the same token, China claims sovereignty over all the South China

Sea, believing it has significant oil and natural gas reserves. China also maintains rights of exploration over the isles around the Spratly and Paracels Islands, but Vietnam, the Philippines, and Taiwan currently challenge the legal status of these islands. The Vietnamese and the Philippines have raised their concerns and as a result have sought to build closer security agreements with the United States.[9]

Constantine Menges, the late scholar and former adviser on Latin American security to U.S. president Ronald Reagan, pointed out that China has displayed a systematically aggressive policy on its territorial disputes with eleven out of fourteen bordering states. Indeed, China has historically used force in order to enforce its territorial and sovereignty claims. In 1974, the Chinese expelled South Vietnam from the Paracel Islands, and in 1979 China invaded the northern region of Vietnam to punish the government for its alliance with the Soviet Union. In 1995, China occupied the Spratly Island's Mischief Reef, which belonged to the Philippines, and established a military naval presence there.[10] China used force against the Philippines and built military structures on the occupied lands of Mischief Reef.[11]

China's most widely known territorial controversy concerns Taiwan. Since 1949 China has pursued a policy aimed at regaining Taiwan. China has used its economic leverage, as much as possible, to sway other countries in the world to recognize the "one China" policy.[12] China seeks to reverse Taiwan's independence mostly by pressuring different governments not to deal with Taiwan if they want China's investments in their countries.

China perceives U.S. military power as an impediment to China's effort to take control of Taiwan. In 1992 when the U.S. government sold missiles to Taiwan, China retaliated by selling missiles to Pakistan and signing a nuclear cooperation agreement with Iran. Even under the conciliatory Obama administration, its announcement to sell $6 billion of weapons to Taiwan early in 2010 angered China, which reacted by threatening to suspend military exchanges with the United States, to review its cooperation on major issues, and to impose sanctions on companies selling arms.[13]

Therefore, if China can make global gains that would enable it to hold a political card that it can use in making an implicit or explicit bargain with the United States over Taiwan or any other claim in China's own backyard (for example, the East or South China Sea), it will do it. Naval power is only one of them. Following the strategic concept of a peaceful naval power helps identify other peaceful strategic means. Economic means are among the most important ones, as they translate into political power.

Under current conditions China perceives a U.S. alliance with a number of countries that surround China as preventing its expansion into territories that China considers as being in its area of influence. Along these lines, China naturally seeks political cards to counter pressure the United States, in a sort of "a political second strike capability." Therefore, against this background, China aims to establish similar alliances and a presence in the backyard of the United States.

China's economic outreach to Latin America thus extends beyond achieving economic gains. It serves China's interest as a "soft power" to make geopolitical gains. Furthermore, in light of the Bolivarian revolution in the area, China's presence in Latin America could turn into a more complex situation, as it could help perpetuate the regimes of Hugo Chávez and his Bolivarian allies.

CHINA'S PRESENCE IN LATIN AMERICA

The Economic Dimension

China's economic offensive in Latin America began in the 1990s, and since then it has astronomically progressed. Trade with Latin America has grown from $10 billion in 2000 to $150 billion in 2008.[14] Moreover, during the 2000s, China increased its investments even more. Its trade with Latin America grew by 40 percent between 2007 and 2008, making 2008's figures three times higher than in 2004. Likewise, Latin American exports to China increased by 41 percent between 2007 and 2008. This growth is substantially higher than any export to the United States. China has signed free trade agreements with Peru and Chile and has improved its access to supplies of copper, zinc, meat, iron ore, and other commodities.[15]

More important, China has increased its economic relations with Hugo Chávez and its allies in the Bolivarian Alternative for the Americas, particularly Ecuador and Bolivia. China also has agreed to develop Bolivia's first communications satellite and a major hydroelectric plant in Ecuador. China's relationship with Venezuela is equally strong as their joint investment fund increased from $6 billion to $12 billion.[16] Venezuela is China's fourth-biggest oil provider and fifth-largest trading partner in Latin America, a year-on-year increase of 68.2 percent.[17] Similarly, China's trade with Cuba has increased, making China the second-largest trading partner of the island after Venezuela. Its $2 billion in trade in 2011, according to Cuban officials, is mostly in the field of biotechnology, machinery, medicine, transportation vehicles, nickel, and computer science.[18]

Brazil is China's major partner in Latin America. China and Brazil have established partnerships in construction, technology, and biotechnology industries and have launched an earth surveillance satellite. As Latin America scholar Susan Kaufman Purcell has pointed out, "China has already de-facto displaced the United States as Brazil's main trade partner. As China's demand for raw materials continues its economic and industrial operation will expand in the continent."[19] There is nothing wrong per se with increasing economic relations between Latin America and China, but as China also has geopolitical strategic interests in the region, the situation becomes complicated for the United States and its regional allies.

It is noteworthy that Chávez and his allies, all sharing a strong anti-American agenda and looking to reduce U.S. influence in the area, already see China as a potential replacement for U.S. technological capabilities. For example, the pro-Chávez government of Rafael Correa in Ecuador did not renew the lease for the U.S. military base of Manta from which the United States monitored drug activity in the area. Indeed, the United States began to withdraw from Manta in July 2009 after ten years of service there. Correa then rushed to call the Chinese to come to Manta.

Early in his presidency President Correa announced his wish to promote more Chinese investments in the area. He not only signed commercial agreements with China in a number of economic areas, such as energy, mining, and agriculture, but also offered China the concession over the Manta airport. In Correa's vision Manta would serve as an important international airport that could be used for trade and international commerce, as well as a key connection hub for other parts of the continent. In economic terms, he also sought a major agreement that would include Venezuela and ALBA countries to develop a refinery.[20] Chinese control of an area that until recently the United States used to control drug trafficking could have far-reaching strategic implications.

Chávez has stated on a number of occasions that China is the new global power. He has urged ALBA members to deepen their relations with China. At the first summit meeting of the Latin American and Caribbean Community of States (Comunidad de Estados Latinoamericanos y Caribeños

[CELAC]), held in Caracas and hosted by Hugo Chávez, the Venezuelan leader read a letter of congratulations and blessings from the Chinese president Hu Jintao. The summit excluded the United States and Canada.

The Bolivarian countries, however, are not the only ones to establish a strong relationship with China. China has also proposed building a multibillion-dollar railway line that would extend across Colombia and connect the Caribbean with the Pacific Ocean.[21]

Chinese companies in the field of telecommunications and space, meanwhile, are penetrating the region as U.S. companies retreat. This development is particularly true in such countries as Argentina and Brazil with whom Chinese companies have signed contracts worth billions of dollars in the field of communication technology.[22] China also began extending its efforts in international space cooperation. Argentina has traditionally cooperated with the United States on space technology, but China has already provided Argentina with a third-generation satellite laser ranger and has signed contracts to manufacture and launch satellites for Venezuela. Likewise, it is cooperating with Brazil in the development and launching of four satellites. The United States apparently is losing in the competition for high technology in Latin America, formerly a traditional partner.[23]

China's economic involvement in the continent has strategic implications as it also provides political leverage. By the same token, its dominance of communications, satellite, and space technology enables it to control a communications network in the continent that has enormous intelligence value. This situation fits the Chinese strategy that they claim to prefer—that is, to achieve domination without resorting to military might.

As a result of its economic activity, China has already scored some strategic gains. Hutchison International Terminals, a Chinese company, has signed a fifty-year lease that gives it control over both ends of the Panama Canal, which is an area of major strategic importance. Several members of Congress denounced the bid through which Hutchison received the contract as being secret and illegitimate, since the Panama government awarded it in an "unorthodox" manner.[24]

Hutchison International Terminals is owned by Hutchison Whampoa Limited. Li Ka-shing, the company's chairman, has close connections with the Chinese government and the Chinese military.[25] The contract that Hutchison International Terminals signed with Panama provides the company with a "first option" to take control over the ports of Rodman Naval Station "as well as an operating area at former U.S. Albrook Air Force

Base."[26] The Rodman Naval Station was the main point for operational and administrational support of all U.S. Navy Forces deployed within the Southern Command area of responsibility before the Panama Canal was given up by the United States in 1999. That played a key role during World War II when the U.S. Navy sought to advance in the Pacific.[27] During the hearing for his confirmation as commander of the United States Southern Command, Lt. Gen. John Kelly pointed out that "the security of the Panama Canal is of critical importance to U.S. regional, and global economic security."[28]

In the economic domain, shipments through the Panama Canal represent about 13 percent of the world trade and about 15–20 percent of the U.S. trade. [29]

The Political Dimension

China's economic power and its demand for natural resources have undoubtedly contributed significantly to the growth Latin America has experienced since 2000. However, China's economic impact could also have geopolitical implications in the region, particularly with regard to the Bolivarian revolution. To comprehend this situation, China's policy toward rogue states is worth reviewing.

China developed strong relationships with such rogue states as Saddam Hussein's Iraq and Ahmadinejad's Iran by selling them weapons. China has also signed deals and strategic alliances with other states that are hostile to the United States, such as Libya, Syria, and Sudan. In exchange for oil, China provided these countries with political support, weapons, and technology, which might also include nuclear technology. Despite international sanctions against Iran, Chinese companies have continued to provide restricted technology to Iran and particularly for its missile program, which is a main concern of the United States and its allies. Chinese companies also continued to sell Iran high-quality materials that could help improve the centrifuges Iran needs to enrich uranium and develop a nuclear weapon.[30] According to the United States, China is the largest buyer of Iran's crude oil and an important provider of gasoline.[31] Likewise, it has also attempted to assist Iran in counteracting the effect of international sanctions by providing it with secret banking facilities.[32]

During the Libyan crisis in 2011, when a rebellion finally toppled the tyrannical rule of Muammar Gadhafi, China abstained from voting in support of a United Nations Security Council resolution aimed at protecting civilians. At the same time China's state-owned weapons manufacturers reportedly conducted meetings with officials in the Gadhafi government.[33] Likewise, as the West demanded sanctions in Sudan because of its genocidal policies against non-Arab minorities in the area of Darfur, China strongly and stubbornly opposed any sanctions. China has also assisted Pakistan with nuclear missile technology, specifically going against the U.S. policy of nonproliferation.[34] Some explain this contrary behavior as stemming solely from China's need for oil, but this motive is only partially true.

In February 2012, China and Russia opposed a United Nations Security Council resolution in support of an Arab League plan that proposed a transition from the al-Assad regime in Syria and called for elections. The veto took place while the Syrian regime furiously carried out massacres and human rights violations against the rebels who challenged it. Syria is not a major oil producer. Therefore, China's policy in this instance was not motivated by a concern over oil supply. Instead, China's actions are political and aimed at counterbalancing U.S. and Western influence.

In addition, China is very suspicious of democracy. Since 1989 when the Chinese crashed the democracy movement that began in their capital's Tiananmen Square, they have continued struggling against internal democratic movements. According to Friedman, what China fears the most and is trying to prevent, is the spread of democracy, which could create a mass uprising in China and risk the regime: "China's military has created the capability for anti-democratic regional interventions. One should expect China to be militantly and militarily opposed to the spread of democracy in its geopolitical neighborhood."[35]

Even though Latin America is not in China's region, China has a major interest in reducing the influence of world democracies and certainly seeks to ease international pressure on the regime on the issue of democracy and human rights. Thus, as Friedman points out, "China is . . . pushing and pulling the world in its authoritarian direction. . . . The CCP [Communist Party of China] intends for authoritarian China to establish itself as a global pole."[36]

Thus, Larry Diamond, a scholar of democracy and democratic studies at Stanford University, has concluded that "democracy is in trouble" today because China's economic growth and increasing influence in the world enables it to support and even bail out authoritarian regimes.[37] Consequently, it is no surprise that China has transferred technology to dictatorships and rogue states.

China finds Venezuela, Cuba, Bolivia, Ecuador, and Nicaragua to be good partners for a number of reasons. First, these countries are not democracies. The dictatorial nature of the Bolivarian regimes might be perpetuated with trade or other types of aid. If the commercial relationships between these countries and China benefit them, likely the Bolivarian regimes will gain strength.

In one clear example, China signed a series of deals in which China agreed to lend Venezuela up to $32 billion at low interest rates in exchange for future oil shipments. Venezuela ships to China half of what it sells to the United States.[38]

Second, given that the Bolivarian countries are, in theory and practice, fervently against the United States, they provide China with opportunities to exercise some influence in what has been the United States' traditional sphere of influence. For that reason alone, China is likely to help these countries stay in power.

Thus, these steps might be more than economically beneficial to both sides. Politically, these relationships will expand the Bolivarian revolution and confirm China's ability to prop up the Bolivarian regime and even protect it from decay. China's soft strategic power, therefore, counts more than its naval or military buildup in expanding its influence worldwide.

▌RUSSIA IN LATIN AMERICA

After the Cold War, Russia sought to integrate with the West and to practice economic liberalism and democracy under the presidency of Boris Yeltsin (1991–1999). Russia tried to stabilize the Russian federation and join a world that was moving more in the direction of Western liberal democracy and renouncing ideology altogether, as outlined in American political scientist Francis Fukuyama's essay "The End of History." In other words, with the collapse of communism, no significant new ideology or idea of the "good life" could compete with what was found in the West. In terms of geopolitics, Russia seemed to have given up its ambitions to exercise influence in the world and focused instead on purely domestic issues.

However, Russia began an economic boom as the price of oil and gas increased in the 2000s. In parallel, a new leader emerged in Russia, Vladimir Putin, who not only revived some of the old antidemocratic practices that had made Russia the largest illiberal democracy but also restored the concept of Russia as being a great world power. Addressing the nation,

Putin pointed out that "the collapse of the Soviet Union was the greatest geopolitical catastrophe of the century."[39] Thus, under Putin, Russia launched a more aggressive foreign policy in 2005.

In 2003 and 2004, pro-Western governments had replaced pro-Russian governments in such countries as Ukraine and Georgia. While the leaders of Ukraine sought more independence from Moscow, Georgia sought to join the North Atlantic Treaty Organization. Along with the former Soviet republics of Lithuania, Latvia, and Estonia, which had already formally joined NATO in 2004, these countries now constituted an important pro-Western belt. U.S. president George W. Bush actively supported Georgia's proposed membership. This development raised the anxiety of the Russians, who were witnessing their influence decline in the same areas that they had dominated for decades.[40]

In August 2008, arguing in favor of the secession of the Georgian provinces of South Ossetia and Abkhazia, which were in conflict with their central government, Russia invaded Georgia. Russia supported the two provinces in their unilateral declaration of independence without international discussion, which a six-point plan agreement negotiated between Russia and the European Union had required. The Russian invasion, however, was basically aimed at preventing Georgia from joining NATO.[41]

Thus, Russia actively seeks to maintain predominance in the regions they consider to be within their sphere of influence.[42] Therefore, using the Venezuelan card against the United States in its hemisphere is also a step that Russia can take to counteract NATO's advance in what used to be Russia's backyard. Consequently, in 2008 Russia offered Chávez $1 billion in credit to buy weapons and nuclear cooperation. At the same time, the Russian and Venezuelan navies conducted joint exercises.[43]

Venezuela had already spent $4.4 billion on twelve contracts for Russian weapons from 2005 to 2007. These deals included purchases of 100,000 Kalashnikov rifles, fifty military helicopters, and twenty-four Su-30 jet fighters.[44] From 2006 to 2008 Russia delivered 472 missiles and launching mechanisms to Venezuela, and in 2009 sent 1,800 shoulder-fired antiaircraft missiles.[45]

In October 2010 Chávez and Russian president Dmitry Medvedev reached an agreement to build two 1,200-megawatt nuclear reactors in Venezuela. This project is similar to the reactor that Iran built with Russia's help and was completed in August 2010. Russia also made a further commitment to send Venezuela sophisticated tanks to replace its old French-made tanks.[46] Venezuela's purchase of Russian weaponry has turned Venezuela into the fourth largest purchaser of Russian military equipment in the world.[47]

Economic relationships between other Latin American countries and Russia have also developed in the last decade, particularly with the former exporting agricultural products. In exchange, Latin American countries, particularly other Bolivarian countries, have imported fertilizers and a large part of its arms purchases from Russia.[48] For instance, Russia lent $100 million to Bolivia to purchase Russian military helicopters.[49] But unlike China, Russia has no economic weight in Latin America, despite the many agreements it has negotiated in energy, agriculture, and other civil sectors.

Yet, Russia's presence in Latin America can have major geopolitical consequences. As pointed out earlier, the crisis in Georgia constituted an important point of conflict between Russia and the United States. As Russia scholar Stephen Blank indicated, "Russian interest in Latin America might be aimed at showing that if the U.S. intervenes in the Commonwealth of Independent States (CIS), Moscow can reciprocate in Latin America."[50] Following this logic, Blank argues that Russian policy in Latin America is aimed at using Latin America as a political bloc to support Russian positions against U.S. dominance in world affairs. Thus, Russia encourages those countries that wish to challenge the United States to rely on Moscow. In this way, Moscow could force the United States to accept a new world that is essentially multipolar, where the United States is not the only superpower but rather one of several world powers. To achieve this goal, Blank says, "multi-polarity remains a policy to enhance Russian standing as a global power." In fact, former Russian president Medvedev conceded that geopolitical calculations primarily motivated his trip to Latin America in 2008.[51] This strategy applies not only to commercial deals, which are mostly on oil- and energy-related projects, but mainly to their arm deals.

▌ RUSSIAN WEAPONS AND THE ASYMMETRIC WAR

The problem with the Russian arms deals has a much more critical dimension. Chapters 5 and 6 pointed out that guerrilla organizations such as FARC or Middle Eastern groups such as Hezbollah could play an important role in Chávez's effort to destabilize countries or in his preparations for an asymmetric war to achieve hegemony in the continent.

If, besides Iran, Moscow also contributes to the Bolivarian attempt to destabilize the region, its involvement constitutes a major danger. Venezuela is believed to have already funneled more than $300 million to FARC and has built a Russia-licensed ammunition plant to supply AK-103 assault rifles, FARC's weapon of choice.[52] These weapons' falling into the hands of revolutionary groups could further aggravate the situation in the continent.

It is important to point out that Viktor Bout, a well-known arms dealer under Moscow's protection, was arrested in 2008 in Thailand for offering weapons to FARC and was later sentenced to twenty-five years in a U.S. prison.[53] At the same time, Russia tends to support Chávez when the Venezuelan president clashes with Colombia.[54] Being that Colombia is a staunch ally of the United States, it makes sense that Russia could be supporting the Chávez agenda. This stance might include not only a business-like, pure-interest-based cooperation with Venezuela or a simple "amoral" weapon transaction but also could well translate into full support of Chávez's agenda with all its implications.[55]

Again, Moscow's position is not clear. In thinking about possible scenarios, one can safely assume that Moscow's actions are likely to strengthen Chávez's asymmetric and subversive objectives with the subsequent destabilizing implications of such policies.

| SUMMARY

In assessing China's and Russia's role in Latin America, the most logical conclusion is that China and Russia will be instrumental in helping perpetuate Chávez and his allies in power. China's economic leverage and its tendency to protect rogue states will serve those regimes. China definitely has more access to the Bolivarian countries than the United States does. China is also becoming influential in the rest of Latin America. Should the forces of democracy be repressed, China will help their suppressors survive by providing either economic assistance or international political support. As noted, as a permanent member of the United Nations Security Council, China and the Russian Federation has opposed sanctions against both Iran and Syria, and it abstained from protecting civilians during the rebellion in Libya. China pursued such policies not only because it purchases Iran's oil and natural gas but also because it has systematically used rogue states to counterbalance the power and leverage of the United States in the world. As China's penetration in Latin America becomes deeper and deeper, its interests will converge with the interests of the Bolivarian revolution. Among other issues, it will protect them from international pressure to democratize. At the same time, in trying to prevent a direct confrontation with China, the United States will have to accept China's protection of Venezuela in the same way China is forced to accept American de facto protection of Taiwan.

For that reason, a rogue leader such as Hugo Chávez, who seeks to destroy U.S. hegemony and wage a major continental revolution in opposition to the United States and its allies in the region, is a gift to China. As such, if a legitimate act of rebellion takes place in Venezuela or an allied country similar to what took place in Iran in June 2009, and to what has been occurring in the Arab world since January 2011, China might undermine international efforts to stop human rights violations and certainly will protect the regime as much as it can.

If in the future the West needs to apply pressure on these Bolivarian regimes over violations of democracy or human rights or over their support for subversive activities or over their dangerous relations with Iran, China will resist such efforts and will stand by the regimes. China will support them even further as it continues both to resent U.S. aid to Taiwan and to nullify Taiwan's independence and take its territory. Thus for this reason, the Chinese white paper on Latin America raised the point of "deepening" military cooperation there.

Even though military missions' visits between China and Latin America have occurred regularly, most weapons sold to Latin America's rogue regimes come from Russia. On a smaller scale, China pledged to deliver six K-8 Karakorum attack planes in 2010 and is lending money to Ecuador to buy aircraft for its air force. Early in 2009, Ecuador signed a contract for $60 million to buy Chinese air defense radars.[56] For the time being, these sales do not represent a real threat, but they could potentially increase in the future. As the relationship between China and the Bolivarian countries strengthens, the latter might move further toward autocratic regime consolidation and tighten the screws on the Bolivarian alliance.

Against this background of an expanded Bolivarian revolutionary trend in alliance with China, the deterioration of U.S. influence in Latin America might aggravate the geopolitical threat outlined in previous chapters. As

Menges has pointed out, "China will not seek a direct confrontation. . . . China still wants the effective support of U.S. business. China's penetration in Latin America is first and foremost economic but contrary to what many analysts believe it carries major geopolitical consequences."[57]

American Scholar Robert Kagan reinforces Menges's observation. According to Kagan, "As the Chinese grow stronger, they worry they will be prevented from fulfilling their ambitions and their destiny, that they will be denied the full extent of the national growth and international standing they believe they need and deserve."[58] Thus, they expand militarily as they do so economically. But most important, the Chinese use their economic leverage to establish themselves strategically. As the United States has a hegemonic and physical presence in China's own backyard, for China, establishing a strategic presence in the U.S. backyard is pivotal.

The Bolivarian revolution, therefore, is naturally allied with Chinese objectives. Bolivarian countries are to China what Japan, the Philippines, and South Korea represent for the United States. At the same time, China might help sustain the autocratic Bolivarian countries, particularly Venezuela. The survival of these regimes might perpetuate their geopolitical danger, as their radicalism will continue to oppress democracy and spread their revolutionary message, as well as their seditious and destabilizing activities, throughout the region. Paraphrasing the Chinese, this "win-win" situation will be achieved by means of soft power. The "peaceful rise" of China, as the Chinese themselves call it, means that China will not have to fight militarily to achieve its goals in the continent but, instead, will succeed quietly using a sophisticated strategic approach. This peaceful approach, however, will not always necessarily serve positive objectives.

The case of Russia is similar but takes a different angle. Russia seeks to diminish the power of the United States, but not being as economically developed as China is, Russia is unable to exercise sufficient influence in this sphere. However, Russia supplies weapons to Venezuela, Bolivia, and potentially other Bolivarian countries. In this case, Russia could help them instigate an arms race with countries like Colombia and perhaps others. Further, given Russia's considerable military technology and nuclear weapons know-how, the possibility that Russia could be involved in an Iranian-Venezuelan nuclear project should not be overlooked.

The most ominous aspect of Russia's involvement in Latin America, meanwhile, is the transfer of Russian-made weapons to FARC that Hugo

Chávez himself has facilitated. This arrangement is a real menace since it not only increases FARC's subversive capability (described in chapter 5) but also serves the drug cartels in their continuous destruction of law, order, and the fabric of society in Latin America. Likewise, these weapons could also fall into the hands of the Iranian-backed Hezbollah in Latin America.

When former U.S. secretary of defense Robert Gates (2006–2011) was asked about the sales of Russian weapons to Venezuela, he dismissed the transaction as a business deal: "The Russians are actually loaning them a fair amount of the money to buy the weapons they're buying."[59] Chapter 8 discusses U.S. policy in the face of these challenges.

8 | REGIONAL AND U.S. REACTIONS TO THE BOLIVARIAN REVOLUTION

The deterioration of democracy, the rise of the Bolivarian revolution, the emergence of non-state actors, the increasing presence of Iran, and other influences have not prompted the countries of the region or the United States to make major policy changes. This chapter describes the policies of the countries in the region and of the United States toward the challenges that Hugo Chávez and the Bolivarian regimes present.

▍REGIONAL POLICIES AND THE ROLE OF THE ORGANIZATION OF AMERICAN STATES

In June 1991, the Organization of American States adopted Resolution 1080, which sets up a series of sanctions and diplomatic pressures in the event democracy in a member state is violated or overthrown by a coup d'état. The resolution also permits the suspension of a member state from the organization if its democratic government is ousted by force.

As former Chilean representative to the OAS Heraldo Muñoz (1990–1994) pointed out, conventional wisdom in Latin America dictated that a democratic breakdown would not be tolerated and that "democratic solidarity has evolved from a moral prescription to an international legal obligation with strong political underpinnings."[1] Since the OAS resolution was approved, the OAS has been called to intervene on several occasions when illegal interruptions of the constitutional order took place.

In Haiti, coups overthrew the government of Jean-Bertrand Aristide on two separate occasions, whereas in Peru and Guatemala the governments rendered self-staged coups. After the Inter-American Development

Bank temporarily suspended loan disbursements to Peru after the self-coup in 1992, President Alberto Fujimori made a commitment to restore democratic order and established an electoral timeline. At the same time, Haiti was subject to an international arms and oil embargo, and its assets were frozen.

In Guatemala, the threat of sanctions alone united civil society and the business community against President Jorge Serrano Elías's self-coup in 1993. Their combined efforts forced the Guatemalan military to withdraw its support from Serrano.[2]

The OAS, along with other countries in the international community, acted in late September 2010 when the Ecuadorian police rebelled against President Rafael Correa and attacked him during a speech with tear gas, which required him to be hospitalized under police siege. The police were protesting cuts in their benefits, but their actions raised fears of a coup d'état. In a matter of hours, Latin American countries rallied around Correa. First regional heads of state gathered in an emergency meeting, expressed its support of Correa, and called the police uprising "a coup d'état." UNASUR, the OAS, and Spanish prime minister José Luis Rodríguez Zapatero followed suit. The next day, they sent their foreign ministers to Quito, the capital. Correa, an ally of Hugo Chávez's who tries to emulate Chávez's regime, received support from countries along a broad ideological spectrum, including not only the Bolivarian nations of Venezuela, Bolivia, and Nicaragua, but also Brazil, Argentina, and the conservative-ruled Colombia and Chile.[3]

Although the OAS with the help of the international community seemed to have been somewhat effective in these cases, it has been totally ineffective, both legally and politically, in dealing with rise of the Bolivarian revolution. Whereas the OAS was able to recognize coups d'état against civilian rule, it did not have the tools or the resolution to identify the deterioration of democracy properly in Venezuela and some of its allied countries.

In the first place, as the Bolivarian countries, despite their highly authoritarian tendencies, continue to hold elections, the non-democratic practices of these regimes are largely ignored. The Inter-American Commission on Human Rights, an arm of the OAS that published a full report on Venezuela, displayed the only exception to this attitude.[4] The 2009 report denounced political intolerance; the subjugation of the legislative and judicial branches to the executive power's authority; the attacks on freedom of expression and on the right to protest government policies peacefully; the existence of a climate hostile to the right of dissent and to human rights organizations; citizen insecurity, with violent acts perpetrated against persons and deprivation of their liberty; and assaults on trade unions and business associations. The report clearly states that democracy in Venezuela is in danger. Yet, OAS secretary-general José Miguel Insulza failed to defend the report against Chávez's verbal attacks against it.[5] Neither the OAS nor the international community made a move to take punitive measures against the Bolivarian regime and failed to issue any warning against its stance on human rights. In September 2012 Venezuela announced that it was withdrawing from the Inter-American Court, a body that hears human rights abuse cases in the region. Such withdrawal from the regional court was initiated by Chávez in order to prevent the victims of human rights violations in Venezuela from bringing complaints before that court.[6]

Still it is important to point out that the OAS leadership has a sluggish attitude toward constitutional issues, democracy, and human rights. When the coup took place in Honduras, the OAS denounced it, and its members voted to expel Honduras from the organization. The OAS proceeded to isolate Honduras through sanctions and demanded Zelaya's return to power. Individual countries, particularly Brazil, actively denounced the new government and even helped smuggle the exiled Zelaya back to Honduras, where he found refuge in the Brazilian Embassy in the capital Tegucigalpa.

The same applies to Paraguay, where its socialist president Fernando Lugo was impeached and ousted by the Paraguayan Congress. Countries of the region reacted harshly to Lugo's ouster. Paraguay has been suspended from Mercosur, a trading block made up of Brazil, Argentina, Paraguay, and Uruguay. Mexico, Brazil, and Argentina have withdrawn their ambassadors.

The case of Nicaragua, another ally of Venezuela's, reflects the same inconsistency but from a different angle. In July 2010 President Daniel Ortega dismissed five mayors and a number of vice mayors and elected councilmen. This action was aimed at subordinating the institutional system of checks and balances to the power of the executive branch and at crushing provincial autonomy. Such policies represent a clear violation of democracy and constitutional rule. President Ortega's actions were carried out after alleged fraud in the municipal elections that enabled him to control 105 of the country's 153 municipalities and after staging a vote by the Nicaraguan Supreme Court to allow him to run for reelection despite a constitutional ban on presidential reelection.[7] The OAS, however, failed to denounce the fraud of the November 2011 presidential elections, the voting irregularities, the manipulation of the courts, the crushing of the opposition, and the harassment of the media. In the face of all these transgressions, the OAS remained silent.

One may understand the power vacuum and lack of precedent in the case of Zelaya's attempt to disobey a judicial and congressional decision or the violations carried out by the Sandinista leader in Nicaragua, where clear instances of infringement of democratic rule occurred. But the OAS could have simply appealed to Article 20 of its democratic charter for guidance. This provision enables the OAS president to convene the Permanent Council "in the event of an unconstitutional alteration of the constitutional regime . . . in a member state" and to proceed with diplomatic steps to restore democracy.[8] In the case of the OAS, apparently the binding power of Resolution 1080 only applies if a president is ousted. The resolution does not seem to apply to elected leaders who destroy democracy from within.

As former ambassador of the Dominican Republic to the OAS Roberto Alvarez has pointed out, "The democratic charter adopted by the OAS was a major step for the strengthening of democratic values in the Americas. Yet the remedies provided by the charter for violations of the democratic process looked more to coups d'état of yesterday than to the gradual erosion of democratic principles of today."[9] Ambassador Alvarez rightly asserted that the OAS lacks mechanisms to detect when a policy alteration might seriously affect or erode the democratic order. Thus, the OAS is not prepared to deal with cases when elected governments violate democratic ideals. Their mere election evidently makes the actions of the governments legitimate. The U.S. government also fell into this trap when it supported constitutional reforms in Bolivia and Ecuador only because they took place through clean elections. Interestingly enough, Alvarez complained that part of the organization's impotence has to do with the will of the individual members. In fact, not only have they demonstrated a lack of political will to denounce violations of human rights by Chávez and his Bolivarian allies, but in fact representatives of several many countries in the region supported certain issues in Chávez's international agenda. Indeed, many Latin American countries sustained language in the OAS resolutions to reinstate Cuba to the OAS without any preconditions.[10] Cuba's inclusion was finalized with the creation of the Latin American and Caribbean Community of States (CELAC) in 2010. The next year Cuba was welcomed and allowed to participate in its first summit in December 2011. If Cuba is not a democracy, why support its inclusion when the OAS charter is very clear about its conditions for membership? Cuba's admittance to CELAC shows that the issue of democracy is not a priority for the countries of the region.

As already noted, many Latin American countries are under the control of left-leaning governments or what is usually known as moderate left-wing governments. Brazil, Chile, and Uruguay, for instance, have maintained social-democratic regimes that stress the need for social justice and redistribution or inclusion but also strive to preserve democracy and the rule of law. Moderate left-wing governments, however, have a complexity of their own.

Jorge Castañeda, a well-known Mexican scholar and former foreign minister, captured the essence of the Left in Latin America. According to Castañeda, the Left has prioritized its issues to include poverty eradication, inequality reduction, and redistribution of and national sovereignty over national resources. The agenda is so oriented to the socioeconomic dimension that such issues as democracy and human rights are downplayed to the point that the moderate Left is increasingly reluctant to criticize those who resort to authoritarian procedures to achieve the agenda's goals.[11] This situation occurs because the Left, including the moderate Left, includes a mixed set of components. Castañeda points out that in Chile, "for every Ricardo Lagos [former Socialist Chilean president] . . . there is a Camilo Escalona [a former president of the Socialist Party], who believes that Chile should stand with Cuba at the United Nations' Human Rights Council in Geneva, that it should stand with Chávez on the RCTV scandal [a case where Chávez closed a radio station critical of the government] in the . . . OAS, that it should maintain solidarity with FARC. . . ." Furthermore, in Mexico, "for every Amalia García—the former president of the Mexican PRD . . . —in the ranks of the Mexican left, there is a *Subcomandante* Marcos [of the indigenous Zapatista movement], who at least ostensibly rose up in arms against the government in 1994. . . ."[12]

According to Castañeda the Latin American Left is far removed from the European Left's acceptance of human rights and taking moral stands. Most countries recognize that the Mercosur, the economic organization that leads the common South American market, has a democracy clause in its founding treaty. Then again, these countries decided to ignore it when Venezuela submitted its application because they viewed it as interfering in the internal affairs of a sovereign country.[13]

These same ambiguities exist in the Latin American countries' interactions with Iran. For instance, in establishing bilateral relations with Iran, the governments of Brazil and Uruguay gave priority to the principle of national sovereignty and saw them as an expression of independence from U.S. foreign policy. The same applies to the memorandum of understanding on the AMIA bombing that was signed between Argentina and Iran. As we have already pointed out in chapter 6, Iran has become a symbol of rebellion against U.S. policy and wishes.

This tendency seems to be strengthened with the emergence of new regional organizations that have been created with the purpose of deepening regional integration in the Americas in order to form a regional bloc. The Union of South American Nations (UNASUR), for instance, was created to promote regional integration. CELAC, as mentioned earlier, not only includes Cuba but also excludes the United States and Canada from membership. Its existence is a symbol of regional independence and serves as an alternative to the OAS, which is seen among the Left as an American-dominated entity created because of the Cold War. Furthermore, every leader in Latin America attended the first CELAC conference. Despite such diversity and the fact that its resolutions were not particularly hostile to the United States, the conference host, Hugo Chávez, received constant praise from the different leaders. Whether leaders attending the conference agreed with the Bolivarian leaders is beyond the point. They were definitely willing to praise them and treat them as comrades with whom they share an interest in regional economic and political strength.

What is even more astonishing is that most countries in Latin America see the presence of Chávez in the region as vital to achieve the goal of regional integration. For example, during the October 2012 Venezuelan presidential elections, countries of the moderate Left wanted Chávez to win the election despite the fact that his opponent ran on an agenda of social democracy echoing the ideas of former Brazilian president Luiz Inácio Lula da Silva.

Argentina's president, Cristina Kirchner, tied Chávez's victory to the future of her own government and political philosophy. Paraphrasing the

Venezuelan national hero Simón Bolívar, Kirchner sent a written note to Chávez stating, "Hugo . . . you have cultivated the land and planted seeds in it; you have watered it and now you have harvested it. . . . Your victory is our victory."[14]

The reaction of the Brazilian government is the most confounding, precisely because it is the Brazilian model that has been most often contrasted with Chávez's. Brazil's president Dilma Rousseff pointed out that the "Venezuelan election is a model of an exemplary democratic process."

Marco Aurelio Garcia—senior advisor to President Rousseff and former senior advisor to President Lula—considered one of the most influential organic intellectuals and foreign policy architects of both governments, praised the democratic character of the Venezuelan elections. Garcia, who was sent by the Rousseff government to observe the election, pointed out, "Venezuela is not a model Brazil should follow, but Chávez, with his own style, implemented a program of social inclusion. In this way, he sought to find equilibrium between political and social democracy. Such equilibrium is something the whole region aspires to achieve."[15]

Garcia then proceeded to complain about the "international support for the Capriles's candidacy and for the attempt to delegitimize the democratic process in Venezuela." In an even more perplexing statement, Garcia suggested that Chávez's victory reinforced democracy, particularly after the region suffered "a democratic interruption with the impeachment of [President] Fernando Lugo in Paraguay."[16] This argument is surprising, particularly given the current deterioration of democracy and human rights, and the increasing political restrictions and political violence promoted by the Venezuelan government for more than a decade. But it makes sense if we continue to listen to what Garcia says.

Echoing Chávez's repeated statements, Garcia said, "right and center-right opposition forces in Latin America supported Capriles." Thus, he was implying that the Venezuelan elections were a point of contention between the right and left wing forces in the region. Therefore, had Chávez lost the elections it would have been a defeat for the Left in general—whether the authoritarian or the democratic wing.[17]

This last point is particularly astonishing since Capriles ran on the platform of the social-democratic Brazilian model. However, the Left could not see Capriles as one of them, because he confronted Chávez, an authentic symbol of the Left. The Bolivarian model may not be the model Brazilian leaders follow, but Chávez remains a symbol of the Left's strength throughout the continent. In other words, they felt that if Chávez lost the election, it might have made the entire left vulnerable.

Garcia acknowledged that there are different types of leftist regimes in the region but "all of them are marching in the direction of translating political democracy into a social factor."[18] Here, he is passionately defending the idea that no political democracy can coexist with inequality or the lack of social inclusion. However, the fact that political democracy, human rights, and judicial independence are sacrificed in the name of social justice is of no concern to the Brazilian leaders.

Brazil's position suggests that its government cares more for regional integration than for democracy. Chávez is seen as a good partner for regional integration, which, along with economic independence, both Brazil and Venezuela have championed. This would not only be good for the region but also for Brazil, as it aspires to be a regional leader and ultimately a world power. The Brazilian government seems to believe that such integration can only work with left-wing governments.

Indeed, Brazilian president Dilma Rousseff expressed concern over the possibility that political forces opposed to Chávez may boycott elections in Venezuela. According to officials in Rousseff's circles, the Brazilian president began to prepare a plan in cooperation with other countries to guarantee "the stabilization of Venezuela" after Chávez's departure. Rousseff also sent Garcia to Cuba and has been in personal contact with Cuban and Brazilian doctors to monitor Chávez's health. Brazil had been also a strong advocate of accepting Venezuela to Mercosur after Paraguay (which objected to Venezuela's membership in the group) was suspended from the organization.[19]

More important, the leadership of Rousseff's Workers party (PT) spoke about the need "to armor the region" and Chávez's legacy. Valter Pomar, an influential leader of the Workers party, said,

> I would recommend the Venezuelan right to think twice before it engages in provocations that may trigger a spontaneous reaction from the people whose consequences are difficult to predict. . . . The Venezuelan right needs to resolve a dilemma. It either understands that Chávismo

is a historical process and accepts its opposition status within the institutional setting or chooses to believe that Chávismo is an accident that depends on its leader and begins an adventure towards a coup d'état."[20]

This statement sounds arrogant and threatening, but it also makes clear that Brazil wishes for a Bolivarian continuity in Venezuela. It views Bolivarianism as a historical necessity not just for Venezuela but also for the region. Therefore, Chávez's legacy needs to be reinforced or "armored."

The idea that regional integration can only come to being through the Left and not through the Right is a myth.

The conservative government of Chile's desire to be part of this regional integration contradicts the idea that integration can take place only through the Left. Likewise, Colombia and Mexico, which also have conservative governments, support regional integration. But yet, Chávez is perceived as an essential piece to building regional integration.

With regard to security issues, regional countries have remained indifferent to the challenges. With the exception of Colombia, Mexico, and Chile, no country has expressed any concern about drugs, terrorism, the deterioration of democracy, or the presence of Iran in the continent.[21]

According to Dan Fisk, a former senior director for Western Hemisphere affairs at the U.S. National Security Council, "Most Latin American countries have not been concerned about the Iranian penetration of the continent. They do not share the same sense of threat that the United States thinks the Iranians represent."[22] They have displayed the same indifference regarding terrorism, even after major attacks occurred in Argentina in the early 1990s.

With respect to transnational crime and drug cartels, countries in the region seem to recognize the problem, but even on this point, their views diverge. Early in 2009, three former presidents of Brazil, Colombia, and Mexico presented a report on the war on drugs.[23] Their proposals included legalizing certain drugs that are as harmful as tobacco and alcohol and launching an educational campaign aimed at reducing consumption. They urged changing the status of addicts from criminals so as not to confuse them with the real elements associated with organized crime and to redirect the police to target organized crime rather than addicts. These leaders also stated that the consumption of drugs in the United States and in Europe needed to be reduced. Consequently, they called on a shared responsibility to address the problems Latin American countries face and to use innovative approaches to reduce the demand for illegal drugs. Indeed, some countries, such as Argentina, Brazil, Chile, Mexico, and Ecuador, are following the report's recommendations and relaxing penalties on consumption.[24]

Guatemala and other countries also have proposed legalizing certain drugs. This idea generated a debate in the April 2012 Summit of the Americas and led to the creation of a special task force to develop alternatives to the war on drugs.

In May 2012, UNASUR conducted a summit where its main declaration called for establishing a regional mechanism aimed at combating organized crime. It resulted in the formation of a council whose responsibility would be to strengthen "citizens' security" and to secure the member countries' collaboration to prevent international crime.[25]

It is far from clear whether Latin American countries will develop a policy that confronts the problem in a comprehensive manner, particularly if such proposals detach the obstacle of official corruption, the colonization of the state by the drug cartels, and other long-term issues. According to former Honduran ambassador to the United States Roberto Flores, drug trafficking should be tackled with comprehensive responses rather than with short-term measures. Long-term measures should include not only police reform but also the strengthening of the judicial systems and the offices of the attorneys general. In Flores's view, drug trafficking does not simply affect one area alone but involves the entire Central American and Caribbean region. He also implicates the United States on the demand side and the producing countries on the supply side, underscoring the need for a highly comprehensive approach to handle the issue. In addition, besides external conditions and the drug trafficking in the region, the domestic situations in the affiliated countries—that is, the high levels of corruption, the poorly funded judiciary system, the lack of public trusts, and the weak law enforcement—facilitate the prevalence of pervasive security threats in this region.[26] (For more on this issue, see chapter 9.)

▌U.S. POLICY TOWARD LATIN AMERICA

In October 2010, Arturo Valenzuela, the assistant secretary of state for the Western Hemisphere (2009–2011) in the Obama administration, delivered a speech at the Latin American Studies Association in which he stated:

"The United States must be a more effective and determined partner in helping countries throughout the Americas achieve their own chosen paths as determined by their own people. In that same vein our policy has to avoid the 'Manichaeism' of previous [U.S.] approaches—of viewing the Hemisphere as divided between friends and enemies."[27]

Valenzuela dismisses previous U.S. policies toward Latin America as being based on dichotomist distinctions between "friend" and "enemy"; however, I assert his comment is only partially true. During the Cold War era, much of U.S. policy was focused on keeping the countries of the region in line with the U.S. policy of containment toward the Soviet Union. Richard Nixon, Gerald Ford, and Ronald Reagan were the last presidents to be concerned with the penetration of Soviet and communist influence in the Latin American continent. In between, there was a hiatus where President Jimmy Carter (1977–1981) broke with that tradition and began promoting human rights in the region with pro-U.S., anti-communist regimes. However, U.S. post–Cold War policies, under either Democratic or Republican administrations, have taken a different path.

President George H. W. Bush (1989–1993) conducted a softer policy based on debt relief and multilateral collaboration. Indeed, his policies were aimed at alleviating Latin America's huge foreign debt in exchange for market reforms and private foreign investment in these countries. His administration also promoted the consolidation of democracy in the region and a policy of reconciliation between the Right and the Left in a very convoluted Central America, particularly in El Salvador and Nicaragua. Eventually national reconciliation was achieved.[28]

During his presidency, Bill Clinton (1993–2000) supported the North American Free Trade Agreement (NAFTA), which included free trade between the United States, Canada, and Mexico. He also initiated the Summit of the Americas in 1994 and proposed a whole free trade zone from Alaska to Tierra del Fuego by 2005. Whereas this policy was difficult to implement for various reasons, including the opposition of U.S. trade unions and environmentalist groups, the idea was to integrate the countries of Latin America into the global economy and help them prosper. The Clinton administration was also concerned about the expansion of drug trafficking. President Clinton, with strong bipartisan encouragement and support, promoted Plan Colombia, which consisted of financial and military aid to Colombia to combat drug trafficking. As discussed in chapter 5, Colombia was then under the threat of disintegration. Plan Colombia succeeded in helping restore the authority of the state to Colombia, thus providing order and improving the security conditions to its citizens.

Under the Bush Administration

During the administration of President George W. Bush (2001–2009), the emphasis focused on promoting economic growth in the region, especially through the expansion of free trade agreements; on supporting friends of the United States, such as Colombia; and on expanding programs to assist countries in consolidating their democratic systems. Further, the administration also pursued efforts at energy cooperation in the area of biofuels and funded initiatives in education and support for small and medium businesses.

The rise of Chávismo and the Bolivarian revolution coincided with the Bush administration, to which fell the responsibility to deal with this new challenge. The administration engaged in a continuing, internal debate on how best to handle and react to this new political and security challenge in Latin America.

To gain a deeper sense of how the United States responded to this new situation, I interviewed three ranking officials in the Bush administration's foreign policy team for the Western Hemisphere: Ambassador Otto Reich, who served as undersecretary of state for the Western Hemisphere (January 2002–November 2002) and as the president's special envoy to the Western Hemisphere until he left the White House in 2004; Roger Noriega and Dan Fisk. My interviews with them focused on the administration's stance on several major issues, including the deterioration of democracy and the Iranian penetration and the increasing presence of terrorist and other destabilizing forces in Latin America.

The Deterioration of Democracy in the Region

Ambassador Reich pointed out that in its initial stages, the Bolivarian revolution was considered a minor irritant, mostly because the administration was focused on the aftermath of the attacks of September 11, 2001. Afghanistan and the Middle East had become priorities. Moreover, Hugo

Chávez's "minor" status seemed to have been justified when compared with such dangerous players as the Taliban or Saddam Hussein. Yet, despite this assessment, Hugo Chávez was still considered to be hostile to U.S. interests.[29] Because the United States was at war, though, no attention was spared for the challenges coming from the Western Hemisphere.

According to Reich, Bush understood the nature of Chávez's threat. However, some key State Department officials who also occupied positions in the National Security Council were able to impose their view that Chávez did not present a threat. The State Department believed that diplomacy as usual was the best way to deal with every conflict. Ambassador Reich pointed out that the United States has remained largely silent on the issue of Venezuela's violation of democratic ideals because such an event did not fall within the tradition of diplomacy. The State Department's philosophy is based on the concept that the United States should not impose its values on other countries. Thus, under Secretary Colin Powell (2001–2005) and Secretary Condoleezza Rice (2005–2009), the department's approach counterbalanced President Bush's relatively hawkish views. Reich mentioned that "although Dr. Rice's views were more akin to President Bush's, she ended up adopting the State Department's view when she became secretary."

Fisk maintained that the Bush administration perceived that Chávez was an anti-American autocrat. In fact, President Bush came into the presidency having taken notice of Chávez's deepening relationship with Fidel Castro and of his visit to Saddam Hussein while the Iraqi regime was under international sanctions. According to Fisk, the administration debated how to deal with Chávez. Some argued for paying less attention to his rhetoric and more toward his actions, based on the assessment that his inflammatory rhetoric was worse than the actions he ultimately took. Moreover, some believed that Chávez wanted nothing more than a war of words with the United States and to be seen as standing up to and provoking the United States, thus bringing him attention and thereby enhancing his position in Venezuela and the region. It was believed that Chávez's own machinations and incompetence would eventually cause his regime to implode. In large part, some administration officials perceived Chávez "as a clown." Those U.S. officials felt that ignoring the Bolivarian Revolution was the better choice, thus denying Chávez the status he sought for himself and his philosophy.

According to Fisk, this point of view, especially the assessment that Chávez sought the attention, had merits but often overlooked the fact that Chávez's words were often translated into corresponding actions. "Foreign and domestic companies were nationalized and democracy deteriorated day to day, with political space being closed and attacks [levied] on independent media. One of the challenges for U.S. policymakers was how to deal with a leader who was democratically-elected and was using democratic instruments for anti-democratic ends." Fisk also pointed out, "Neither the administration nor the inter-American system knew how to deal with a situation where democracy is dismantled via apparent democratic means." Even though "support for democracy was a priority for us and an important component of the Organization of American States—under the Inter-American Democratic Charter—the concept of 'sovereignty' stood above support for 'democracy' for Latin American countries." According to Fisk, the realistic policy options toward Venezuela were limited to begin with, and the reluctance of the regional leaders to pressure Chávez was a factor in the administration's policy deliberations and implementation.

Despite the general regional tendency to dismiss Chávez's antidemocratic actions, the administration sought to encourage other countries to take a more active and responsible role. Specifically it undertook an effort to encourage Brazil, under President da Silva, to be more active in counterbalancing the Bolivarian agenda in Latin America. This strategy—and the assumption that the best antidote to the extreme Left was the moderate, democratic Left—was undoubtedly creative. This tactic, however, also had its limitations and ultimately failed to work. "President Lula eventually never restrained Chávez's behavior but rather became an enabler of Chávez," claimed Fisk. With the election of Chávez's allies in Bolivia, Ecuador, and Nicaragua, the U.S. administration then developed a modus vivendi with Presidents Morales, Correa, and Ortega.[30]

Ambassador Roger Noriega pointed out that during his tenure, U.S. policy attempted to keep the region in some sort of constitutional and democratic track and within this framework sought opportunities to hold Chávez accountable. Thus, the United States supported diplomatic multilateral institutions, putting its efforts in upholding the electoral process. The administration hoped that involving the OAS would lead to regional accountability. This strategy failed, in Noriega's view, because Chávez "showed no respect whatsoever for the OAS democratic charter."[31]

Noriega also admitted that the United States underestimated Chávez's willingness to establish a dictatorship. Noriega confirms that President Bush was "clearheaded. The President saw what Chávez was capable of doing, but at most senior levels, we were unprepared to use the U.S. leverage to counteract Chávez." Moreover, added Noriega, "after the 2002 failed coup attempt against Chávez we were on the defensive because the general perception was that the U.S. supported the coup. Yet, our own top leaders like Secretary of State Condoleezza Rice did not feel that dealing with Chávez should be a priority for the Administration."[32]

Furthermore, building a case against Chávez was tough because proving that he had cheated in the multiple elections and referendums that he called was difficult. That elections and referendums have been conducted in Venezuela has created both a misleading perception and a shield for Chávez against those who criticized him for undemocratic behavior. In addition, Noriega pointed out that "no country in Latin America wanted to put its bilateral relation with Venezuela at risk." Thus, the policy of thwarting Chávez through the OAS failed.

Many people interested in U.S. foreign policy in the region widely believe that the main reason why the United States has remained paralyzed in the face of Chávez and the Bolivarian revolution is because Venezuela is a major oil supplier to the United States. Both Fisk and Ambassador Reich have maintained that the issue of Venezuelan oil was never fully discussed in the meetings.

According to Fisk, some in the State Department favored policies that consequently accommodated the consensus approach on the region to ignore Chávez's antidemocratic activities at home and abroad. In his view, at moments, concerns about either Chávez's or the region's reaction unnecessarily silenced the voice of the United States. Consequently, some countries were uncertain about the U.S. commitment to democracy while others, including elements of Venezuela's democratic opposition, took U.S. silence as evidence that oil was more important than democracy. Further, as Fisk concluded, "the U.S. administration's silence did not generate a greater regional responsibility to fulfill the Inter-American Democratic Charter or to diminish Chávez's assault on Venezuelan human and political rights or to extend his influence in the region."[33] Yet, this silence and inaction neither slowed down Chávez's actions nor diminished his outreach in Latin

America, particularly his attempts to influence the outcome of the Peruvian elections and to bolster antidemocratic forces in Bolivia.

The Influence of Iran and Other Destabilizing Forces

Fisk asserted that the U.S. administration recognized that Chávez was
opening the doors to Iran in the continent. In 2004 and 2005 the administration began collecting data about Venezuelan-Iranian relations. Once
the data was compiled, the idea was to share this information with other
countries in the region and even make it public; however, this attempt was
also a disappointment.

According to Reich, even though today Chávez is no longer seen as a
minor irritant, he is not regarded as a threat either. As noted previously,
under the Obama administration, former chief of the Southern Command
General Fraser seemed to confirm this point when he stated that Iran had
no military presence in Latin America. Fraser saw Iran's interests in Latin
America as focused on commercial and diplomatic goals. A year earlier,
Defense Secretary Robert Gates supported this view when he stated that,
from a military standpoint, "I see no military threat to the United States
from Venezuela. . . . I do not see any potential for a conflict."[34]

Gen. John Kelly, who assumed duties as commander of the U.S. Southern Command in November 2012, acknowledged the role of Venezuela in
promoting the drug trade and also the extent of involvement of top political and military leaders.[35] He also understands the damage drug cartels
can inflict on the integrity and authority of state institutions and the rule
of law.[36] However, Kelly pointed out that "Iran's overtures to the region
are primarily undertaken to circumvent international sanctions, and, with
like-minded nations, attempt to undermine U.S. influence in the region. I
do not see evidence of an increase in uniformed Iranian military presence
in the region. . . . Iran's engagement strategy has primarily been centered
on diplomatic and economic endeavors with sympathetic countries like
Venezuela and Bolivia."[37] With regard to Hezbollah's presence in the area
Kelly pointed out that Hezbollah's "supporters and sympathizers in the
region are focused on licit and illicit fundraising, although proselytizing,
recruitment, and some elements of radicalization exist as well."[38] Likewise
Kelly acknowledged the dangerous interaction between Hezbollah and
drug traffickers. However, Kelly sees Hezbollah as a money launderer and

a fundraiser and defines the threat of Hezbollah in the region as "low to medium."[39]

There is no question that General Kelly understands many aspects of the potential security threat, but again there is an underestimation of Hezbollah and Iran's capability to do harm. There is no mention of the presence of Iranian Revolutionary Guard or Iran's nuclear cooperation with Venezuela or uranium mining. FARC is mentioned only in the context of Colombia's internal struggle, and not in its connection to the Bolivarian revolution.[40] Ambassador Reich observed, "Venezuela's lack of offensive [conventional] capability has caused the defense establishment to totally ignore the damage an asymmetric war can cause."

In the Bush era, the United States faced a dilemma regarding Chávez's relationships with terrorist organizations. If Venezuela were declared a state sponsor of terrorism, what price would the U.S. and the American oil corporations pay? What would be the overall ramifications, including the question of oil supply? Fisk explains that the administration confronted uncertainty over the repercussions of declaring Venezuela a state sponsor of terrorism. In addition, many experts gauged aspects of the issue differently; the actions of the Venezuelan leader fell in a gray area, which pushed the United States into a situation of inaction. Fisk explained that Latin American countries, in general, were not concerned with terrorism and did not see themselves as a target.

Meanwhile, Reich believed that the United States could have lived with an oil boycott of Venezuela.[41] On his part, Noriega argued that the United States did not want to exploit the oil sanctions for fear of increasing world oil prices, but at the same time the administration recognized that U.S. businesses have a right to do business in Venezuela. Noriega believed that the prevailing strategy has been to try to avoid provoking Chávez, "as if Chávez would not pursue his agenda regardless of our provocations." Noriega added that former assistant secretary of state for Western Hemisphere affairs Thomas Shannon (2005–2009) began a policy that has remained until this very day: "The situation in Latin America was accepted as a fait accompli. . . . We kept things quiet, hoping for an internal rebellion in Venezuela. We did not think things through."[42]

In 2008 John Walters, director of the National Drug Control Policy Office, raised an alarm that Chávez was becoming a major facilitator of cocaine trafficking to Europe and other parts of the hemisphere.[43] Former

U.S. ambassador to Colombia Myles Frechette confirmed this assertion and stated that the U.S. government had clear evidence, based on information provided by radar technology, that airplanes loaded with heroin departed from Venezuela for the United States.[44] U.S. government officials did not deny the truth of Walter's and Frechette's revelations, but the administration, through Shannon, responded to these events by calling for strengthening Venezuelan-U.S. relations. Shannon offered Chávez U.S. cooperation on drug-trafficking control efforts.[45] What is curious in this episode is that the assistant secretary of state spoke forcefully of cooperating with Hugo Chávez on matters related to drug trafficking when Chávez himself was suspected of enabling it.[46] This example clearly illustrates that the main thrust of U.S. policy was conciliation and acceptance of the situation in Latin America. Or, as Noriega insinuated, the philosophy was to remain passive until some internal dynamics in Venezuela would change the course of events. Perhaps the result of the Venezuelans' constitutional referendum in December 2007 encouraged U.S. policymakers to think this way. But instead the threat continued to rise.

Regarding drug policy, the Bush administration proposed the Mérida Initiative, which the Obama administration chose to implement. This program includes funding to fight drug cartels in Mexico and Central America and could be seen as the primary U.S. response to this serious problem. This plan is positively designed as a security agreement between the United States and Mexico and Central American countries to combat drug trafficking, money laundering, and organized crime. It includes not only technical assistance, training, and equipment, but also aid in strengthening the mechanisms of law enforcement and the rule of law in all the participating countries. One of the limitations of this initiative is that it is underfunded, particularly for the countries of Central America, which are suffering a collapse of their legal systems in the face of increasing crime. Former Guatemalan president Alvaro Colom complained that drug cartels have more money and are better equipped than the governments are and can counter this response.[47] The Mexican allocation is four times larger than that for Central America, with $450 million going to Mexico and $100 million for all Central America and the Dominican Republic.[48]

Dan Fisk, who was deeply involved in creating the Mérida Initiative, pointed out that it was precisely inspired by a meeting between President

Bush and Guatemalan president Oscar Berger. The latter conveyed the sense of fragility that Guatemala and the other Central American countries felt facing gang and drug cartel activity. Guatemala felt the threat, but lacked a strategy to counter it.

The Mérida Initiative was carried out in Central America through the Central American Integration System (SICA), an organization that brings together Central American countries to strengthen regional security. The United States built a comprehensive public security proposal that responds directly to the needs identified by the leaders of the countries of the region. Thus, Mérida provided funds to these countries in order to help them complement the efforts they were already undertaking and thus help them manage their own budgets and resources more effectively.[49]

However, according to Shannon, Central American countries were less resourceful than their own adversaries. While drug traffickers enjoy large amounts of cash and more sophisticated technology including jets, submarines, and semi-submersible vessels, Central American countries "are barely able to keep operational their basic law enforcement and counternarcotics vehicles, boats, or Vietnam-era aircraft."[50] The Mérida Initiative in Central America has remained underfunded and undeveloped.[51]

Under the Obama Administration

The Obama administration began its tenure believing that the Bush administration's foreign policy failed since it had been influenced by an aggressive, neoconservative approach. Senior Director for Latin American Affairs at the National Security Council Dan Restrepo stated in October 2009—a few weeks after Chávez acknowledged he was cooperating with Iran in trying to build a "nuclear village" in Venezuela—that President Obama did not see Venezuela as a challenge to U.S. national security. According to Restrepo, "There is no cold war. There is no hot war. Those days are over. We need to look at the present and see how we can work constructively with those countries that have an interest in working with us. Maybe not everyone is interested but the majority of the nations and the countries in Latin America are indeed interested in working with us."[52]

A few months earlier, during the Summit of the Americas in April 2009, President Obama indicated that the United States had nothing to fear from a country whose defense budget was six hundred times smaller than that of the Pentagon.[53] This remark was curious, taking into account that al Qaeda's assets are substantially smaller than oil-rich Venezuela's or that Iran's economy is not comparable to the American economy (even in times of recession and economic crisis). As noted earlier, asymmetric war is a device aimed at causing damage to an enemy from a position of inferiority. Therefore, in his dismissal of the Venezuelan threat, the president seemed to be thinking in conventional terms without taking into account the more comprehensive set of factors at work in Venezuela.

The Obama administration's innovation in terms of Latin America policy has consisted mainly of a public relations strategy, aimed at opening a new page in U.S.–Latin American relations. At the Summit of the Americas in 2009, President Obama said:

> All of us must now renew the common stake that we have in one another. I know that promises of partnership have gone unfulfilled in the past, and that trust has to be earned over time. While the United States has done much to promote peace and prosperity in the hemisphere, we have at times been disengaged, and at times we sought to dictate our terms. But I pledge to you that we seek an equal partnership. There is no senior partner and junior partner in our relations; there is simply engagement based on mutual respect and common interests and shared values. So I'm here to launch a new chapter of engagement that will be sustained throughout my administration.[54]

This speech failed to address issues of security or democracy and instead focused on issues of economic development, energy cooperation, and drug interdiction enforcement. By no means do I underestimate the importance of those issues, particularly the last, which represents one of the central concerns of this book. However, President Obama's speech, on the one hand, displays his conviction that the source of turmoil in Latin America is social and economic and does not acknowledge any ideological and revolutionary movement in Latin America with the potential to threaten regional security. On the other hand, he does admit that the United States has been disengaged and has treated Latin American countries as junior partners in the past.

In 2010, Arturo Valenzuela referred briefly and indirectly to the Chávez phenomenon in a speech to the Latin American Studies Association. In Valenzuela's own words:

> We need to be clear eyed and proactive in addressing risks to our common agenda, and those include attempts to expand majority or populist

rule at the expense of fundamental minority rights and effective democratic governance based on dialogue and consensus within the rule of law. Though our agenda remains manifestly inclusive and seeks points of convergence even in difficult cases, we remain steadfast in our commitment to core principles and recognition of key values like human and labor rights, press freedom, and the importance of robust democratic institutions.[55]

Most of Valenzuela's speech refers to such important issues as the role of the United States in building effective institutions of democratic governance and in helping to promote social and economic opportunity for everyone. However, Valenzuela's speech remains diplomatic and does not translate to any action. U.S. soft policies toward the Bolivarian revolution will remain unchanged.

Abraham Lowenthal, a recognized authority on Latin America and U.S.–Latin American relations, confirms this point. According to Lowenthal, in the Bush years, once Thomas Shannon became assistant secretary of state for the Western Hemisphere in 2005, policies focused less on radicalism and more on the social origins of left-wing radicalism.[56]

As already noted, socioeconomic and other causes brought about the emergence of radical regimes. I do not object to the economic development and energy policies instituted in U.S. foreign policy. To the contrary, I believe it is extremely important to consider regional socioeconomic problems in formulating a foreign policy strategy. However, the policies that the State Department under the Bush and the Obama administrations pursued did not transcend these economic-oriented ideas. They did not develop any successful strategies to counterbalance the spread of the Bolivarian revolution.

At the same time, they engaged in an active effort to change the image of the United States in Latin American countries. Obama openly shifted the discussion from the war on drugs to the need to reduce Americans' demand for drugs and offer treatment to addicts.[57] The administration also made overtures to Cuba, offering to alleviate restrictions on Americans traveling to Cuba and pledges of future engagement in exchange for political prisoners. Initially Obama ignored Chávez, expecting that a policy of nonconfrontation would bring better results. This assumption becomes clear in a statement that an Obama aid made to a journalist from *El Nuevo*

Herald: "Chávez's life turns more complicated when we do not behave like a typical gringo [American]."[58]

U.S. policy was further highlighted in the events in Honduras in the summer of 2009, when many widely perceived that Manuel Zelaya, a Chávez ally, attempted to create a Bolivarian state in his country. The Obama administration's immediate reaction was to join multilateral efforts in the OAS to restore Zelaya to power. (Later the administration softened this position and supported elections in Honduras without Zelaya.)

Regarding reports of Iran's penetration in Latin America, President Obama and Secretary of State Hillary Clinton showed occasional signs of concern. Perhaps the most important step was the president's sanctions against Venezuelan oil giant Petróleos de Venezuela SA in May 2011 over its exports to Iran. As sanctions against Iran and companies doing business with the country's energy sectors were intensified, the PDVSA was affected by the president's decision to bar the company from access to U.S. government contracts and export financing. However, these sanctions were far from severe in that they avoided such tougher measures as stopping the purchase of crude oil to the United States.[59] The United States remains the largest buyer of Venezuelan oil, and those purchases were neither stopped nor significantly restricted.

▌ SUMMARY

It would be fair to say that the Obama administration, as well as the Bush administration before it, has not been able or willing to take a harsh line against the security and stability threats in Latin America. The Bush administration understood the challenges that the Bolivarian revolution posed but expected to use other countries in Latin America to counterbalance Chávez's authoritarian advance. It expected Brazil to fulfill that role; instead, President Lula enabled Hugo Chávez while pursuing a foreign policy independent of the United States. Lula embraced Chávez though Lula never joined his revolution, and the Brazilian option collapsed under Lula's multipolarity. Next, the OAS option did not fare any better as the spirit of its democratic charter surrendered to the principle of national sovereignty and noninterference in countries' internal affairs. In fact, the member countries of the OAS failed to denounce violations of democracy and showed total indifference or inaction toward the other threats described here. The Bush administration also failed to condemn violations of democracy in the region.

Meanwhile, most U.S. policy was focused on economic and social development and paid less attention to the effects and dangers of the Bolivarian revolution altogether. The Bush administration's Mérida Initiative, which the Obama administration implemented, reinforces the U.S. drug interdiction policies. This plan is significant in Mexico but is less effective in Central America, where it is underfunded and deals softly with the problem of the collapse of the state governments. Chapter 9 discusses the need to expand Mérida in Central America as the failure to do so will contribute to the further "Afghanization" of the region.

Next, the Obama administration carried the trauma of George W. Bush's interventionism in Iraq and the perception that the United States is an aggressive country. The Obama administration's unwillingness to interfere in other countries' internal affairs, however, has encouraged the Bolivarian revolution and aggravated the problem. The administration has not formulated a strategy to stop an authoritarianism wave either.

In both administrations, the State Department's insistence on focusing on the socioeconomic roots of the region's problems and the need to help the continent economically constituted good policies, but they were insufficient given the gravity of the threat unfolding in the continent. Furthermore, the Obama administration failed to make the Bolivarian leaders accountable for their connections to drug cartels and for undermining the U.S. war on drugs. The most telling example is the report that the Government Accountability Office issued in 2009 that disclosed the activities of drug cartels and FARC, as well as their connections with Chávez (see chapter 5). Despite the credible report, the U.S. government has taken no real action even though the criminal activities clearly affect U.S. interests in the region. The same applies to the administration's inaction in the face of Colombia's multiple public and private charges that Venezuela harbors FARC and guerrillas in its territory. Finally with regard to the Iranians' presence in Latin America and their close and ominous ties with Venezuela, the U.S. reaction seems to be even more alarmingly passive.

Latin American countries are undergoing a confusing period. On the one hand, they claim victory since they have been experiencing economic growth and increasing political independence in the international realm.

Their relationships with the United States are perceived almost as something of the past. On the other hand, these countries have created their own organizations in pursuit of a "regional nationalism" that have permitted the Bolivarian revolution to proceed with its authoritarian tendencies and its associations with Iran, guerrilla and terrorist groups, and drug cartels.

Chapter 9 presents general ideas about short- and long-term policies that could serve as guides for future U.S. regional policy.

9 | HALTING THE ADVANCE OF THE BOLIVARIAN REVOLUTION AND ITS ALLIES

Dan Fisk accurately observed that U.S. policies regarding Hugo Chávez have made Chávez stronger. As Fisk said, "The threat has now become disproportional to the risks of any action we could have taken to stop him. We now have less leverage than ever before."[1] Whether Fisk is too pessimistic remains to be seen; however, I believe it is not too late to reverse the course of events in Latin America.

This chapter provides some direction in designing short- and long-term policies for confronting the Bolivarian revolution. The short-term policies need to weaken the advance of the Bolivarian revolution, the radicalization in the area, and the involvement of non-state actors and Iran. The long-term policies provide general guidelines on how to achieve long-standing stability in the region. They are aimed at consolidating strong democratic regimes and setting the conditions to prevent the destruction of state authority and to reduce the possibility of revolutionary situations.

In considering the short-term policies, focusing on the internal developments in Venezuela is crucial. Venezuela has been pivotal in inspiring continental radicalism and encouraging the spread of authoritarianism, fostering the presence of Iran, revitalizing the Revolutionary Armed Forces of Colombia, and facilitating the work of the drug cartels. Changing the course of events in that country is a critical component to halting the expansion of these threats.

Another important part is to strengthen those alliances in the continent that are performing better economically and experiencing economic growth. Encouraged by this growth, Latin American countries have sought to achieve regional integration while becoming more independent from Washington. These countries appear to be unconcerned about the threats to their security that arise from the radical elements, non-state actors, and

Iran. In the context of current Latin America, therefore, the United States must seek alliances with countries that potentially share its concerns and values for human rights and democracy.

Brazil seems to be an important country to target. Not only is Brazil the fastest-growing and most developed economy in the area, but it is also consolidating a stable democracy and is a rising regional and world power. Despite its proud insistence on being autonomous and often running a foreign policy contrary to the interests of the United States and its Western allies, Brazil can be a potential U.S. ally on key issues.

Next, I provide some suggestions on approaches to halt the presence of Iran and terrorist groups in Latin America. I connect this effort to the existing policies dealing with drug cartels. This last point is also linked to the long-term policies required to consolidate a strong democratic and legal state that will advance the rule of law across the continent. The premise is that a strong democratic state achieves legitimacy by helping to integrate and protect the rights of a maximum number of citizens and by imposing the rule of law. Beyond this capacity, democracy also fulfills a geopolitical role in that a democratic state rejects tyranny with all its implications. Thus, democracy and security are interwoven.

▌SHORT-TERM STRATEGIES
REGARDING THE BOLIVARIAN REVOLUTION

Since the revolution began more than a decade ago, many have speculated a great deal about the possible collapse of the Bolivarian regime in Venezuela. First, some observers, such as former Venezuelan congressman Gustavo Coronel, believe that because the Venezuelan regime depends so much on oil revenues, the collapse of this regime is necessarily tied to the fall of oil prices. The oil factor has indeed created crises in Venezuela and economic discontent, particularly when budgets were calculated on certain expenses that oil revenue was unable to meet. When Venezuela undermined the Petróleos de Venezuela SA's production capabilities as a result of politically dictated changes in personnel and the decline of oil prices, astronomical public spending and high inflation significantly reduced Venezuela's economic growth after 2008.[2]

Yet, history teaches that a country's inability to deliver on welfare policies may bring about general discontent but not necessarily the downfall of a regime and certainly not if the regime resorts more and more to authoritarianism as is the case with the Bolivarian regime. The Bolivarian regime can obtain additional revenue from drug income and thus continue its welfare policies. Second, and more important, the regime can survive by establishing a coercive infrastructural mechanism. After all, many repressive regimes have survived for a long time without legitimacy, by ruling with an iron fist. Among examples of these regimes are all those that Chávez deeply admires: the Islamic Republic of Iran, various Arab dictatorships, and, of course, Fidel Castro's Cuba.

Opposition forces in Venezuela finally achieved unity for the October 2012 presidential elections. Following the primary election in February of that year, and after many years of conflicts and divisions, the opposition finally united around one candidate, Henrique Capriles Radonski. However, Chávez defeated Capriles Radonski by 800,000 votes in an election not devoid of violence, intimidation, and fear. Capriles Radonski quickly recognized the results, effectively aborting massive social protests. His declarations conceding Chávez's victory in the elections also provided legitimacy to a process that was far from pure and helped protect Chávez and his supporters from international criticism.

At the same time, Capriles reaffirmed his commitment to an electoral process and urged people to believe in the future. How this conciliatory attitude will play in the future is not clear. Although Capriles's benevolent and pacifist approach received praise, I do not see the forces of the Bolivarian revolution following his example should they lose in the future. I cannot envision any possibility other than the further consolidation of the Bolivarian revolution in its socialist and authoritarian form.

Chávez's campaign against Capriles Radonski was aggressive. It included virulent anti-Semitic language, which the official media promoted. Chávez's rhetoric was polarizing and insulting. Chávez's antagonism toward those who oppose or criticize him has succeeded in causing panic, particularly after the 2002 failed coup and the 2004 recall referendum. Fear of losing one's job, of persecution, and of retaliation and other types of intimidation have had a tremendous impact. Likewise, through its welfare policies, the government has widely used state resources to bribe voters. Besides the allegations of electoral fraud, this state largesse could be a factor in explaining Chávez's victory in the October 2012 presidential elections.

The expectation that Capriles Radonski could unseat the Bolivarian government derived from the idea that the democratic process was still viable in Venezuela despite the multiple acts of manipulation and use of state resources especially before the elections. However, a dictator is after all a dictator. Chávez's ambition from the outset was to remain in power; therefore, for him to renounce his national and regional leadership was not in his plans.

But what would happen in Venezuela after the death of Hugo Chávez? What impact would his demise have on the presidential succession?

After his death, Hugo Chávez will leave behind a revolutionary process that has not only domestic but also transnational ramifications. His years in power have provided him with sufficient time to purge members of the military and to replace them with loyal officers, many of whom live in luxurious homes and enjoy a comfortable life. Thus, an important sector of the military is likely to resist change unless a new government furnishes the same conditions (assuming that these officers are opportunists and are not necessarily identified with the Bolivarian ideology). But even if these officers are true democrats and reject Chávez, the Bolivarian regime already has in place paramilitary groups, such as the Bolivarian Circles and a militia, that respond directly to the executive branch. These paramilitary forces and even militias might be filled with "fighters" from other groups such as FARC and Hezbollah—two groups Chávez has embraced. Furthermore, the regime has also created a network of people who have benefitted from his regime and would like to see it continue. This group includes the Boliburguesías, businesspeople and activists who have made their wealth not from hard work and devotion but by virtue of their connections to the state.

Henry Rangel Silva, former chief of the Strategic Operational Command of the National Armed Forces, said late in 2010 that the "National Armed Forces are fully loyal to the people, a life project, and a Commander in Chief." Referring to the Bolivarian Revolution, he pointed out that the armed forces "are married with this Project."[3]

Nelson Bocaranda, a columnist for the Venezuelan daily *El Universal*, revealed in April 2012 that Hugo Chávez, Raúl Castro, six Cuban generals, and eight pro-Chávez Venezuelan generals, including Minister of Defense Rangel Silva, met in Cuba. Their discussion focused on possible scenarios after the death of the Bolivarian leader. Bocaranda reports that among the issues they considered was the possibility of creating chaos, including violence and looting, to provide an excuse for the military and other nonmilitary security forces to carry out a self-coup, or to impose an authoritarian de facto regime that would disregard the electoral process altogether.[4] This view seems to be confirmed by Wilmar Castro Soteldo, who is the coordinator of the electoral campaign of the ruling party, the United Socialist Party of Venezuela (PSUV), who publicly declared that Venezuela should consider suppressing elections as an option in case Chávez died before the next election.[5]

Of course, some people, such as Professor Aníbal Romero, formerly of Universidad Simón Bolívar in Caracas, believe that the military, even those officers who support Chávez, may not be willing to confront the people in order to defend the Bolivarian regime. Moreover, according to Romero, the Venezuelan military resents the presence of Cubans in the National Armed Forces and its security apparatus.[6] Furthermore, Maria Teresa Romero, another Venezuelan academic and expert on national politics, argues that a self-coup would place Venezuela in a very difficult position in the international arena. She also believes that the military is loyal to the law and not to the Bolivarian revolution.[7] Thus, if Chávez dies, the PSUV candidate who would succeed him may not enjoy the same degree of popularity. This possibility leads Maria Romero to point out that there is no "Chávismo without Chávez."[8]

However, both of these academics' scenarios are too optimistic. I vehemently dispute their arguments.

Carlos Peñaloza, a former chief of the National Armed Forces from 1989 to 1991, estimates that a handful of military officers might support a self-coup, but he also acknowledges divisions and conflicts exist within the military, including among the Chávistas themselves. General Peñaloza also confirmed Aníbal Romero's point that the presence of Cubans in the military and the existence of a militia that is not subjected to the armed forces' authority have caused resentment among the officers.[9] However, the assumption that the military will not defend the Bolivarian regime in case of a self-coup is likely incorrect, and I would not count on it. Neither would I count on the assumption that the foundation of the Bolivarian Revolution rests solely on Chávez.

Certainly, those who support Chávez and those who oppose him—and even among these groups themselves—experience multiple conflicts and differences. However, the Bolivarian revolution has benefited a whole network of individuals and institutions that has enjoyed a special connection to the Bolivarian state, including a handful of military men, the Boliburguesías, and the recipients of Bolivarian welfare. The latter group has been a determining factor in securing Chávez's popularity and his multiple victories in elections and referendums. Likewise, the revolutionary wave of Bolivarianism has generated a special excitement in the masses not only in Venezuela but also among leaders and grassroots groups outside the country.

At the domestic and regional level, Chávez has earned an image as the father of the oppressed, thus his followers believe he is the only leader in the region who has the ability to unite different and diverse sectors of the population.

The landslide victory of Chávez's PSUV candidates in the gubernatorial elections of December 2012 supports Chávez's political strength. In those elections, where Chávez was absent and signs of his imminent death were conspicuous, the PSUV won overwhelmingly and now holds twenty out of the twenty-three state governments in the nation. The opposition lost important states such as oil-rich Zulia, which it had controlled for more than eight years. It also lost Carabobo, a state that has never been in the hands of a pro-Chávez government. Even the state of Táchira, which was the only state the opposition won in the October 7 presidential election, was lost to Chávez's political loyalists.[10]

Those who think that Chávez's movement will not survive his death should be dissuaded from this belief given the results of this gubernatorial election. Following the thought of scholars Hannah Fenichel Pitkin and Ernesto Laclau, we can say that how the constituent is kept satisfied matters less than the symbol the government or the leader represent.

As Fenichel has pointed out, "a monarch or a dictator may be a more successful and dramatic leader, and therefore a better representative, than an elected member of parliament. Such a leader calls forth emotional loyalties and identification in his followers . . . representation seen in this light need have little or nothing to do with accurate reflection of the popular will, or with enacting laws desired by the people."[11]

Whether or not the Bolivarian Revolution succeeded in fulfilling its promises or whether it has created a fiscal cliff has less weight than the loyalties and identification of its followers. One of the great accomplishments of Chávismo has been its ability to homogenize and bring together a diverse group of people, who now have a sense of representation, unknown to them prior to the revolution.

The collective perception that Chávez and his revolution represent the oppressed and disadvantaged is crucial, regardless of whether people truly are better off now than they were fourteen years ago or whether democracy and constitutionalism are being respected. The revolution has also succeeded in blaming the opposition for the problems it has created. The Chávez regime has adopted a patronizing attitude toward the opposition, accusing it of polarization, when in truth, the larger polarizing force is the regime itself.

As I am completing this book, Chávez seems to be very close to death. His vice president, Nicolás Maduro, and others seem to try to ride over the mandate Chávez received in the October 2012 presidential elections. Chávez was supposed to be sworn in for a new mandate on January 10. The Chávez-loyal Supreme Court sworn in Chávez in absentia and Maduro continues to fill the role of president. The opposition, however, is demanding that the letter of the constitution (most specifically article 233) be followed so that in the president's absolute absence or physical or mental disability, a new election should be called within thirty days. The Maduro government has not acknowledged that Chávez is incapable of governing and has given optimistic but highly dubious reports about Chávez's health condition. The purpose seems to be to avoid a new election.

According to article 234 of the constitution if the president is temporarily unable to serve, he/she shall be replaced by the executive vice president for a period of up to ninety days, which may be extended by resolution of the National Assembly for an additional ninety days. But since the PSUV controls the majority of the National Assembly, it can extend the period of temporary absence every ninety days almost limitlessly.[12]

The Bolivarian revolution has excited the masses, not only in Venezuela, but also across Latin America. It has expanded the revolution to Bolivia, Ecuador, and Nicaragua. It is a symbol among the grassroots of the ruling Workers and Peronist Parties in Brazil and Argentina respectively, and the Movement of Popular Participation (MPP), one of the largest sectors in Uruguay's ruling party, the Broad Front. The Bolivarian revolution is also popular among indigenous grassroots and has also fascinated important sectors of the intellectual Left.

Chávez and his revolution are so powerful that various governments in South America, including that of Brazil, a rising world power, viewed Chávez's victory in the October elections as a necessary condition for the continuity of regional integration. Even Uruguayan president José Mujica, a proud atheist, took time out of his schedule to pray in a church for Chávez's health.[13]

The success of the Bolivarian revolution provides no incentive to the new leadership in Venezuela to change its course, whether there is economic bankruptcy or internal divisions. Contrary to the Fascist or the Communist revolutions, the Bolivarian revolution has neither been challenged nor contained.

What is not clear to me is why Maduro and his associates are fearful. If Chávez won a gubernatorial election in absentia, I see no reason why another pro-Chávez presidential candidate should lose. Their fear may not be rational but it is clear that Chávez's successors wish to continue to perpetuate themselves in power.

While multiple scenarios are possible after Chávez's death, the intensity of the Bolivarian revolution may cool off but probably not by very much. Although the Bolivarian revolution is relatively young—little more than a decade old—the structures, institutions, networks, habits, and customs that Chávismo have built likely will continue after Chávez's passing. In Iran, for instance, the death of Ayatollah Ruhollah Khomeini ten years after he inspired the Islamic Revolution not only failed to lead to a transition but also saw reformers, such as President Muhammad Khatami (1997–2005), fail in their attempts to make the regime more open and flexible. Even though Khatami advocated for freedom of expression, foreign investment, free markets, and better foreign relations, Supreme Leader Khomeini had gathered a group of hard-liners that provided continuity to the regime and undermined Khatami's efforts. The Islamic Revolution in Iran has remained alive and highly repressive more than twenty years after its charismatic leader vanished from the scene. By the same token, in the Soviet Union, Joseph Stalin's death in 1953 did not lead to a transition. Authoritarian structures—censorship and state control of society—remained in place. Moreover, despite the repudiation of Stalin by his immediate successor, Nikita Khrushchev, the state nonetheless persisted. Although less murderous, it still employed the tools of repression and the gulag for a long time. Only Mikhail Gorbachev's initiative in the 1980s, seventy years after the revolution, sparked the transformation that led to the Soviet Union's collapse. Following these examples, after Chávez's death, Venezuela might very well continue its path toward authoritarian socialism.

It is important to point out that in Venezuela, the paramilitary presence, corruption at all levels of government, state-sponsored murder, and criminality are widespread. As we have noted, political turmoil could start a civil war in Venezuela that could involve armed groups.

Dissident Venezuelan Supreme Court justice Luis Velásquez Alvaray has confirmed links between Chávez's regime and drug trafficking and corruption.[14] In May 2012, Velásquez Alvaray revealed that the former vice president of the Bolivarian republic of Venezuela, José Vicente Rangel, leads a gang that controls judges' decisions to secure support for the government. Called the Gang of the Dwarfs (Banda de los Enanos), the group of judges, prosecutors, security officers, and others bribes judges to promote verdicts and blackmails those who refuse. Public servants, including prosecutors and governors, have also been murdered. According to Velásquez Alvaray, drug trafficking has managed to penetrate the courts and obtain their protection. He also has claimed that a Venezuelan judge serves as FARC's attorney and that FARC keeps an office in the Miraflores Palace, or the house of government. According to Velásquez Alvaray's revelations, China pays for its Venezuela oil shipments in part with weapons that are destined not only to Venezuela but to guerrillas as well. This faction could include not only FARC, but also paramilitary groups. Velásquez reports that Cubans and FARC have already trained thirty-five thousand members of a Venezuelan group called Brigada Juvenil Francisco de Miranda.

If all these allegations are found to be true, it would be more than reasonable to assume that this corruption serves the purpose of the Bolivarian revolution, including its defense if needed. Thus, should a situation of anarchy develop in Venezuela, it might invite the involvement of foreign elements, such as Iranians or other foreign terrorists, as well as drug traffickers. The Chávez regime has created a whole corrupt infrastructure designed to perpetuate the regime in power. Those who think that the military will side with the people are not taking this factor into account.

The Bolivarian regime is arming paramilitary forces and FARC guerrillas, and it might even be recruiting the drug-trafficking criminal machine to exercise its regime of terror. These allies of the Bolivarian revolution—

the FARC members and drug cartels—need the Bolivarian regime that allows them to move and carry out their activities freely. They will fight alongside the Bolivarian regime for ideological reasons or for reasons of convenience; they all have a vested interest in this struggle.

▌U.S. POLICY ON VENEZUELA

A civil war or a state of anarchy in Venezuela would prove a very serious challenge to the United States. The administration could not treat such a conflict in the same way it would a war taking place farther away. It could not possibly remain passive as a civil war in Venezuela could spiral out of control quite quickly. Nor could the United States rely on an international forum to resolve the hostilities since Russia and China might side with the Bolivarian countries and thus lead to a similar impasse as the one plaguing Syria.

Instead, the United States should take a strong stand in favor of democracy and constitutionalism. If a self-coup takes place or a civil war breaks out in Venezuela, the U.S. government needs to side with and support the opposition. Past ambiguities where Chávez was considered to be a legitimately elected president of Venezuela should no longer apply, and the United States should recognize the Bolivarian revolution as a threat to regional security. The United States also should reach out to the democratic countries of the region and perhaps beyond and demand the resignation of the Bolivarian government and the restoration of the democratic regime. Although the U.S. position on human rights has been poor and disappointing in the past, the United States should enlist the help of regional allies. Together they could ensure that a firmly consistent policy of democracy and human rights promotion in the area would force Venezuela to rule in a more democratic way, one that follows the spirit of the OAS charter. As I have described, the attitude of the countries of the region, particularly Brazil, is that this task seems to be an uphill battle unless the Workers party loses the next election in Brazil. Yet, it is important for the U.S. government to invest thought and energy in these contingencies.

By the same token, Venezuela's special connections to FARC cannot go unpunished. If the State Department defines FARC as a terrorist organization, then logically it should list a country—in this case, Venezuela—that has such a close connection with the organization as a sponsor of terrorism. Although U.S. congressmen have introduced different resolutions to designate Venezuela as a sponsor of terrorism, these proposals did not move forward in Congress.[15] The U.S. government's consideration of classifying Venezuela as a sponsor of terrorism could help at least raise international awareness of the nature of the regime and help isolate it.

The same applies to the alliance between the Venezuelan regime and the drug cartels. As noted in chapter 5, the Bolivarian countries and particularly Venezuela have strengthened their connections to the cartels. Most of these countries have expelled the DEA from their territories and view the war against drugs as part of a U.S. hegemonic agenda.[16] Meanwhile, Venezuela has placed its airports and ports at the disposal of the drug cartels. When countries of the region discussed the drug problem, they have avoided any discussion of this issue. What is worse, the United States has done the same. Instead, the United States needs either to apply forceful sanctions against Venezuela or to find mechanisms that send a clear message to Venezuela that its links to drug trafficking constitute a real threat and that it needs to find creative ways to stop the smuggling. The United States and other countries in the region should not tolerate the current situation.

Diminishing the intensity and strength of the Bolivarian revolution is vital. Venezuela is the head of the Bolivarian snake that extends from Ecuador and Bolivia all the way up to Nicaragua and Cuba. If the PSUV government in Venezuela is weakened, it will undermine those that depend on Venezuela's deeds and leadership. Certainly, in a Latin American continent that aims at further integration, any measure that erodes the authoritarian government—whether it focuses on democracy or human rights or drug- or terrorism-related policy—could be more effective with substantial regional support.

Reaching Out to Brazil

Brazil is the largest and fastest-growing economy and democracy in the region. Consequently, Brazil has tended, particularly under the government of former president Lula Da Silva, to conduct a foreign policy independent of the United States. Its policy often has been diametrically opposed to that of the United States (per the discussion of Iran's presence in the continent in chapter 6).

As noted previously, Lula's Brazilian government did not wish to counteract the radical forces in Latin America and Hugo Chávez in particular.

Brazil has also become self-conscious regarding its position as an emerging economic power and as such has demanded a greater global political status. Thus, Brazil's policies at times sharply contradicted U.S. policy as President Lula aimed to counterbalance U.S. power in the region and to certain extent at the global level.

As Susan Kaufman Purcell, Director of the University of Miami Center for Hemispheric Policy has pointed out, Lula viewed the invasion of Iraq through a third world lens and criticized the United States.[17] As we have seen in chapter 6, the Brazilian president himself was identified with the third world as he pursued South-South relations. Brazil then played a more supportive role for Iran, downplaying its human rights record, recognizing the results of its fraudulent 2009 elections, and trying to reach an agreement that would have allowed it to pursue its nuclear program.

In May 2005, Brazil hosted the first South American–Arab Summit, where the attendees adopted ambiguous resolutions typical of the Arab world that included downplaying the Sudanese genocide and condemning Western sanctions against rogue states like Syria. Then, in December 2010, shortly before leaving office, Lula unexpectedly announced Brazil's recognition of a Palestinian state based on the 1967 border. He argued that the declaration was intended to restart the stagnated peace process. About a week after making this move, Brazil openly declared that peace in the Middle East would not be achieved as long as the United States was the mediator.[18] A number of countries in the region followed suit after Brazil openly challenged the honesty, credibility, and ability of the United States to solve the Middle East conflict.

With regard to Latin America, the Brazilian attitude was similar. Although Lula had signed bilateral agreements of cooperation with the United States to develop alternative energy for the region, his foreign policy openly continued to oppose that of the United States in the continent. Brazil's strong support for regional independence has led it to help create alternative groups to the OAS that excluded the United States and Canada from its membership—the Union of South American Nations, a regional defense organization, and the Latin American and Caribbean Community of States. In 2009, Lula also took the lead in supporting Chávez's ally Manuel Zelaya during the crisis in Honduras and provided refuge to the ousted president at Brazil's embassy in Tegucigalpa. Also, Brazil has not criticized the Venezuelan regime in light of human rights and democracy violation.

Another instance of high tension between Brazil and the United States was registered again in the summer of 2009 when Colombia agreed to allow the United States to use seven Colombian military bases to fight drug trafficking. Brazil expressed discomfort and anger over the failure of the United States to inform Brazil about such step. Brazil also felt that this arrangement could pose a challenge to its sovereignty.[19] UNASUR urgently convened to deal with this issue, but its final compromise resolution simply stated that "the presence of foreign forces in the continent shall not threaten either the sovereignty of any South American nation or security in the region." It also stressed "the importance of respecting the principle of noninterference in the internal affairs of the nations or the self-determination of the (South American) people."[20]

Nevertheless, Brazil might not remain in this posture. In fact, it has slightly changed its foreign policy under the government of Dilma Rousseff, whose tenure began in January 2011.

Brazil in Perspective

Shortly after Dilma Rousseff took the reins of power in Brazil, she announced her willingness to increase trade with the United States, very much in contrast to Lula's insistence in developing South-South relations. Likewise, she took a stronger stance toward China over what she considered an unbalanced trade between the two countries that favored China.[21] Brazil also began to react to domestic protests regarding China's keeping its currency, the yuan, artificially low. Similarly, Brazil raised several complaints against China in the World Trade Organization. Rousseff's moves created a tension between China and Brazil and is a clear sign that her government is willing to sacrifice ideological alliances and apply more pragmatic calculations.

This pragmatism is also reflected in some changes Rousseff made in foreign policy. Contrary to Lula, she was willing to criticize Iran over its human right violations and stoning practices, asserting that she would not compromise on these issues. Rousseff supported a United Nations investigation of Iran over its human rights violations, a stance that Lula would not have supported. Likewise, Rousseff abstained when President Obama sought authorization from the United Nations Security Council to use force to support the rebels in Libya.[22] Lula might have done exactly as Chávez did and vehemently opposed such a move.

Moreover, Rousseff has expressed interest in expanding bilateral relations with the United States. At her invitation, President Obama visited Brazil in March 2011 and signed an agreement to share technological knowledge on alternative energy and to conduct educational interchanges between the two countries.[23]

During the Summit of the Americas that took place in Cartagena, Colombia, in April 2012, Rousseff made an extremely significant point: "In our region, we have to recognize the importance of the United States. [The United States] has features that are crucial in this emerging multi-polar world: it has flexibility; it has leadership in science, technology and innovation; and it also has democratic roots."[24] Rousseff has indicated that Brazil wants to be a U.S. partner and that she is committed to promoting democracy.

Brazil has a special attraction to the countries of the region. Its model of economic growth and social inclusion has attracted the attention of many leaders in Latin America, including Peruvian president Ollanta Humala, Venezuelan opposition candidate Henrique Capriles Radonski, and Uruguayan president José Mujica.[25]

Thus, it is extremely important that the United States continue to cultivate Brazil as a regional and global partner even if its current behavior is disappointing.

Brazil may offer a window of opportunity in the near future. As Brazil develops as a strong economic power with regional influence and a strong democracy, it could turn into an ally of the United States, and its regional reputation could be very helpful.

On its part, the United States may need to accept the idea that it will no longer have the same type of hegemonic influence in Latin America that it has enjoyed in the past. Establishing alliances with Brazil on the basis of shared values could be advantageous not only at the regional level but also at the global level. In this sense, the U.S. relationship with the European Union could serve as a model. The European Union does not always share the same views with the United States, and occasionally tensions between the two surface. However, the European Union is a natural ally, particularly when key security challenges such as terrorism or a nuclear Iran arise. Nothing proves this point better than the solidity of the North Atlantic Treaty Organization.

U.S. goals should be to strengthen its relations with Brazil, a country that has the potential to become another Western superpower, and at the same time to seek its cooperation in confronting the many challenges that are described in this book: the drug cartels, FARC and other insurgent or terrorist groups, Iran, and, most important, the Bolivarian alliance. On this last point, the more Brazil grows democratically, the more it needs to be persuaded that the Bolivarian revolution and the Bolivarian alliance, as well as Iran and other nefarious groups, are a threat to the region. It must see that allowing these forces to proliferate undermines the stability of the region and presents a threat to democracy. The United States must also explain that as much as Brazil may seek to flex its muscles and be a regional and global player, the ominous reality is that these elements are working against its interests. To counter them, the United States must convince Brazil to pursue a policy that supports democracy and human rights in the region.

If Brazil moves closer to the position of the United States, the rest of the continent is more likely to follow suit for the Brazilians' success is having a major impact on the other countries of the region. Further, if Brazil makes a commitment to help reinforce democracy, it can be a major force in driving the OAS back to the principles outlined in the organization's democratic charter and Resolution 1080, which stipulates sanctions and diplomatic pressures when democracy is violated.

In turn, the United States' recognizing the authority of Brazil and its immense influence in the region, as well as supporting its quest for a permanent seat in the United Nations Security Council, could be a positive incentive for Brazil to offer its cooperation and move to the West's side on political and international matters. In a nutshell, Brazil can play a leadership role that could potentially veto the political power of the Bolivarian bloc.

Likewise, as Latin American scholar and editor of the *Americas Quarterly* Christopher Sabatini suggests, the United States can recast the Group of Twenty Finance Ministers and Central Bank Governors (or G-20) and the International Monetary Fund in a way that reflects the rise of Brazil.[26] The United States can also increase its trade and make other gestures to Brazil, such as making it a partner of NATO and making it a military ally, as former NATO commander Adm. James Stavridis has suggested.[27] It is crucial, however, that the United States ensures these deeds are politically reciprocated.

Democracy and Human Rights

Although the Organization of American States and countries of the region became nothing but enablers of authoritarian tendencies in Latin America, a few signs of change have appeared. The OAS Inter-American Court of Human Rights did challenge an Ecuadorian Supreme Court decision in favor of President Rafael Correa when he sued the country's leading opposition newspaper over an opinion piece that called him a dictator and accused him of giving troops permission to fire on a hospital full of people during the September 2010 police uprising. After the Inter-American Court disputed the Ecuadorian rule, international pressure mounted and forced Correa to pardon the convicted defendants, effectively archiving the cases and dismissing the penalties.[28]

Through its political leadership and its Inter-American Court, the OAS could exercise the role of being an effective democracy watch, which would be a positive development. Further, with Brazil's strong leadership, the OAS could implement one of the organization's proposals and send political observers to countries where democracy has deteriorated (whether the affected countries requested them or not), notify them that the international community is watching their behavior, and facilitate solutions.[29] The OAS must also be able to impose proper punitive measures to those countries that ignore its warnings and recommendations.

Likewise, speaking up for political prisoners' rights, against violations of democracy and attacks on the press, and other measures of this kind is extremely important. So far, however, U.S. policy has been timid on this score and has played into the hands of the Bolivarian revolution.

Although every year the U.S. State Department publishes a thorough and comprehensive human rights report, it has not demanded that the Venezuelan government release prisoners or stop human rights abuses. In fact, in my informal conversations with State Department officials, they have claimed that it was not appropriate for them to denounce human rights violations or to demand the release of political prisoners. Instead, they preferred that such organizations as Amnesty International or Human Rights Watch do so. I assume that this policy was intended to avoid provoking the irascible Bolivarian leader and to prevent further confrontations with him.

U.S. Policy on Iran's Regional Presence

As examined in chapter 8, Iran's presence in Latin America is not seen as a threat yet. Its presence has been detected, but as U.S. officials have expressed, Iran's potential menace is still viewed as speculative. It will be extremely important, therefore, for the U.S. government to create a special security task force comprising a diverse group of people who could examine different angles and, of course, seek the crucial cooperation of other countries in the region.

First, the United States must recognize that the main danger that Iran poses is not found in its economic relationships with countries in Latin America but in its alliance with Bolivarian countries, its asymmetric warfare capability, and its likely possession of a nuclear weapon in the near future. The critical element that intensifies these dangers is that the Bolivarian revolution and the Islamic republic have shared interests. Therefore, the weakening of the Bolivarian regimes could be a key piece in diminishing Iran's presence in the region.

However, many non-Bolivarian countries' dealings with Iran also have given the Islamic republic political clout in Latin America. This status increases the Middle Eastern country's legitimacy and distorts the true nature of the Islamic regime. If the United States succeeds in cultivating Brazil as an ally and reaches out to the rest of the countries, emphasizing the issue of Iran and raising awareness of the risks that it presents to the region will be crucial.

Meanwhile, it is still unconceivable that U.S. policy toward Iran is based on general statements of concern or on estimations of threats measured in conventional terms. Likewise, U.S. policy should not accept the comfortable notion that commercial agreements between Iran and the Bolivarian countries have not been actually implemented. Therefore, the aforementioned U.S. government special task force should cover all possible aspects when looking into the Iranian presence in Latin America. That task force should include not only security experts and members of the defense establishment but also academics and other experts who could give a real assessment and project future scenarios regarding the threat of Iran, its Revolutionary Guard, and its proxy, Hezbollah.

While other perils, such as waging asymmetric warfare or consolidating repressive Bolivarian regimes, are highly problematic, the most important issue that the task force can address is the potential scenario where a nuclear Iran either places missiles on Venezuelan soil or assists Venezuela in obtaining nuclear weapons. Even if this threat is not actually possible now or imminent, it should be treated as a definite potential threat.

Furthermore, the U.S. government must develop a contingency plan in case Iran's nuclear cooperation with Venezuela develops in a dangerous direction. One of the most immediate actions that it could take is to apply sanctions on those countries that ignore the U.S. and international sanctions against Iran and deal with Iran's energy sector. The sanctions that have been applied to PDVSA are largely symbolic and far from being crippling or exercising any significant pressure. If the United States stopped doing business with PDVSA, however, it could cause a significantly negative impact on the Venezuelan economy.

▌LONG-TERM STRATEGIES: THE QUESTION OF DEMOCRACY

Yet, as this book has shown, the continent faces multiple problems. Hugo Chávez and the Bolivarian revolution pose a substantial number of pressing issues; therefore, neutralizing the Bolivarian revolution could be a very important first step in moving the continent toward democracy. This work cannot be done through military intervention because that effort would be deemed illegal and illegitimate, and thus would hurt the image of the United States in Latin America. Therefore, the best tool to countervail the impact of the Bolivarian revolution is to reaffirm and strengthen the concept of democracy in the rest of the continent.

Here I subscribe to Immanuel Kant's premise, which U.S. president Woodrow Wilson (1913–1921) adopted: in democracies, by virtue of creating a system where the law prevails and conflict is resolved in a peaceful and civilized way while seeking consensus, a culture will follow where such practice extends also to the international arena. Wilson found inspiration in Kant's assumption that the republican form of government is the most conducive to peace because in light of potential civil war, it leaves people no choice but to enter legal restrictions while maintaining their freedom. Therefore, the multiplication of republican governments should lead to a situation that would maximize international peace.[30] Wilson also saw the promotion of democracy in Latin America as an antidote against violent uprisings, revolutions, and regional international warfare. Thus, the Wilson Doctrine of self-determination and rule by the people's consent refused to recognize unconstitutional governments in Latin America.[31]

Democracy is not merely a better, freer, or more humane regime than dictatorship is. Democracy is a system that enables a modus vivendi where people with diverse ideas and interests resolve their differences peacefully. As democracy generates a political culture of "civilized confrontation," the expansion of this culture can play an important geopolitical role. Thus, democracy becomes a crucial component of international relations. At the same time, the more countries that practice democracy, the more likely they will embrace the Western side as they share the values of freedom. In an increasingly multipolar world, where countries such as China and Russia play important international roles and where rogue states and jihadists continue to proliferate, democracy can serve as an important geopolitical tool to counteract these elements.

Thus, democracy is not only a geopolitical antidote to the Bolivarian alliance but also serves as an answer to the growing influence of China and other nondemocratic actors in the continent. Of course, the United States can encourage economic competition and free–trade agreements to counteract China's influence. This is indeed a very important factor in Latin America. However, it is insufficient to guarantee an effective political counterbalance. Consequently, helping to strengthen democracy so that its institutions and legal systems grow stronger and its rule prevails above forms of authoritarian government or chaotic anarchy is extremely important.

Strengthening and Consolidating Democracy

The United States' strategy on democracy promotion cannot be aimed only at securing a formal elections-based democracy. Revisiting the discussion in chapters 1 and 4, leaders must focus on the roots of revolutionary regimes and the mobilization of grassroots groups.

As noted earlier, elements in civil society are disconnected from the political parties and their leaders. When parties do not respond directly to their constituencies and when political leaders believe that winning the vote gives them an automatic mandate to act without further consulting participants in civil society, alienation between civil society and elected officials take place. Such estrangement leads to a situation where society cannot advance its diverse interests and becomes marginalized while the state and the political elite remain unaccountable and experience a rapidly expanding corruption. If the state happens to rule by the powers of a formal democracy, then the whole regime suffers a crisis of legitimacy. This case has occurred in several countries in Latin America.

This precedent demonstrates the need to prevent the conditions that have brought other authoritarian regimes to power. Therefore, the challenge is to promote a sound democracy based on freedom and pluralism, on the one hand, and to build a strong state that is capable of credibly exercising governability and imposing the rule of law while remaining a legitimate democracy, on the other hand. Certainly, the goal is not a contradiction. Achieving this form of government is possible, as the American and the Western experiences have shown. In Latin America this work is a challenge but certainly not impossible in the long run.

"Maintaining a Democratic Legal System"

Distinguishing a democratic regime from a democratic state is important, as scholar Guillermo O'Donnell has suggested.[32] *Democratic regimes* are mainly characterized by electoral politics. They hold regular and fair elections and conduct peaceful transitions of power at all levels of government. Likewise, these elections are universal. All citizens have the right to vote and to run for office. By the same token, their societies enjoy the freedom of expression and of association. The majority of Latin American countries can be defined as having democratic regimes.

A *democratic state* includes all of these elements and a legal system that both backs the rights and freedoms that exist in a democratic regime and prevents anyone from monopolizing the power to legislate (*legibus solutus*).[33] To be effective, the democratic state's legal system must allow its legal actors, or judges, to be independent and follow an inclusive and fair procedure that takes into account police, prosecutors, defense lawyers, and higher courts. Similarly, the legal system should apply to all across the territory and treat everyone equally regardless of class, ethnicity, gender, and race.[34]

The democratic state's institutions must support a democratic legal system. Maintaining citizens' civil and human rights, as well as their ability to air their individual or group demands, justifies the art of government. Elected officials cannot view themselves as having a mandate from the electorate and legislate simply by virtue of having been voted to office. They must respond mainly to the people rather than to a party boss or other authority. Likewise, the institutional and legal frameworks of the state must be designed for the people to be a representative "government of the people, by the people, and for the people."

The laws of the state must be created with the input and participation of civil society—that is, the individuals, movements, interest groups, trade unions, religious groups, and associations of all kinds that seek to advance their interests whether they are material or ideal. Whether the people seek new labor policies, corporate advantages, the advancement of women's rights, or any other interest, the state's legislative branch serves as a channel for their demands and enacts laws that are likely the result of compromises. The laws, those who enforce them, and those who regulate them must be part of the state's institutional setting, which should not be subject to manipulation by political authorities or economic minority groups. Instead, making changes to these institutions should require legislative procedures and consensus. By the same token, political parties cannot solely represent party notables whose only connection to civil society is the act of voting; they must reflect the constituencies that elected them and direct their actions to respond to their needs. Thus, the democratic state is an arena where compromises between different constituencies are made and legislation is the natural outcome. It is the real rule of law and the foundation of a robust state democracy. In this sense a democratic state can govern better and more efficiently than can an authoritarian state or a government that ignores republican procedure or the division of powers altogether.

Latin American states are still far from being consolidated democratic states. They have not substantially reformed their legal institutions since the downfall of previous authoritarian regimes. The security apparatuses and other state institutions continue to abuse their power and are often unaccountable, as prosecuting the perpetrators is often virtually impossible. Regardless of the good will of elected officials, the criminal system still uses torture, and state violence often runs out of control. Likewise, in large portions of the territory, local ruling classes have sway over the police and the judiciary, effectively preventing them from becoming independent. In some cases, the legal system does not reach the entirety of the national territory. In large parts of Latin America, police officers see the rule of law as an obstacle rather than as a guarantee of social control, and they still view the poor and members of the marginalized sectors of society as if they were not citizens.[35] As scholar Paulo Sérgio Pinheiro has pointed out, "Although the fundamental guarantees are well-defined by most of the democratic constitutions, the exercise of full citizenship is practically nonexistent for certain sectors of the population. These societies, which are based on exclusion in civil and social terms, could be considered 'democracies without citizenship.'"[36]

In some countries in Latin America, advances made on political rights and parliamentary representation have not necessarily corresponded with improvements in civil and minority rights. In Guatemala, the government has often treated popular organizations that demanded agrarian reform like subversive elements. Peasants also often have been evicted from the land, and the judicial system was perceived as favoring the landowners. Even in such countries as Brazil, dominant families in local states still hold political control.[37] This inability of the state to absorb social forces is a serious problem. If these groups are driven outside the system, they can become available masses for anti-system movements. Therefore, it is important to build a strong democratic state that goes beyond the status of a democratic regime.

Building a Strong Representative Government

In Latin America, the third wave of democratization has reached states that are weak. We are witnessing in the region the unprecedented emergence of democracies in weak states.[38] The task now is to build democratic states.

As previously noted, democracy must be tied to a representative, deliberative, and open parliament. From this process the law will derive. In a legitimate representative government, those parties that do not win the battle for their interests accept the outcome. On the other side in this argument, law without democracy is not nurtured by society but is the result of government decrees with little or no input from civil society.

As discussed in chapter 1, Latin American countries faced a crisis of legitimacy during the early democratic period because the integration of civil society and government did not take place. Parliaments were mere instruments of government decrees. Parties sought votes but did not maintain relationships with those who voted for them. When the state ignores the rule of law and its civil institutions, society turns into angry masses that see in the promises of charismatic leaders their only hope for stability. One could suggest this insecurity is what enabled Hugo Chávez, Rafael Correa, and Evo Morales to take power and re-found their respective states. In those cases, the authoritarians' charisma and the people's messianic hope replaced the absence of a strong legitimate law.

Parliament, however, should not be a place where behind-the-scenes agreements with the most powerful elements in society take place at the expense of other sectors in civil society. A clear and well-defined division of powers can serve the purpose of representing different inputs, reflect these different interests, channel the dialogue between them, and legislate based on the compromises the representatives make. When the state legislates merely based on political decisions that do not include input from civil society, the law will be weak. The resulting deficient legislative, judicial, and administrative institutions leave the state vulnerable to corruption. This breach of the public trust opens the door for a crisis of legitimacy, the rise of authoritarianism, or the takeover of the state by non-state actors such as drug cartels (as is clearly the case in several Central American countries).

Latin America countries have been characterized by weak parliaments and strong executive branches. A 2010 report from the Organization of American States clearly notes that a key problem in Latin America is the fact that the executive power has overrun the legislative and the judicial power. Half of the region's eighteen presidents had assumed functions usually designated to members of parliament or the legislative brunch. According to this report, the weakness of republicanism "is the result of an exacerbated Presidentialism that makes the Latin American State, a Ceasarist state," or one that is ruled by commands from above.[39] This situation comes at the expense of a functional legislative power, which provides sectors in a civil society their political voice.

A typical example of this phenomenon is the control of the budget. In Latin America, issues related to budget cuts or increases, taxation, and other types of decisions generally fall within the realm of executive or presidential authority.[40] In the United States, Congress plays a key role in those and many other decisions, including multiple issues related to foreign policy, which by law is the responsibility of the president. Rule by decree also continues to be a problem in Latin American countries. In some cases—for example, that of former president Carlos Menem of Argentina—civilian presidents have issued more decrees than military rulers have. In another example, Peruvian president Alberto Fujimori dissolved Congress in 1992 over what he viewed as congressional obstructionism in carrying out his policies. With some exceptions, these governments with strong presidents have generally weakened their democratic practices and thus their respective states as well.

In many parts of Latin America, young people feel that political parties only represent themselves, thus the youth have no confidence in them. They believe that politicians are corrupt, that they come and go, and that elections do not change the status quo. In many sectors across the continent, they feel more propensity to participate in street protests. By the same token young people, particularly in Central America, are less inclined to support democracy as a system of government than adults are.[41]

Parties and elected officials continue to operate on the basis of patronage rather than on representation, leading to greater corruption and less actual leadership. Yet popular participation does not necessarily vanish, but acquires new forms of mobilization that reject the parties as vehicles of political representation. The people instead follow charismatic leaders who, in turn, see themselves not only above regular mechanisms of representation but also use these mechanisms—party and parliament—as instruments of their personal political power.[42]

Indeed, as an OAS analyst has pointed out, the breakdown of representation is often translated as a breakdown of the democratic state. It is a democratic crisis generated within democracy itself.[43] On a positive note, some have observed that the legislative power in Latin American countries has gained some strength in the last few decades.[44] But certainly they still have a long way to go.

Confronting Inequality

Latin American leaders and academics consider inequality as a key element that affects democracy and democratic rule. This very real issue has long been discussed in Latin America.

Moderate left-wing governments, such as that in Brazil, have stressed the matter of social inequality as a key problem and acted upon it. Under the slogan "Economic growth and social inclusion," Brazil has helped improve the condition of many people. According to the World Bank, poverty has fallen from 21 percent of the population in 2003 to 11 percent in 2009. Extreme poverty (measured in purchasing power parity of US$1.25 per day) also dropped dramatically, from 10 percent in 2004 to 2.2 percent in 2009. More than 22 million Brazilians were lifted out of poverty.[45]

However, one could suggest the issue of inequality is often ill defined. Many refer to inequality as an uneven distribution of income and resources. Whereas this situation is a legitimate concern, such inequality can be further accentuated at times of economic growth. Certainly in such countries as the United States, inequality is definitely a problem according to that definition.

The issue of inequality must also be recognized as a problem when, as noted previously, large sectors of society remain outside the law and outside the system. As the OAS report clearly points out: "For many inhabitants in large parts of Latin America the problem is one of legal poverty and the loss of participation in the legal system. Even the problem of crime often involves a confrontation between two people whose participation in the legal system has been blocked. . . . [Therefore] the ultimate goal should be to allow citizens to fully participate in the legal system, and that rights not be denied to them."[46]

If in Latin America citizenship is not expanded, the chances to overcome inequality are weakened. If a correct form of republicanism with a division of powers that enables participation from below is not in place, the state will be incapable of distributing power properly. A good system of checks and balances not only limits the power that the state itself can exert over individuals but also prevents a powerful and resourceful minority from gaining control of the state.

As pointed out in chapter 1, the Left, including the moderate Left in Latin America, has responded to the problem of inequality. Thanks to economic growth, several Latin American countries, mainly Brazil and Argentina, have been able to promote social programs aimed at helping poor families and the most needy sectors. Lula's slogan acknowledged the good in integrating and providing for the marginalized and poor sectors; however, if this problem is viewed as purely a matter of economics, these achievements will fade away as soon as the next economic crisis comes into sight.

One example is the Brazilian social program Bolsa Familia (family grant). It provides economic benefits to the poor under the condition that beneficiaries send their children to school. In addition, beneficiaries must seek special preventive medical exams. The welfare program's goal is also intended to enhance human capital.[47] Further, the Bolsa Familia program can be a catalyst in expanding citizenship since the children are required to attend school, which works to make them into productive members of society. The program benefits millions of people and has an accountability mechanism; therefore, it also expands the state's access to areas where it was previously absent.

Although programs such as Bolsa Familia are great steps in improving social inclusion and citizenship, the key to good integration is to provide proper representational mechanisms for these groups and marginal sectors. If governments in Latin America do not solve the structural problems associated with legal representation and citizenship, clearly the democratic states could face another legitimacy crisis with the first economic crunch. Extending citizenship and representation, meanwhile, should empower people within mainstream channels and allow the previously disenfranchised sectors at least to have some input or access to resources that would provide equal opportunities. Latin America has remained a classist society, among other reasons, because the state and its laws have failed to treat citizens uniformly and equally. This disparity is no less important than economic inequality.

However, it is important to make the distinction between inequality that stems from a lack of income or resources and the inequality of opportunities and citizenship that have consequently marginalized certain sectors of society. Economic growth and prosperity strengthen democracy only if the state successfully integrates as many sectors of society as possible.

This issue is vital, particularly in light of the enfranchisement of new grassroots movements and traditionally marginalized groups that look now for a political voice (see chapter 4). The Latin American states need to absorb these many social forces, because—as Chávez's outreach has shown—if they are not properly integrated, they will constitute a ticking political time bomb that nefarious forces are ready to exploit.

Furthermore, a weakened state will have to face greater security consequences. By virtue of having inadequate legal institutions, a lack of legitimacy, and poor governance, the leadership will succumb to corruption and to dangerous non-state actors, as evidenced in Mexico and Central America. Weak democratic regimes and states are prone to being taken over by drug cartels and other elements.

Engaging the United States

Reinforcing democracy beyond the electoral dimension into a real and legitimate form of representative government is the goal that needs to be achieved. The United States can contribute a great deal to this process, for example, by supporting nongovernment organizations and other organized groups that promote democratic practices. Likewise, in the past U.S. funds have sustained several measures to strengthen democracy, including in the areas of the rule of law, governance, human rights, and elections.

According to a 2003 Government Accountability Office report, these assistance programs have helped a number of countries in Latin America, including Bolivia, Colombia, El Salvador, Guatemala, Nicaragua, and Peru.[48] Some areas have reported positive results: new criminal procedures and codes have been adopted that have made the justice system more efficient and transparent, some municipalities have improved their budgeting and planning of public expenditures, governments have become more involved in protecting human rights, and elections have been conducted in a fair manner.

According to Ambassador Paul Trivelli, who served as the U.S. State Department's director of Central American affairs and as director of the Office of Planning for Latin America, U.S. programs have given priority to issues related to fair elections, human rights, improvement of transparency, and efforts against corruption.[49] They have offered training to political parties and national assemblies (Congress or parliament) to teach how a modern party and a modern legislative power work. Likewise, judges, lawyers, and prosecutors received training, and there were attempts to change the old-fashioned French Civil Codes to common law (particularly regarding the oral trial and the concept of juries). U.S. programs also have worked with police departments to improve their communications with the local community and to avoid abuses. European countries also developed similar programs.[50]

Programs were successful at the municipal local levels and attracted significant citizen participation. However, many of these programs have had limited results, mostly attributed to the inability or unwillingness of host governments to participate. Sometimes the state has not provided the right resources, and at other times, changes in governments have led to different attitudes regarding U.S. attempts to reform the state. Institutional weaknesses and a lack of human and financial resources have prevented some of the host governments from implementing or expanding the U.S. programs.

Likewise, given budget constraints, the extensive legal training centers cannot operate independently of U.S. aid. By the same token, there is concern that the region's law schools may not be providing adequate training. In certain countries, the credentials of judges and attorneys have come into question. Meanwhile, in such countries as Colombia, Peru, El Salvador, and Guatemala, "houses of justice" have been established in order to provide legal services to the poor and for the state to establish a presence in remote places.[51]

One important issue that still needs to be addressed is legislative reform, since it affects the core of civil society and a break with the authoritarian president–oriented style of the Latin American political system.

In such countries as El Salvador the legislature developed a master modernization plan to facilitate consensus building with regard to public participation in the legislative process. Except modernizing the offices and providing equipment, however, the government has not made substantial progress in overhauling legislative procedures or other issues relating to representation. Establishing these offices has helped decrease partisanship in El Salvador and in Guatemala, though; these offices have carried out civic education initiatives, organized public hearings, and handled constituent casework.[52]

This area is where the American experience can be helpful to Latin American countries and serve as a model to build a strong democratic legal state. Empowering civil society and strengthening the legislative and judicial powers are key goals for most Latin American countries, including not only the failed states, such as Guatemala, but also countries like Argentina. Of course, these countries need to be willing to do the necessary work.

Continuing to offer U.S. programs on building civil society and governance, on public debate, and on legislative and judicial reform is important regardless of the sometimes-disappointing results. More so, additional experts should share the American institutional experience with countries seeking to reinforce democratic institutions.

Strong democracies develop democratic cultures and moral awareness. Accountable governments reduce cynicism and encourage constructive attitudes. Well-rooted democratic cultures reject authoritarianism and provide moral judgment with regard to rogue states, terrorism, and certainly human rights. Currently, Latin American political culture gives priority to economics and social rights and thus widely admires China's model, despite its disregard for democratic procedures and human rights. It sees China as a developing economy that rose out of the ashes of poverty and underdevelopment to become an economic giant. Meanwhile, most of Latin America views the United States more and more as a declining power and its global role as a democratic power as diminished.

Thus, Brazilian president Dilma Rousseff's praise of American democracy in 2012 has special significance. The approbation could serve as a foundation for developing a special relationship with Brazil and possibly sway other Latin American leaders' opinions.

Restoring State Authority amid the Drug Problem

Regarding state authority, a legitimate question of course can be asked: how can one possibly speak about building a strong democratic state when the state has lost its power and ability to govern its territory, as is the case in several Central American countries?

As I pointed out in chapter 5, northern Mexico and countries in Central America have already fallen into a near state of anarchy. These countries have attracted dangerous non-state actors and proxies of rogue states that negatively affect the security of both the region and the United States even though they are not in the immediate border of the United States. This phenomenon represents the Afghanization of Latin America.

How can the foundations of a democratic state be established when violent armed groups and powerful illegal businesses rule the country? It is crucial to attach the future of a democratic state to defeating these groups. Such programs as Plan Colombia or the Mérida Initiative that are aimed at defeating drug trafficking are also implemented as a way to build the state's rule of law.

One of the challenges of executing these plans is the risk of human rights violations, which could occur as the state attempts to regain control from dangerous elements. The state must take this risk seriously and ensure such violations do not happen. The Colombian experience confirms this problem to certain extent. Indeed, in combating drug trafficking, human rights violations have taken place as well as state and paramilitary violence. The Colombian experience, however, also teaches that drug cartels can be weakened and at the same time democracy can be restored. The leadership of Colombia—including Presidents Virgilio Barco Vargas (1986–1990), César Gaviria (1990–1994), Andrés Pastrana (1998–2002), and Alvaro Uribe (2002–2010)—pursued an unprecedented political path. Instead of abolishing democracy, they remained committed to it. Indeed, a bill of rights was passed in 1991 as well as an actual mechanism of protecting citizens' rights. The Office of the Ombudsman (a public defender or *defensor del pueblo*) was formed in 1992 with the purpose of handling public complaints and protecting civil rights. The government also created popular forms of participation, such as referendums, consultations, and the direct election of mayors and other local public officials. Businesses, universities, and other organizations also incorporated democratization and bottom-up participation. In order to strengthen the judicial system, the government established a constitutional court with the authority to revoke unconstitutional laws and government decrees. Likewise, it introduced a mechanism to enable former guerrillas to repent, to be integrated in society, and to participate in the formulation of the new constitution. It also adopted new methods of negotiating with the guerrillas.[53]

As government forces worked to defeat the FARC, Uribe moved to demobilize the paramilitary groups that initially played a role in fighting FARC as the Colombian state collapsed. With the Colombian state back to functioning properly, thanks to Plan Colombia and Uribe's strong will, the demobilization of the paramilitary constituted an important step in advancing a strong state authority, a strong democracy, and a rule of constitutional law. Late in 2006, dozens of paramilitary leaders were jailed with full support of Colombian constitutional courts. In addition, more than thirty thousand individuals belonging to paramilitary groups were peacefully disarmed in an agreement signed with the Uribe government.[54] That pockets of paramilitary groups still exist in Colombia should not downplay this significant achievement. Moreover, politicians associated with the paramilitary were successfully prosecuted. The Colombian government also successfully fought the drug cartels and eliminated high-level drug lords like Pablo Escobar. In addition, it has succeeded in considerably weakening FARC even though the group still manages to control a portion of Colombian territory.

The fact that even under the most adverse circumstances in the early 1990s Colombia still aspired to strengthen its democracy and called for negotiations with guerrilla groups has no precedent. The country's military and security strengthened under Plan Colombia, yet this development did not transform the government into a highly repressive and authoritarian state as its counterparts in the Southern Cone—Argentina, Chile, Paraguay, Uruguay, and southern Brazil—did several decades ago. Indeed, in the countries of the Southern Cone, the fight against insurgency served as an excuse to impose an authoritarian rule that in some cases lasted decades.

Ambassador Trivelli, who served in Latin America during those years, explains that Colombia's success had to do with a number of factors.[55] First, President Uribe was fully committed to restoring order and authority in Colombia and to defeating the cartels. Next, all sectors of Colombian society gave the project overwhelming support. In addition, the Colombians themselves provided 90 percent of the funding for Plan Colombia and were willing to pay taxes to achieve the program's goal. The majority of Colombians found the presence of the guerrillas and drug cartels intolerable. Even though Colombia cooperated with the U.S. Drug Enforcement Administration, local police did most of the work.

Governance has been gradually restored in Colombia, and groups that challenged the state's authority have been substantially curbed. These actions represent an enormous accomplishment, one that observers wish for Mexico and countries in Central America that are facing the weakening of their states. In their efforts to strengthen their respective governments, these states could also use lessons learned from the Colombian experience to prevent human rights violations.

Furthermore, Central American countries could use the Mérida Initiative as a mechanism to help defeat drug cartels and counter anarchic forces. This significant and important initiative could be expanded and become more effective. As pointed out in chapter 8, this program is underfunded, but it could be subjected to reevaluation.

Trivelli agreed that the Mérida Initiative for Central America needs to be two or three times larger in order to defeat the cartels and restore state authority. Under current circumstances for every three illegal activities taking place in Central America, the available resources can only respond to one instance. In some cases, authorities detect illegal drug trafficking activities but lack the resources to counteract them. Countries such as Guatemala have never been able to collect taxes, not even from the wealthiest citizens, to develop any antiguerrilla and antidrug programs. The state in Guatemala is in such disarray, moreover, that in 2008 the United Nations began administering a parallel judicial system.

The goal should be to restore state authority and democracy simultaneously. Colombia could be a good model even if it cannot be fully replicated. The United States needs to devote time and creativity to support countries in Central America and other parts of Latin America as they attempt to build and fortify their states. This work needs to be done also in case the Bolivarian regimes collapse, because the governments will remain vulnerable regardless of the state of the Bolivarian revolution. This activity needs to be constant and not given up simply because the initial results are not satisfactory.

▌SUMMARY

In order to develop a workable foreign policy regarding Latin America, the United States should focus on both short-term and long-term goals. Since the Bolivarian revolution constitutes a large part of the political and security challenges discussed throughout this book, it is extremely important to conduct a policy aimed at weakening this revolution and, in turn, diminishing the intensity of other actors, such as FARC, Iran, and, to certain extent, the drug cartels.

In particular, the death of Hugo Chávez would present a unique opportunity to speak up in support of a true democracy in Venezuela and generate regional pressure to implement the Inter-American Democratic Charter of the OAS, including levying punitive measures in case Chávez's successors violate democratic standards. The United States must be ready with a contingency plan and take an active role in trying to influence the course of events in Venezuela. The ultimate goal should be restoring democracy and constitutionalism to Venezuela and its allies in the Bolivarian alliance.

Taking a strong pro-democracy and pro–human rights stand is crucial. The United States needs to use its leadership and influence on the OAS so that this organization applies public pressure on countries that violate civil liberties, democracy, and human rights. Transgressions also need to be denounced and cases of individuals imprisoned by the regime need to be brought to light. Countries such as Venezuela and Cuba hold a large number of political prisoners whose names remain largely unknown to the public.

The concept of restoring democracy needs to be expanded beyond the narrow definition of a coup d'état. It needs to address the problem of elected governments' engaging in activities that lead to the deterioration of democratic governance. Support for true democracy not only limits the authoritarian practices of elected leaders that contravene democracy—acts that the Venezuelan leader purposely encourages—but may also prevent their expansion throughout the continent.

It is imperative that the United States enlist the international community, governments, nongovernmental organizations, and human rights organizations to denounce and pressure those countries that make use of their electoral mandate to violate individual, human, and political rights, as well as the freedom of the press. The United States should enlist the crucial help of the OAS and especially such countries as Brazil, the largest democracy in the region. If this campaign becomes an international effort, these countries' authoritarian tendencies most likely will be contained.

Insisting on the sacredness of democratic practices can open the way to alternatives to Chávez and his allies from perpetuating their power and their aggressive expansion throughout the continent. Furthermore, upholding sound democratic governments will protect regional and national security because sound democracies will stop the advance of tyrants. This crusade is particularly essential when the creation of authoritarian Bolivarian regimes in the region is a prelude for an ominous international agenda that aims at entering into alliances with rogue states, such as Iran, drug cartels, and terrorist groups.

While democracy is a powerful antidote to counteract the political (but not the economical) influence of China, with regard to Iran, upholding democracy is crucial to check Iran's multilevel presence in Latin America. A task force comprising a number of experts—including advisers from the Pentagon and the U.S. State Department—should be created seriously to assess and compile reports on the nonconventional security threat coming from Latin America. Participants should first send a strong message to Latin American leaders that Iran's presence should not be tolerated and then solicit their support in countering the threat that Iran poses. Further, countries such as Venezuela that openly violate the sanctions levied against Iran should be subjected to proper punitive measures. Likewise, pressure should be applied on Venezuela and other countries in Latin America to eliminate military, nuclear, or any criminal activity that Iran or its proxies may have going in the continent.

In the long run, helping Latin American countries in addressing their problems of weak governments and constitutions, of powerful party oligarchies, and of corruption is important. In many of these countries, a detachment has existed between political leaders and civil society because the political parties fail to represent their constituencies. A strong democracy and a sound legal system may prevent situations and conditions similar to those that existed before Chávez and his allies took the reins of power and inspired their revolution. Given the mobilization of so many grassroots groups and indigenous movements, having a democratic system capable of absorbing diverse and emerging sectors in civil society is a crucial step. Strengthening the state can be a means to prevent anarchy and circumstances that facilitate a revolutionary authoritarian phenomenon such as the Bolivarian revolution.

Electoral democracy is a necessary but not sufficient condition for the creation of a stable and consolidated representative democracy. The United States has a role to play in providing real assistance for institution building. As it does so, it must insist that the states continue the programs to train civil society groups, public officials, judges, law enforcement officials, and state administrators to run a democratic, transparent, and uncorrupted state.

A strong democratic state structure will not only enable a stronger interaction with civil society but also, as a result of this association, will be viewed as more legitimate. Thus, the state will be less vulnerable to corruptibility, to its power being usurped by minority groups, and to becoming impotent in the face of drug cartels.

In geopolitical terms, a multiplicity of strong democratic states in the continent will generate a political culture whereby the system and common sense will automatically reject nondemocratic and authoritarian forces. This reaction, however, might not be possible when a state's authority is broken. Therefore, it is imperative that the United States help rebuild state authority in countries that experience governability problems before they fall into anarchy.

CONCLUSION

The challenges that Latin America poses today are not all the direct result of the Bolivarian revolution. Indeed, outside pernicious forces—the drug cartels—existed before the Bolivarian revolution, and they had been a major challenge in the region for two decades before Chávez's rise to power in 1999.

But the Bolivarian revolution has promoted the destruction of democracy and has set afoot an authoritarian socialist movement throughout Latin America that despises the market economy, liberal democracy, and U.S. political and cultural hegemony. It has inspired governments to follow its model and has gained admirers among groups and movements throughout Latin America. Chávez has made alliances with all anti-U.S. elements in the region and now around the globe.

Indeed, the Bolivarian leader has deepened his relationship with the FARC guerrillas in Colombia and has made alliances with Iran. His financial and material assistance has revitalized a moribund FARC and incorporated it with the insurgent force of the Bolivarian revolution. He has promoted Iran's presence in Latin America, including its most ominous aspects—asymmetric warfare and nuclear cooperation. Further, the Bolivarian leadership expanded its relations with drug cartels and has facilitated their hunt for more territory, giving them an outlet in the midst of the U.S. war on drugs and enabling them to continue destroying the social fabric of society and state authority in the region. The leadership expected that such lawlessness could precipitate the rise to power of other revolutionary leaders.

These partners of the Bolivarian revolution, however, still follow their own interests and objectives. All together, they create chaos in a region that in the future will see the proliferation of nothing but more adverse conditions: authoritarianism, further anarchy, insurgency, local and international terrorism, rogue states' involvement, and other negative elements such as an arms race and nuclear activity.

The continent's current economic prosperity, about which many Latin American leaders rejoice and brag, is not enough to counteract the detrimental effects of the Bolivarian revolution in some countries. Further, attempts to counter the negative repercussions have met with the indifference and impotence of other non-Bolivarian countries in the region. Being that the majority of these countries are left leaning, where the push for social rights and appeals to the poor are stronger than that for liberal democracy, Chávez's actions did not disturb their leaders. In fact, countries like Brazil rushed to view Chávez as a key to regional integration. Moreover, many of them joined Chávez in his anti-American fervor. They did not embrace it with the same fury that Chávez and his allies did, but the moderate Left certainly still carries the anti-American baggage of the past.

Brazilian president Lula's foreign policy toward Iran is a case in point. As we have seen, many other countries of the moderate Left also developed warmer relations with Iran. Argentina is moving toward conciliation with Iran despite the fact that its own courts declared Iran responsible for the most lethal terrorist attacks on Argentinean soil. Iran therefore became a symbol of resistance to American influence in the region.

For those who look at the facts with a technical perspective—for example, a general in the armed forces whose specialty is conventional warfare—they might not perceive the threat of the Bolivarian revolution and its actions as imminent. For those who seek hard evidence beyond reasonable doubt, predicting what may happen in the future is impossible; however, the current situation provides enough signs to require a serious look at the rise of authoritarian governments in the region and their connections.

For one, the breakdown of democracy in the continent is alarming, but it cannot be reduced to a crisis of democracy per se. Instead, it is the inevitable result when a state's government fails to consolidate its powers, to include its citizens in policymaking and represent their interests, and to strengthen the rule of law so that it can prevent external elements from corrupting it. Simply, a weak democracy becomes a weak state. A weak state is vulnerable to corruption. Corruption leads to colonization of the state by powerful groups that have enough purchasing power. As noted throughout the book, the deterioration of democracy to this extent has security implications insofar as external forces can penetrate it.

The United States has remained impotent in the face of these developments because it took a defensive position. In addition, the war in Iraq hurt its image in Latin America and exacerbated negative feelings toward the United States. Consequently, the United States could not confront Chávez and his revolution directly, leading to its position of compliance with Latin American countries. Thus, the United States lost the ability to pursue its agenda actively and ended up accepting a passive role in the continent.

As stated in chapter 9, however, the Bolivarian revolution will not die along with Chávez. It will endure and survive because of the structures and practices he has left in place, not just in Venezuela but in the region as well. The United States should not have any illusions about it: The challenge will continue. The effects of authoritarianism, the destruction of the state, and the proliferation of non-state actors and rogue states are likely to continue their course if no one moves to counter them. As time goes by, these circumstances will further aggravate Latin American relationships with the United States.

U.S. foreign policy, therefore, cannot be guided by traumas of the past, appeasement, fear, or guilt. Its security and foreign policy needs to serve the interests and goals of the region, as well as those of the United States, particularly when a threat to national security is raised.

EPILOGUE

Hugo Chávez passed away on March 5, 2013, after the main production of this book was completed. This book was written precisely to help think about a post-Chávez era; therefore, his confirmed passing does not change the premises, the analyses, the conclusions, or the recommendations of this book.

Chávez's death has left a legacy in Venezuela similar to that of Juan Perón. He's being lauded as a mythical figure who will be remembered by those sectors that have materially benefited from his rule, by those who see him as a symbol of redemption and independence, and by those who are less concerned for constitutional democracy.

Meanwhile, acting president and Chávez's heir Nicolas Maduro is imitating Chávez's governing style. The day Chávez died Maduro expelled two American diplomats. Later he accused the country's enemies of having injected cancer into the body of Hugo Chávez and killing him. Like his boss and mentor, Maduro feels the need to find enemies and thus he has accused two former assistants of secretary of state for the Western Hemisphere—Otto Reich and Roger Noriega—of plotting the assassination of opposition leader Capriles in order to create chaos and then blame the government of Venezuela for it.

However, a very interesting development has happened since Chávez's forever vanishing from the scene was confirmed.

The official results of the April 14 presidential elections show that Nicolas Maduro, Chávez's chosen successor and protégé, won by a margin of less than 2 percent.

Once again the party of Chávez won because it took advantage of huge state resources that include mass media, intimidation of public employees, the use of the oil giant PDVSA to fund the political campaign, and the use of all public resources to support Maduro. Moreover, there have been denunciations of irregularities that include claims that on election day more than 500 voting machines were damaged, affecting almost 190,000 voters. Moreover, there has been a claim that votes coming from outside Venezuela were not counted.

However, the opposition leader Henrique Capriles Radonski refused to recognize the results, demanded a recount, and mobilized his supporters to protest peacefully. This could be a sign that as Chávez is gone, fear might be gone as well. During the campaign, Capriles engaged in a more aggressive discourse, mocking Maduro and campaigning with determination.

Maduro and the government-controlled National Council of Elections (CNE) refused to allow the recount. This shows that fraud may indeed have taken place, perhaps not only in this election but in previous elections as well. But most importantly, the government of the PSUV is being challenged as illegitimate for the first time in many years.

As the personal charisma of Chávez disappeared, the Venezuelan people are likely to become more conscious of the situation they have lived in for a decade and a half, which has included political intimidation and economic hardship including inflation, power outages, food shortages, deterioration of the middle class, a war against the private sector, and other elements.

However, even if the results announced by the CNE remain unchanged, the fact that, scarcely a month after Chávez's death, his successor received far fewer votes than Chávez received in the October 2012 presidential elections is significant. This clearly indicates that Maduro's uncharismatic personality and his often ridiculous attempt to be a Chávez was only slightly successful and did not convince many of Chávez's followers.

If the PSUV represents the poor and Chávez was their savior, why would they not overwhelmingly support his successor? This shows the irrational power of Chávez and his discourse. For many years those who criticized Chávez' policies thought that the Venezuelan government's awful waste of money and resources plus its mismanagement of the oil sector would end badly for Venezuelans. However, as long as Chávez was in power, the effervescence of his charisma, his ability to communicate with the masses, and his image as the protector of the poor overcame the reality of the conditions in which they were living. That Venezuela is one of the few countries in Latin America that has not grown economically and expects more unemployment and even higher inflation and decline matters more now than ever before. Maduro can no longer rely on his charisma but on improving the economy.

However, this could prove to be very difficult. Can Maduro act rationally and make the economy flourish? Does he possess the power to change the course of the revolution? It is unlikely. After all, the Bolivarian government and its companies, such as PDVSA, are populated with political loyalists that include a plethora of inept and corrupt people. The professionals are long gone. Maduro is likely to continue the course of the revolution and follow in Chávez's footsteps. Since he lacks the charisma and ability to galvanize the public, this will put him at the mercy of all the elements that were empowered under Chávez: the Cubans, the co-opted military officers, the Boliburguesía, the Bolivarian circles, the militias, and the paramilitary.

Under these circumstances, a highly polarized society will bring about protests and government violence. The Bolivarian paramilitary will be quickly mobilized, and the whole state apparatus will increase its repression.

Support also for the Bolivarian revolution still prevails in the region as this book demonstrates. Rafael Correa won reelection overwhelmingly in February 2013 in Ecuador. He may even have the energy and effervescence to lead the Bolivarian revolution at the regional level and fill the international role that Chávez had. Likewise, I do not see any change coming up either in the enabling attitudes of the Workers' Party government in Brazil or in the Argentinean Peronist government's enthusiastic support for the Bolivarian government.

The number of leaders from the region that attended Chávez's funeral confirms the unfortunate fact that the late tyrant and his Bolivarian doctrine are still putative and admired in the region. Perhaps Chávez's death and Venezuela's economic deterioration will slow down the Bolivarian enthusiasm.

The peoples of Latin America need to understand that the geopolitical challenges described in this work not only affect the United States but mainly affect them. The geopolitical challenges of the region require them to act, think, and reevaluate conducting business as usual. Change needs the work and consciousness of civil society in Latin America. The people must value freedom and fight for it too, particularly when anarchy, chaos, terror, and fear are not unfamiliar feelings for Latin Americans. Civil society, as well as its political leaders, needs to stop thinking in terms of immediate economic reward or welfare and start showing a commitment to building pluralistic democratic institutions, checks and balances, the rule of law, as well as respect for rights and freedoms.

NOTES

INTRODUCTION

1. Romina Mazzaferri, "Latin America After Obama's 'Countering Iran in the Western Hemisphere Act,'" *Asian World,* February 12, 2013, http://www.the asianworld.co.uk/index.php/latin-america-after-obamas-countering-iran-in -the-western-hemisphere-act.

2. Michael Reid, *Forgotten Continent: The Battle for Latin America's Soul* (New Haven, CT: Yale University Press, 2007), 255.

3. René Antonio Mayorga, "Outsiders and Neopopulism: The Road to Plesbic-itary Democracy," in *The Crisis of Democratic Representation in the Andes,* ed. Scott Mainwaring, Ana Maria Bejarano, and Eduardo Pizarro Leongómez (Stanford, CA: Stanford University Press, 2006), 132–70.

4. Fareed Zakaria, *The Future of Freedom: Illiberal Democracy at Home and Abroad* (New York: W. W. Norton, 2003).

5. Douglas E. Schoen and Michael Rowan, *The Threat Closer to Home: Hugo Chávez and the War against America* (New York: Free Press, 2009), 105.

6. Max G. Manwaring, "Venezuela's Hugo Chávez, Bolivarian Socialism, and Asymmetric Warfare" (Carlisle, PA: The Strategic Studies Institute, U.S. Army War College, October 2005), 9–10, http://www.strategicstudiesinstitute .army.mil/pubs/display.cfm?pubID=628.

1. WHAT TRIGGERED THE REVOLUTIONARY FORCES IN LATIN AMERICA?

1. Gretchen Helmke and Steven Levitsky, eds., *Informal Institutions and Democracy: Lessons from Latin America* (Baltimore, MD: John Hopkins University Press, 2006).

2. Jorge Dominguez and Jeanne Kinney Giraldo, "Conclusion: Parties, Institutions, and Market Reforms in Constructing Democracies," in *Constructing Democratic Governance: South America in the 1990s,* ed. Jorge Dominguez and Abraham Lowenthal (Baltimore, MD: John Hopkins University Press, 1996), 28.

3. Ibid., 31.

4. Ibid., 29.
5. See Horacio Verbitsky, *Robo para la Corona* (Buenos Aires: Ed. Planeta, 1991).
6. Fernando Henrique Cardozo, "More than Ideology: The Conflation of Populism with the Left in Latin America," *Harvard International Review*, Summer 2006.
7. Steven Levitsky and Kenneth Roberts, "Introduction: Latin America's Left Turn; a Framework for Analysis," in *The Resurgence of the Latin American Left*, ed. Steven Levitsky and Kenneth Roberts (Baltimore, MD: John Hopkins University Press, 2011), 8.
8. Ibid., 7.
9. George Philip, *Democracy in Latin America: Surviving Conflict and Crisis* (Cambridge, UK: Polity Press, 2003).
10. Michael Coppedge, "Venezuela: The Rise and Fall of Patriarchy," in Dominguez and Lowenthal, *Constructing Democratic Governance*, 5.
11. Ibid., 6–7.
12. Cristina Marcano and Alberto Barrera Tyszka, *Hugo Chávez: Sin Uniforme* (Buenos Aires: Editorial Sudamericana, 2005).
13. Coppedge, "Venezuela," 13–14.
14. Marcano and Tyszka, *Hugo Chávez*, 16–19.
15. Anita Isaacs, "Ecuador: Democracy Standing the Test of Time?," in Dominguez and Lowenthal, *Constructing Democratic Governance*, 42–57.
16. Ibid., 45.
17. Ibid., 47.
18. Ibid., 49–54.
19. José Natanson, *La Nueva Izquierda* (Buenos Aires: Editorial Sudamericana, 2008).
20. Ibid., 47.
21. Luis Fleischman and Nicole Ferrand, "The Latin American Grassroots III," *The Americas Report*, May 10, 2007.
22. Guillermo O'Donnell, "Delegative Democracy," *Journal of Democracy*, 1993, 59–60.
23. See the CONAEI website, http://www.conaie.org/sobre-nosotros/que-es-la-conaie.
24. Catherine Conaghan, "Ecuador: Rafael Correa and the Citizens' Revolution," in Levitsky and Roberts, *Resurgence of the Latin American Left*, 260–82.
25. Eduardo Gamarra, "Bolivia: Managing Democracy in the 1990s," in Dominguez and Lowenthal, *Constructing Democratic Governance*, 73–74.
26. Ibid., 81.
27. Ibid., 92–93.

28. René Antonio Mayorga, "Bolivia's Democracy at the Crossroads," in *The Third Wave of Democratization in Latin America: Advances and Setbacks*, ed. Frances Hagopian and Scott Mainwaring (New York: Cambridge University Press, 2005), 149–78.

29. Natanson, *La Nueva Izquierda*, 78–79.

30. Mayorga, "Bolivia's Democracy," 177.

31. Luis Tapia, "Bolivia: The Left and the Social Movements," in *The New American Left: Utopia Reborn*, ed. Patrick Barrett, Daniel Chávez, and Cesar Rodriguez-Garavito (Amsterdam: Pluto Press, 2008), 215–31.

32. Ibid., 221.

33. Raúl Madrid, "Bolivia: Origins and Policies of Movimiento al Socialismo," in Levitsky and Roberts, *Resurgence of the Latin American Left*, 239–59.

34. David Close, "Nicaragua: The Return of Daniel Ortega," in *Reclaiming Latin America: Experiments in Radical Social Democracy*, ed. Geraldine Lievesley and Steven Ludlam (New York: Zed Books, 2009), 110–11.

35. Jaime Daremblum, "Democracy is under Attack in Nicaragua," *Journal of the American Enterprise Institute*, February 2, 2009.

36. Randall Wood, "Democratic Consolidation in Nicaragua: 1979–2003," Johns Hopkins School of Advanced International Studies (SAIS) Seminar on Latin American Politics, November 2003, http://therandymon.com/papers/nica-democracy.pdf.

2. THE ORIGINS OF THE CHÁVEZ (BOLIVARIAN) REVOLUTION

1. A discussion of historical models of populism can be found in María Moira Mackinnon and Mario Alberto Petrone, eds., *Populismo y Neopopulismo en América Latina* (Buenos Aires: Editorial Universitaria de Buenos Aires, 1998), 13–58.

2. "Illiberal democracy" refers to a regime that is formally democratic insofar as it holds elections and elects public officials; however, the regime also contains nondemocratic elements such as excessive power in the hands of the president at the expense of other branches of government. Parliaments are weak and courts are not fully independent. Likewise, the power of regional and local authorities, businesses, and the press is diminished. See Zakaria, *Future of Freedom*, chapter 3.

3. Edgardo Lander, "Venezuela, Populism and the Left: Alternatives to Neo-Liberalism," in Barrett, Chávez, and Rodriguez-Garavito, *New Latin American Left*, 79.

4. Minister Ali Rodriguez, Thirty-Fifth OAS General Assembly, Ft. Lauderdale, Florida, June 7, 2005.

5. John Lynch, "Conclusion," *Latin American Revolutions, 1808–1826: Old and New World Origins*, ed. John Lynch (Norman: University of Oklahoma Press, 1994), 373–84.

6. Simón Bolivar, "An American's Conviction," in Lynch, *Latin American Revolutions*, 308–20.

7. Enrique Krauze, *El Poder y el Delirio* (Barcelona: Tusquets Editores, 2008).

8. Julia Buxton, "Venezuela: The Political Evolution of Bolivarianism," in Lievesley and Ludman, *Reclaiming Latin America*, 57–74.

9. Heinz Dieterich, "The Socialism of the 21st Century," November 2006, video transcript, Rotenburg, Germany, European Institute for Progressive Cultural Policies (2007), http://eipcp.net/transversal/0805/dieterich/en.

10. Buxton, "Venezuela."

11. Marcano and Tyszka also share this view. Ceresole's expulsion from Venezuela does not necessarily mean that his influence was removed. The authors point out, "Despite Ceresole's apparent defeat, he has influenced not only the Venezuelan political process but also Chávez' personal development." See Marcano and Tyszka, *Hugo Chávez*, 361.

12. Norberto Ceresole, *Caudillo, Ejército, Pueblo: La Venezuela del Presidente Chávez* (Caracas, February 1999), http://www.analitica.com/bitblioteca/ceresole/caudillo.asp.

13. Ibid., 18; and Lander, "Venezuela, Populism, and the Left."

14. Marcano and Tyszka, *Hugo Chávez*, 234.

15. Muammar al Gathafi, *The Green Book* (Berkshire, UK: Ithaca Press, 2005), http:\\books.google.com/books?id=5HrjbDUQk9UC&dq=gaddafi+the+green+book&printsce=frontcover&source=bn&hl=en&ci=CU13TOGTHs HO8Aa.J45yMBQ&sa=X&oi=book result &ct=resultresnum=4&ved=OCC YQ6AEwAw#v=onepage&q&f=false.

16. Marcano and Tyszka, *Hugo Chávez*.

17. Enrique Krauze, "Looking at Them: A Mexican Perspective on the Gap with the United States," in *Falling Behind: Explaining the Development Gap between Latin America and the United States*, ed. Franics Fukuyama (New York: Oxford University Press, 2008), 48–71.

18. Ibid.

19. Andre Gunder Frank, *Latin America: Underdevelopment or Revolution: Essays on the Development of Underdevelopment and the Immediate Enemy* (New York: New York Monthly Review Press, 1969).

20. In an interview with CNN host Larry King on September 25, 2009, Chávez claimed that during the failed April 2002 coup, the administration of George W. Bush tried to assassinate him. When King asked Chávez how he knew the

Americans had tried to kill him, Chávez replied, "I saw my assassins. I was a prisoner. . . . They received the order to kill me until a group of soldiers prevented this from happening. The order came from the White House, I have no doubt because this is what the White House did to [former Chilean president] Salvador Allende; what it did to 'Che' Guevara, and what they did to [former Panamanian president] Omar Torrijos. The U.S. bombarded Panama, Nicaragua, and the Dominican Republic. This is our history." Thus, Chávez has no evidence to prove that indeed anyone attempted to assassinate him except what he interprets historically as business as usual in U.S. policy in Latin America. "Larry King Interview Chávez Says Bush Tried to Kill Him," WorldNews, September 25, 2009, http://www.youtube.com/watch?v =gk3lSCPhy4k.

21. Constantine Menges, *Venezuela: Overview of Politically Active Groups and Current Trends* (Washington, DC: Hudson Institute, 2002).

22. Constitución de la República Bolivariana de Venezuela Publicada en Gaceta Oficial del jueves 30 de diciembre de 1999, N° 36.860, http://www.inpsasel.gob .ve/moo_doc/ConstitucionRBV1999-ES.pdf.

23. Speech by Hugo Chávez delivered at Palacio Municipal, Montevideo, Uruguay, March 2, 2005.

24. Brian A. Nelson, *The Silence and the Scorpion: The Coup Against Chávez and the Making of Modern Venezuela* (New York: Nation Books, 2009), 283.

25. Ibid., 211–14.

26. Ibid., 284.

27. "Boliburguesía" is a term informally coined in Venezuela. According to public policy professor Jose Manuel Puente, its members constitute a new class of people that mixes political activists and militants with entrepreneurs whose businesses profit as a result of opportunities that arise from their connections to the new Bolivarian revolution and the Bolivarian state. Yolanda Valery, "Boliburguesía: nueva clase venezolana," BBC Mundo, Venezuela, December 2, 2009, http://www.bbc.co.uk/mundo/economia/2009/12/091202_1045_ venezuela_boliburguesia_wbm.shtml.

28. Walden Bello, "Militares Radicales en Venezuela: ¿Cual es su Relevancia para el Resto de los Países en Desarrollo?," *Focus on the Global South* (Bangkok), March 15, 2006, http://focusweb.org/node/900.

29. Nelson, *Silence and the Scorpion*, 131–33.

30. Karl Marx, *The Eighteenth Brumaire of Louis Bonaparte* (New York: International Publishers, 1984), 75–76.

31. For a complete chronology of how Chávez tried to challenge and manipulate the process of the recall referendum, see Constantine Menges, "Venezuela-Chávez

Obstruction of the Presidential Recall Referendum," Hudson Institute, Washington, DC, March 2004.

32. Javier Corrales and Michael Penfold-Becerra, "Venezuela: Crowding Out of the Opposition," *Journal of Democracy* 16, no. 2 (2007): 99–112; and Reporters Without Borders, "Venezuela: Criminal Code Ammendments Pose Threats to Press Freedom," March 24, 2005, http://vcrisis.com/index.php?content=letters/200503240637.

33. Asdrúbal Aguiar, "La Revolución Bolivariana al Descubierto," August 19, 2005, http://www.analitica.com/va/politica/opinion/7819867.asp.

34. Reporters Without Borders, "Venezuela."

35. Aguiar, "La Revolución."

36. "Venezuela: Hugo Chávez Declares as Enemy of the Country to the Fedecámeras Union," M24Digital.com, June 24, 2010, http://m24digital.com/en/2010/06/16/venezuela-hugo-Chávez-declares-as-enemy-of-the-country-to-the-fedecameras-union/.

37. Fabiola Sanchez, "Venezuela Decrees Expropriation of 11 Rigs Owned by U.S. Oil Driller Helmerich & Payne," Associated Press, July 1, 2010; and Christopher Toothaker, "Chávez Orders Takeover of French Hypermarket Chain," Associated Press, January 17, 2010.

38. Jonathan Hartlyn, Jennifer McCoy, and Thomas M. Mustillo, "Electoral Governance Matters: Explaining the Quality of Elections in Contemporary Latin America," *Comparative Political Studies* 41, no. 1 (January 2008): 82.

39. Genaro Mosquera, "Hacernos Trampa es mas Difícil porque hemos aprendido mucho," *Boletin Digital Universitario*, Universidad de Carabobo, November 6, 2010.

40. Ibid.

41. Zakaria, *The Future of Freedom*, 93–96.

42. This definition is provided by Zbigniew Brzezinski. See Juan Linz, *Totalitarian and Autoritarian Regimes* (Boulder, CO: Lynne Rienner Publishers, 2000).

43. U.S. Department of State, "2010 Human Rights Report: Venezuela," Bureau of Democracy, Human Rights, and Labor, April 8, 2011, http://www.state.gov/j/drl/rls/hrrpt/2010/wha/154523.htm.

44. Ibid.

45. Raul Sanchez Urribarri, "Venezuela, Turning Further Left?," in *Leftovers: Tales of the Latin American Left*, ed. Jorge Castañeda and Marco Morales (New York: Routledge, 2008), 187.

46. Phil Gunson, "Critics of Venezuelan Education Law Vow to Defy It," *Miami Herald*, August 15, 2009.

47. Jesus E. Machado, "Estudio de los Consejos Comunales en Venezuela," *Function Centro Gumilla* (May 2008): 12, http://gumilla.org/files/documents/Estudio-Consejos-Comunales01.pdf.

48. Sanchez Urribarri, "Venezuela," 187.

49. Ricardo Sidicaro, "Consideraciones Sociológicas Sobre las Relaciones entre el Peronismo y la Clase Obrera en la Argentina, 1943–1955," in Mackinnon and Petrone, *Populismo y neopopulismo*, 153–72; and Francisco Weffort, "El Populismo en la Política Brasilera," in Mackinnon amd Petrone, *Populismo y neopopulismo*, 135–52.

50. Human Rights Watch, "A Decade under Chávez," September 22, 2009, www .hrw.org/reports/2008/09/22/decade-undre-ch-vez.

51. U.S. Department of State. "2010 Human Rights Report: Venezuela."

52. Human Rights Watch, "A Decade under Chávez."

53. Aleksander Boyd, "The Irrefutable Proof of the Existence of Political Persecution in Venezuela," September 15, 2005, http://www.vcrisis.com/index.php ?content=letters/200509152101.

54. "U.N. Rights Envoy Urges Chávez to Leave Globovision Alone," Reuters, June 17, 2010, http://in.reuters.com/article/2010/06/17/idINIndia -49388720100617.

55. Alicia De La Rosa, "Suspendido el juicio de la jueza Afiuni para enero," *El Universal*, Caracas, December 19, 2012.

56. "La juez Afiuni revela que fue violada en prisión y luego tuvo un aborto en Venezuela," ABC.es, November 25, 2012, http://www.abc.es/internacional/ 20121125/abci-venezuela-afiuni-violada-prision-201211241844.html.

57. "U.N. Rights Envoy," Reuters.

58. Hanna Arendt, *The Origins of Totalitarianism* (New York: Harcourt Brace Jovanovich, 1998), 394.

59. Simon Romero, "New Laws in Venezuela Aim to Limit Dissent," *New York Times*, December 24, 2010.

60. "Constitución de la Republica Bolivariana de Venezuela," chapter 1, Article 19, venezuelanalysis.com, http://venezuelananalysis.com/constitution/title/3.

61. Ibid., chapter 1, Article 27.

62. Ibid., chapter 1, Article 29.

63. Hannah Arendt, *On Revolution* (London: Penguin Books, 1998), 394–95.

64. Mayorga, "Outsiders and Neopopulism," 170.

65. Samuel Blixen, *Chávez: 48 Horas en la Vida de Hugo Chávez* (Montevideo, Uruguay: Ediciones Trilce, 2005), 57–58.

66. Harold Trinkunas, "Venezuela: The Remilitarization of Politics," in *Armed Actors: Organised Violence and State Failure in Latin America*, ed. D. Kees Kooning and Dirk Kruijt (London: Zed Books, 2004), 106–12.

67. Ibid., 111.

68. Ibid., 114–15.

69. Simon Romero, "Chávez Seeks Tighter Grip on Military," *New York Times*, May 29, 2009.

70. Linz, *Totalitarian and Autoritarian Regimes*, 98.
71. "Informe que presenta la comisión permanente de defensa y seguridad de la asamblea nacional sobre el proyecto de ley de reforma parcial del decreto No 6,239 con rango, valor y fuerza de ley orgánica de la fuerza armada nacional Bolivariana a los efectos de su segunda discusión," October 1, 2009, Art. 23–25.
72. Ibid., Art. 5.
73. Ibid., Art. 46 and Art. 49.
74. Ibid., Art. 50.
75. Ibid., Art. 60.
76. Simon Romero, "Venezuela's Military Ties with Cuba Stir Concerns," *New York Times*, June 14, 2010.
77. Arendt, *On Revolution*, 417–18.

3. THE CONTINENTAL EXPANSION OF THE CHÁVEZ REVOLUTION

1. Speech at Palacio Municipal, March 2, 2005, in Blixen, *Chávez*.
2. Raúl Isaias Baduel, *Venezuela, Crisis y Salvación* (Caracas: Libros Marcados, 2008), 109–16.
3. Javier Corrales, "Venezuela: Petro-Politics and the Promotion of Disorder," in *Undermining Democracy: 21st Century Authoritarians* (Washington, DC: Freedom House, Radio Free Europe/Radio Liberty, Radio Free Asia, June 2009), 75–76.
4. Eduardo Gamarra, "Bolivia on the Brink," Council on Foreign Relations, CSR no. 24, February 2007.
5. Matias Franchini, "Asamblea Constituyente en Bolivia: Génesis, evolución y conflicto en el cambio," *Centro Para la Apertura y el Desarrollo América Latina*, June 5, 2007.
6. Luis Fleischman and Nicole Ferrand, "Quietly Following Chávez's Lead," *The Americas Report*, December 12, 2007, http://www.theamericasreport.com/2007/12/12/quietly-following-Chávezs-lead/.
7. Alain Rouquie, *A la Sombra de las Dictaduras* (Buenos Aires: Fondo de Cultura Económica, 2011), 222–23.
8. Rubén Ferrufino G., "Análisis crítico de los preceptos económicos establecidos en la Nueva Constitución Política del Estado," in *Reflexión Crítica a la Nueva Constitución Política del Estado* (La Paz, Bolivia: Konrad Adenauer Stiftung, 2009), 517–55.
9. Jimena Costa Benavides, "Los cambios en la estructura y organización del Poder Ejecutivo ante la nueva estructura y organización territorial del Estado," in ibid., 267–96.
10. Madrid, "Bolivia," in Levitsky and Roberts, *Resurgence of the Latin American Left*.

11. Rory Carroll and Andres Schipani, "Evo Morales Wins Landslide Victory in Bolivian Presidential Elections," *The Guardian*, December 7, 2009, http://www.guardian.co.uk/world/2009/dec/07/morales-presidential-victory.
12. Madrid, "Bolivia," 256.
13. In "Bolivia, paralizada por protestas contra Evo," *El Universo*, December 31, 2010.
14. "1.500 indígenas protestan por construcción de vía en el Amazonas," *El Mundo*, August 20, 2011, http://www.elespectador.com/noticias/elmundo/articulo-293219-1500-indigenas-protestan-construccion-de-via-el-amazonas.
15. "MundoBolivia: Gobierno e indígenas logran acuerdo por construcción de carretera," *El Comercio*, October 24, 2011.
16. Emily Achtenberg, "Bolivia: End of the Road for TIPNIS Consulta," North American Congress on Latin America, December 13, 2012, https://nacla.org/blog/2012/12/13/bolivia-end-road-tipnis-consulta.
17. Emily Achtenberg, "Battle of Reports Sustains Bolivia's TIPNIS Conflict," January 18, 2013, http://www.nacla.org/blog/2013/1/18/battle-reports-sustains-bolivia's-tipnis-conflict.
18. Alvaro García Linera, "Bolivia: Estrategias para Destruir la Dominación K'hara en Bolivia," *eju!*, February 2007.
19. U.S. Department of State, "2009 Human Rights Report: Bolivia," March 11, 2010, www.state.gov/j/drl/rls/hrrtp/2009/wha/136102.htm.
20. Ibid., Section 1 C.
21. Ibid., Section 1 C.
22. Ibid., Section 2 A.
23. Ibid., Section 7 A.
24. Sonia Alda Mejías, "La Alianza del Pueblo y las Fuerzas Armadas en el proyecto de transformación social de Evo Morales," Instituto Universitario Gutiérrez Mellado, January 17, 2007, 2.
25. Ibid. See also Andean Information Network, "The Bolivian Armed Forces' Growing Mission," Center for International Policy's Colombia Program, June 1, 2008, www.cipcol.org/?p=608.
26. Hans Hansen, "Nuevo lema militar y la relación con Chile marcarán el 'Día del Mar' boliviano," *El Mostrador.mundo*, March 22, 2010, http://www.elmostrador.cl/noticias/mundo/2010/03/22/nuevo-lema-militar-y-la-relacion-con-chile-marcaran-el-dia-del-mar-boliviano/.
27. Simon Romero, "Amid Growing Unrest, Bolivia Orders U.S. Ambassador to Leave," *New York Times*, September 10, 2008, http://www.nytimes.com/2008/09/11/world/americas/11bolivia.html?_r=1&.
28. Morales's speech to the Latin American and Caribbean Community of States (CELAC) took place in December 2011. Also see Luis Fleischman, "The Meaning and Implications of the Latin American–Caribbean Summit,"

The Americas Report, December 20, 2011, http://www.theamericasreport.com/2011/12/20/the-meaning-and-implications-of-the-latin-american-caribbean-summitt/.

29. Nicole Ferrand, "Ecuador's Democracy at Risk," *The Americas Report*, May 3, 2007, http://www.theamericasreport.com/2007/05/03/ecuadors-democracy-at-risk/.

30. Luis Fleischman, "Chávez's Repression Continues," *The Americas Report*, October 10, 2008, http://www.theamericasreport.com/2008/10/10/Chávezs-repression-continues/.

31. Constitución de la República del Ecuador, Capitulo Segundo, sección primera.

32. Ibid.

33. Conaghan, "Ecuador," 260–82.

34. Article 144 of the Ecuadorian Constitution, quoted in Rouquie, *A la Sombra de las Dictaduras*, 227.

35. Constitución de la República del Ecuador, Capítulo Quinto, Artículo 313.

36. "ICSID in Crisis: Straight-jacket or Investment Protection?," News, Bretton Woods Project, July 10, 2009.

37. Douglas Farah and Glenn Simpson, "Ecuador at Risk: Drugs, Thugs, Guerrillas, and the Citizens Revolution" (Alexandria, VA: International Assessment and Strategic Center, January 24, 2009).

38. Luis Fleischman, "Is Ecuador Lawsuit against Chevron 'Messianic Justice'?," *The Americas Report*, September 11, 2009, http://www.theamericasreport.com/2009/09/11/is-ecuadors-lawsuit-against-chevron-messianic-justice/.

39. Brent Kendall, "High Court Rejects Chevron Challenge in Ecuador Case," *Wall Street Journal*, October 9, 2012, http://online.wsj.com/article/SB10000872396390443982904578046393789075594.html.

40. U.S. Department of State, "2009 Human Rights Report: Ecuador," March 11, 2010, www.state.gov/g/drl/rls/hrrpt/2009/wha/136111.htm.

41. Ibid.

42. "Ecuador: El supuesto golpe de estado, la democracia y las organización indígenas," *kaosenlared.net*, October 6, 2010, www.kaosenlared.net/noticia/ecuador-supuesto-golpe-estado-democracia-organizaciones-indigenas.

43. Pablo Dávalos, "Alianza País: De la teoría de la conspiración a la real politik," *Alainet.org*, October 4, 2010, http://alainet.org/active/41384&lang=es.

44. Alonso Soto, "Ecuador Military Crisis to Test Correa's Mettle," Reuters, April 10, 2008.

45. "After re-election, Correa wants big legislative win," Agence France Press, February 18, 2013, http://www.globalpost.com/dispatch/news/afp/130218/after-re-election-correa-wants-big-legislative-win-0.

46. "Nicaragua: How to Steal an Election," *The Economist*, November 13, 2008, http://www.economist.com/node/12607338.

47. Ibid.

48. Luis Fleischman, "Nicaraguan Election, Venezuelan Fraud," *The Americas Report*, November 20, 2008, http://www.centerforsecuritypolicy.org/p17802 .xml?genre_id=5.

49. Edmundo Jarkin, "Sobre el Futuro Democratico en America Latina," *La Democracia en America Latina,* The Democracy Papers No. 2, Interamerican Institute For Democracy, February 2010, 35–56.

50. C. Blake Schmidt, "In Nicaragua, Opposition Sees an End Run," *New York Times*, November 15, 2009.

51. Javier Hernandez, "Nicaragua Is Poised to Re-elect Ortega," *New York Times*, November 6, 2011, http://www.nytimes.com/2011/11/07/world/ americas/president-daniel-ortega-poised-to-win-third-term-in-nicaragua .html?_r=1&ref=danielortega.

52. "Editorials: Electoral Transparency Needed in Nicaragua," Voice of America, November 14, 2011, http://editorials.voa.gov/content/electoral-transparency --133814478/1482821.html.

53. Richard Feinberg, "Daniel Ortega and Nicaragua's Soft Authoritarianism: The Story of the Sandinista Survivor," *Foreign Affairs*, November 2, 2011, http://www.foreignaffairs.com/features/letters-from/daniel-ortega-and -nicaraguas-soft-auhoritarianim.

54. Rocio San Miguel quoted in Romero, "Venezuela's Military Ties."

55. Marifelli Pérez Stable, deputy director of the Interamerican Dialogue, as cited in Carlos Chirinos, "Venezuela y Cuba como referencia" BBC Mundo, June 29, 2005, http://news.bbc.co.uk/hi/spanish/latin_america/newsid_4636000 /4636005.stm.

56. Alternativa Bolivarian para los Pueblos de Nuestra América at http://www .alianzabolivariana.org/modules.php?name=Content&pa=showpage&pid =2080.

57. Ibid.

58. Ibid.

59. Ibid.

60. Ibid.

61. Joel Hirst, "A Guide to ALBA," *Americas Quarterly*, http://www.americas quarterly.org/hirst/article.

62. Ali Rodríguez, *Petroamérica vs. ALCA* (Buenos Aires: Capital Intelectual S.A., 2004), 13. See also http://www.petrocaribe.org/.

63. These are the words of PDVSA president Rafael Ramirez, quoted in Blixen, *Chávez*, 88.

64. Venezuelan Government, "Presidente Chávez: Sólo unidos podemos salir del atraso y la miseria," press reléase, December 17, 2005.

65. "Antonini Wilson confirmó que dinero de la maleta salió de PDVSA e iba para la campaña de Cristina Kirchner," *Globovision*, March 11, 2008, http://globovision.com/articulo/antonini-wilson-confirmo-que-dinero-de-la -maleta-salio-de-pdvsa-e-iba-para-la-campana-de-cristina-kirchner-2.

66. Rouquie, *A la Sombra de las Dictaduras*, 89.

67. "Zelaya enfrenta denuncias por propuesta de reforma constitucional," Diario las Américas, May 16, 2009, http://www.diariolasamericas.com noticia/ 78147/pda.

68. Kathleen Bruhn, "The Evolution of the Mexican Left," in Castañeda and Morales, *Leftovers*, 223–24.

69. Robert Kozack, "Venezuela Contributed to Peru Humala's 2006 Campaign— Report," *Wall Street Journal*, May 12, 2011.

70. Nicole Ferrand, "Chávez Moves into Peru," *The Americas Report*, April 7, 2008.

71. Matthew Walter, "Chávez's Military Plan in Bolivia Cost Him UN Support (Update 1)," Bloomberg News, October 13, 2006, http://www.bloomberg.com /apps/news?pid=newsarchive&sid=at2Zb4U71pH8&refer=latin_america.

4. THE EMERGENCE OF INDIGENOUS AND NEW GRASSROOTS MOVEMENTS IN LATIN AMERICA

1. Jorge Dandler, "Indigenous People and the Rule of Law in Latin America: Do They Have a Chance?," in *The (Un)Rule of Law: The Underprivileged in Latin America*, ed. Juan Mendez, Guillermo O'Donnell, and Paulo Sergio Pinheiro (University of Notre Dame Press, 1999), 146.

2. Isaacs, "Ecuador," 47.

3. Ibid.

4. Felipe Quispe Huanca, "We Want To Govern Ourselves," IV *Online Magazine*, IV331, May 3, 2001, http://www.internationalviewpoint.org/spip.php? article658.

5. Enrique Vera, "Ollanta Humala selló pacto político con partidos de izquierda radical cuyo nombre será Gana Perú," *El Comercio*, December 16, 2010, http:// elcomercio.pe/politica/685344/noticia-ollanta-humala-sello-pacto-politico -partidos-izquierda-radical-cuyo-nombre-gana-peru.

6. Jaime Cordero, "Humala opta por la vía polítca de Lula," *El País*, July 21, 2011, http://internacional.elpais.com/internacional/2011/07/21/actualidad/ 1311199204_850215.html.

7. Feliciano Gutiérrez, "Ex reclusos etnocaceristas anuncian protestas contra gobierno de Humala," *La Republica*, April 10, 2012, http://www.larepublica

.pe/10-04-2012/ex-reclusos-etnocaceristas-anuncian-protestas-contra
-gobierno-de-humala.

8. "Humala acepta diálogo tras 5 muertos y 40 días de paro por proyecto Conga,"
   Hoy.com.ec, July 12, 2012, http://www.hoy.com.ec/noticias-ecuador/humala
   -acepta-dialogo-tras-5-muertos-y-40-dias-de-paro-por-proyecto-conga
   -555260.html.

9. Andrés Benavente Urbina and Julio Alberto Cirino, *La democracia defraudada: populismo revolucionario en América Latina* (Buenos Aires: Grito
   Sagrado, 2005), 255–59.

10. Ibid., 267.

11. Ibid., 269.

12. To clarify this point Antonio Gramsci distinguishes civil society and the state
    as two dimensions of hegemony. According to Gramsci's view, the dominant
    class exercises direct domination through the administrative and juridical
    state apparatuses and cultural domination through civil society. The latter
    consists of the "spontaneous" consent "given by the great masses of the pop-
    ulation to the general direction imposed by on social life by the dominant
    fundamental group." This group gains prestige through its position in the
    productive apparatus and by the acceptance of the supremacy of its values. In
    other words, those values penetrate the individual's mind at the level of prej-
    udice and instinctual reaction. Gramsci points out, "A social group can and
    must exercise leadership before winning government power." See Antonio
    Gramsci, *Selections from Prison Notebooks* (New York: International Publish-
    ers, 1985), 12 and 56. The idea of the Brazilian landless movement under the
    influence of Gramsci's writings is precisely that this social dominant group
    first dominates the minds of the people.

13. Urbina and Cirino, *democracia defraudada*, 270.

14. Ibid., 299.

15. Urbina and Cirino, *democracia defraudada*, 299–328.

16. Gramsci, *Selections from Prison Notebooks*, 18.

17. Dandler, "Indigenous People and the Rule of Law," 127–36.

18. Alexis de Tocqueville, *The Old Regime and the French Revolution* (New York:
    Anchor Books, Doubleday, 1955), 119.

19. Leonardo Curzio, "La transicion a la democracia y la construccion de la ciu-
    dadania en Mexico," in *La Democracia en America Latina, un Barco a la deriva*,
    ed. Waldo Ansaldi (Buenos Aires: Fondo de Cultura Economica, 2007), 315.

20. I consulted www.congresobolivariano.org. This website is no longer active
    as the organization has been integrated in the Bolivarian Continental Move-
    ment, whose website is www.conbolivar.org. I retrieved much of the informa-
    tion before the previous website was deactivated.

21. Ibid.

22. Ibid.

23. Maria Kienast, "En Argentina el mercado es el chivo expiatorio," Cato.org, December 14, 2005, http://www.elcato.org/publicaciones/articulos/art-2005 -12-14.html.

24. See Quebracho's website, http://www.quebracho.org.ar/.

25. Ely Karmon, "Hezbollah America Latina: Strange Group or Real Threat?," Institute for Counter-Terrorism, November 14, 2006, http://www.freerepublic .com/focus/f-news/1773483/posts.

26. Ibid.

27. http://www.quebracho.org.ar/.

28. Ramy Wurgat, "Quebracho, los encapuchados que siembran Buenos Aires de violencia," El Mundo.es, April 4, 2010, http://www.elmundo.es/america/ 2010/03/31/argentina/1269987797.html.

29. Mauricio Caminos, "Quebracho negó participar de los incidentes frente a la embajada británica," *La Nacion*, April 3, 2012.

30. http://www.quebracho.org.ar/.

31. Daniel Gallo, "Controvertida agenda Política del embajador de Venezuela," *La Nacion*, November 16, 2006.

32. Karmon, "Hezbollah America Latina."

33. "Kirchner y Piqueteros tenian un 'matrimonio por conveniencia,'" *Perfil.com*, February 12, 2011.

34. "D'Elia Admits He Met AMIA Attack Suspect," *Buenos Aires Herald*, March 8, 2010.

35. Nicole Ferrand, "Chávez's Dangerous Intervention in Peru," *The Americas Report*, July 30, 2007.

36. Reported in *Diario Expreso* on July 24, 2007, and quoted in Ferrand, "Chávez's Dangerous Intervention."

37. "ALBA tiene aspiraciones de llegar al poder," *La Republica*, July 8, 2007, http:// www.larepublica.pe/08-07-2007/alba-tiene-aspiraciones-de-llegar-al-poder.

38. Nicole Ferrand, "Chávez Moves into Peru," *The Americas Report*, April 7, 2008, http://www.centerforsecuritypolicy.org/2008/04/07/Chávez-moves-into -peru-2/.

39. Patrick McDonnell, "In Peru's High Plains, Chávez Is Exalted," *Los Angeles Times*, March 9, 2008.

40. Confederación de Nacionalidades Indígenas del Ecuador, "Resoluciones del III Congreso de las Nacionalidades y Pueblos del Ecuador," CONAIE .org, January 2008, http://www.conaie.org/congresos-de-la-conaie/iii-congreso -de-la-conaie/90-resoluciones-del-iii-congreso-de-las-nacionalidades-y- pueblos-del-ecuador-.

41. See Friends of the MST (website), www.mstbrazil.org/.

42. Felix Sanchez, Joao Machado Borges Neto, and Rosa Maria Marquez, "Lula's Government: A Critical Appraisal," in Barrett, Chávez, and Rodriguez-Garavito, *New American Left*, 44.

43. "Resistência líbia cria agência de notícias alternativa: Iniciativa fortalece a batalha midiática contra o bombardeio desinformativo da OTAN," CUT (Central Unica Dos Trabalhadores) Brasil, September 19, 2011, http://www.cut.org.br/destaque-central/46073/resistencia-libia-cria-agencia-de-noticias-alternativa.

44. Érika Hernández, "Respaldan PRD y PT a Chávez," Medias Mexico, July 25, 2012, http://mediosenmexico.blogspot.com/2012/07/respaldan-prd-y-pt-chavez.html.

45. Bruhn, "The Evolution of the American Left," in Castañeda and Morales, *Leftovers*, 231–28.

46. Ibid., 223–24.

47. "Entrevista con Fernando Bossi, Secretario de Organization del Congreso Bolivariano de los Pueblos," Noticias Bolivarianas, January 17, 2008, http://vulcano.wordpress.com/2008/01/17/entrevista-con-fernando-bossi-secretario-de-organizacion-del-congreso-bolivariano-de-los-pueblos/#more-2633.

48. "Declaracion al pie del tata imbambura y mama cotacachi, los pueblos y nacionalidades indigenas del Ecuador frente a la cumbre de los presidentes del ALBA-TCP con "Autoridades Indigeneas y Afro-Descendientes," June 25, 2010, http://ebookbrowse.com/conaie-ante-cumbre-del-alba-pdf-d142719706.

5. CHÁVEZ'S DANGEROUS LIAISONS
WITH GUERRILLAS AND DRUG CARTELS

1. Manwaring, "Venezuela's Hugo Chávez," 9.

2. Ibid., 16. Francisco Gutierrez Sanin, "Criminal Rebels? A Discussion of Civil War and Criminality from the Colombia Experience," *Politics & Society* 32 (2004): 257–85.

3. Che Guevara, Brian Loveman, and Thomas M. Davies, Jr., *Guerrilla Warfare*, 3d ed. (Wilmington, DE: Scholarly Resources Books, 1997), 253–62.

4. John Hartlyn and Jonathan Dugas, "Colombia: The Politics of Violence and Democratic Transformation," in *Democracy in Developing Countries: Latin America*, ed. Larry Diamond, Juan J. Linz, and Seymour Martin Lipset (Boulder, CO: Lynne Rienner Publishers, 1999), 279.

5. Guevara et al., *Guerrilla Warfare*.

6. Hartlyn and Dugas, "Colombia," 279.

7. Jorge Salcedo, "What I saw inside the Cali drug cartel," CNN, January 18, 2012, http://www.cnn.com/2012/01/18/opinion/salcedo-first-person-account-drug-corruption.

8. Sam Dillon, "Colombian President Is Charged with Fraud," *New York Times*, February 15, 1996, http://www.nytimes.com/1996/02/15/world/colombian president-is-charged-with-fraud.html.

9. Sandra Viviana Giraldo, "Decisionismo y Democracia: La Amenaza de crisis bajo el gobierno de Ernesto Samper," *Revista de Ciencia Política* no. 13 (August 2011), http://www.revcienciapolitica.com.ar/num13art6.php.

10. Reid, *Forgotten Continent*, 255.

11. Ibid., 258–59.

12. Hartlyn and Dugas, "Colombia," 283.

13. Reid, *Forgotten Continent*, 260.

14. Ibid., 261.

15. U.S. Government Accountability Office, "Drug Control: U.S. Counternarcotics Cooperation with Venezuela Has Declined," July 20, 2009, http://www.gao.gov/assets/300/292722.pdf.

16. Ibid., 5.

17. Ibid., 7.

18. Ibid., 9–11.

19. Ibid., 12.

20. Ibid.

21. International Institute of Strategic Studies (IISS), *The FARC Files: Venezuela, Ecuador, and the Secret Archives of "Raúl Reyes"* (London: IISS, 2011), 148.

22. Ibid., 60.

23. "Chávez: Take FARC off terror list," CNN, January 11, 2008, http://www.cnn.com/2008/WORLD/americas/01/11/Chávez.farc/.

24. IISS, *The FARC Files*, 90–95.

25. Ibid., 90.

26. Ibid., 215.

27. Ibid., 138.

28. Adrian Alsema, "FARC Admit Financing Presidential Campaign of Rafael Correa," Colombia Reports, July 17, 2009, http://colombiareports.com/colombia-news/news/5050-farc-admit-financing-presidential-campaign-of-rafael-correa.html.

29. IISS, *The FARC Files*, 192.

30. Farah and Simpson, "Ecuador at Risk," 28–30; and see IISS, *The FARC Files*, chapter 7.

31. Ibid., 30–34.

32. Douglas Farah quoted in Norman Bailey, Nancy Menges, and Brian Bilbray, *Malign Neglect: Misguided U.S. Foreign Policy in Latin America* (Washington, DC: Menges Hemispheric Security Project, Center for Security Policy Press, 2011), 40.

33. IISS, *The FARC Files*, 164.

34. Douglas Farah, "Into the Abyss: Bolivia Under Evo Morales and the Mas," International Assesment and Strategy Center, June 2009, http://www.strategy center.net/docLib/20090618_IASCIntoTheAbyss061709.pdf, 25–27.

35. Douglas Farah, "The FARC's International Relations: A Network of Deception," NEFA Foundation, September 22, 2008, http://www.nefafoundation .org/miscellaneous/FeaturedDocs/nefafarcirnetworkdeception0908.pdf.

36. "Conclusiones del II Congreso de la Coordinadora Continental Bolivariana," Aporrea.org, February 29, 2008, http://www.aporrea.org/tiburon/n109960 .html.

37. IISS, The Reyes Files, 106.

38. Ibid.

39. "La Coorinadora Continental Bolivariana no es una Organizacion Clandestina, es un Movimiento Politico-social Publico/Entrevista a Carlos Casanueva," Mariátegui (blog), July 2009, http://mariategui.blogspot.com/2009/07/ la-coordinadora-continental-Institutebolivariana.html.

40. "Saludo de las FARC-EP, Marzo de 2012," YouTube.com, http://www .youtube.com/watch?feature=player_embedded&v=g9Gbk_RCopM#!.

41. Douglas Farah, "Venezuela Hosts Terrorist Central in Caracas," December 8, 2008, http://www.douglasfarah.com/article/517/venezuela-hosts-terrorist -central-in-caracas.

42. Coordinadora Continental Bolivariana, "Declaración Bolivariana de Caracas," *Noticias de la Rebelion,* December 17, 2009, http://www.noticiasdela rebelion.info/?p=4931.

43. "The World of the FARC (Part II: America)," Semana, January 6, 2009.

44. "Fluidos Contactos con las FARC antes del Secuestro de Cecilia Cubas," ABC Color, Asunción, September 15, 2009.

45. Hanna Stone, "Paraguay's EPP: Phantom or Rebel Army?," InSightCrime.org, May 2, 2011, http://insightcrime.org/insight-latest-news/item/852-paraguays -epp-phantom-or-rebel-army.

46. "World of the FARC"; and ibid.

47. Nigel Inkster, "Los Archivos de las FARC: Venezuela, Ecuador y el archivo secreto de 'Raúl Reyes,'" director of Transnational Threats and Political Risk, IISS, May 10, 2011.

48. "Bolivia Drug Makers Speed Ahead," *Die Welt*, March 11, 2009, http://www .welt.de/english-news/article3359104/Bolivias-drug-makers-speed-ahead .html.

49. Martin Arostegui, "Former Bolivia Anti-Drug Chief Sentenced to 15 Years," *Wall Street Journal,* September 23, 2011.

50. Samuel Rubenfeld, "Nicaragua Government Took Bribes from Drug Traffickers, Cable Says," *Wall Street Journal,* December 13, 2010.

51. Ricardo Ravelo, *Herencia Maldita: El Reto de Calderón y el Nuevo Mapa del Narcotráfico* (Chapultepec Morales, Mexico: Grijalbo, 2007).

52. Ibid., chapters 2 and 7.

53. Max Weber, "Politics as a Vocation," in *From Max Weber: Essays in Sociology*, ed. and trans. H. H. Gerth and C. Wright Mills (New York: Oxford University Press, 1946), 78.

54. "Memorandum to the Secretary of State: Major Drug Transit or Major Illicit Drug Producing Countries for Fiscal Year 2009," September 16, 2008, http://www.state.gov/j/inl/rls/rpt/109777.htm.

55. "Guatemalan Drug Traffickers Flaunt Local Support," *Reuters*, August 6, 2009.

56. Steven Boraz, "Case Study: The Guatemala-Chiapas Border," in *Ungoverned Territories: Understanding and Reducing Terrorism Risks*, ed. Angel Rabasa et al. (Santa Monica, CA: Rand Corporation, 2007), 277; and Sgt. Lou Savelli, "Gangs and Terrorists Together in the Streets of America!," SRA International, n.d., http://www.gangsacrossamerica.com/gangs_and_terrorists.php.

57. Boraz, "Case Study," 281.

58. Ibid., 282.

59. Ibid., 286–87.

60. Savelli, "Gangs and Terrorists Together."

61. Boraz, "Case Study," 289.

62. Simon Romero, "Cocaine Trade Helps Rebels Reignite War in Peru," *New York Times*, March 17, 2009.

63. "Drug Trafficking Grows in Peru, Newspaper Says," *Latin American Herald Tribune*, January 23, 2010.

64. Arthur Brice, "Dominican Leader Keeps Up Crackdown on Corruption," CNN, March 3, 2009.

65. Manwaring, "Venezuela's Hugo Chávez," 22.

66. Ibid., 23.

6. THE BOLIVARIAN REVOLUTION'S LINKS TO IRAN AND HEZBOLLAH

1. John Williams Hoyt, "Cuba: Havana's Military Machine," *The Atlantic*, August 1988.

2. Eugene Pons, "Castro and Terrorism: A Chronology, 1959–1967," Institute of Cuban & Cuban-American Studies, September 2001.

3. Ibid.

4. Bruce Hoffman, *The PLO and Israel in Central America: The Geopolitical Dimension*, (Santa Monica, CA: Rand Corporation, 1988), 4, http://www.rand.org/content/dam/rand/pubs/notes/2009/N2685.pdf.

5. Ibid., 5.

6. Eileen Scully, "The PLO's Growing Latin American Base," Backgrounder (Washington, DC: Heritage Foundation, August 2, 1983).

7. Hoffman, *PLO and Israel,* 7.
8. Bill Varner and Blake Schmidt, "Former Nicaragua Sandinista Leader Named Libya's UN Envoy," Bloomberg News, March 31, 2011, www.bloomberg .com/news/2011-03-30/former-nicaragua-sandinista-minister-named-libya -s-un-envoy.html.
9. Arturo Wallace, "Los Vínculos de la Libia de Gadafi con las guerrillas de América Latina," *BBC Mundo,* May 25, 2011, www.semana.com/mundo/ vinculos-libia-gadafi-guerrillas-america-latina/157321-3.aspx.
10. See Cristina Zuker, ed., *El Tren de la Victoria* (Buenos Aires: Editorial Sudamericana, 2003); Marcelo Larraquy and Roberto Caballero, *Galimberti: De Perón a Susana, de Montoneros a la CIA* (Buenos Aires: Grupo Editorial Norma, 2000); and Rodolfo Walsh, "La Revolución Palestina," in *El Violento Oficio de Escribir: Obra Periodística, 1953–1977,* ed. Rodolfo Walsh (Buenos Aires: Planeta, 1995), 373–406.
11. Comité de Solidaridad con la Causa Arabe, "La XI Reunión del Foro de Sao Paulo muestra su Oposición a la Guerra contra Iraq y su solidaridad con el Pueblo Palestino," December 5, 2002, www.nodo50org/csca.
12. Nadim Lacki, "Venezuelan President Meets Saddam Hussein," August 1, 2000, http://abcnews.go.com/International/story?id=82924&page=1#.T4mg ZHM2qrA.
13. Schoen and Rowan, *Threat Closer to Home,* 105.
14. NewsMax, "Chávez: A New Danger to America," September 21, 2001, http://archive.newsmax.com/archives/articles/2001/9/24/191722.shtml; and Schoen and Rowan, *Threat Closer to Home,* 105.
15. Nasser Karimi, "Hugo Chávez Receives Iran's Highest Honor," *Washington Post,* July 30, 2006, www.washingtonpost.com/wp-dyn/content/article /2006/07/30/AR2006073001026.html.
16. Ely Karmon, *Iran and Its Proxy Hezbollah: Strategic Penetration in Latin America* (Madrid: Real Instituto Elcano, 2009), 2–3.
17. Norman Bailey, "Iranian Penetration in the Western Hemisphere through Venezuela," paper presented at Center for Hemispheric Policy, University of Miami, Miami, 2009. See also Robert Morgenthau, "The Emergent Axis between Iran and Venezuela," *Wall Street Journal,* September 8, 2009.
18. Andrew Quinn and Frank Jack Daniel, "U.S. Sanctions Venezuelan Oil Giant for Iran Trade," Reuters, May 24, 2011, http://www.reuters.com /article/2011/05/24/us-iran-usa-sanctions-idUSTRE74N47R20110524.
19. Elodie Brune, "Iran's Place in Venezuelan Foreign Policy," in *Iran in Latin America: Threat or "Axis of Annoyance"?,* ed. Cynthia Arnson, Halch Esfandiari, and Adam Stubits (Washington, DC: Woodrow Wilson Center, 2009), 38.
20. Karmon, *Iran and Its Proxy Hezbollah,* 5–6.

21. Ilan Berman, "Iran Woos Bolivia for Influence in Latin America," *Daily Beast*, May 20, 2012, http://www.thedailybeast.com/articles/2012/05/20/iran-woos-bolivia-for-influence-in-latin-america.html.

22. "Iran launches Spanish TV channel," Associated Press, January 31, 2012, http://www.guardian.co.uk/world/2012/jan/31/iran-launches-spanish-tv-channel.

23. Berman, "Iran Woos Bolivia."

24. Gustavo Fernandez, "Bolivian Foreign Policy: Observations on the Bolivia-Iran Relationship," in Arnson et al., *Iran in Latin America*, 94.

25. Ibid., 95.

26. Karmon, *Iran and Its Proxy Hezbollah*, 6–7.

27. Javier Melendez and Felix Maradiaga, "Iranian-Nicaraguan Relations under the Sandinista Government: Rhetoric or Anti-Establishment Foreign Policy?," in Arnson et al., *Iran in Latin America*, 65–82.

28. Karmon, *Iran and Its Proxy Hezbollah*, 7–8.

29. Cesar Montufar, "Recent Diplomatic Developments between Ecuador and Iran: A Gesture of Sovereign Affirmation or Lukewarm Geopolitical Alignment?," in Arnson et al., *Iran in Latin America*, 101–14.

30. "Iran signs nuclear fuel-swap deal with Turkey," BBC News, May 17, 2010, http://news.bbc.co.uk/2/hi/8685846.stm.

31. Aylin Gürzel, "Turkey's Role in Defusing the Iranian Nuclear Issue," *The Washington Quarterly* 35 no. 3 (Summer 2012): 142.

32. Jorge Castañeda, "Not Ready for Prime Time," *Foreign Affairs*, no. 3 (September/October 2010): 112.

33. "Irán Fortalece Relacion con Uruguay: Relaciones enriquecidas, como el uranio," Montevideo.com, January 18, 2011, http://www.montevideo.com.uy/notnoticias_129191_1.html.

34. "Sanctions in Iran Force Uruguay to Propose Teheran Rice for Oil Barter Deal," Mercopress, April 1, 2012, http://en.mercopress.com/2012/04/01/sanctions-on-iran-force-uruguay-to-propose-teheran-rice-for-oil-barter-deal.

35. "Iran Daily: Latin American Trade on the Rise," Latin Business Chronicle, December 7, 2009, http://www.latinbusinesschronicle.com/app/article.aspx?id=3855.

36. "Iran's annual trade with Latin America stands at $945m," *Tehran Times*, August 26, 2012, http://tehrantimes.com/economy-and-business/100806-irans-annual-trade-with-latin-america-stands-at-945m.

37. The full text of the memorandum can be found in Spanish at "Argentina: Preocupante memorandum de entendimiento entre el régimen de Cristina Fernández de Kirchner y el de Irán—Urgente24," February 12, 2013, http://www.hacer.org/latam/?p=24151.

38. "Irán niega la indagatoria de su ministro de Defensa por la justicia argentina," AFP, February 12, 2013, http://www.afp.com/es/node/824692.

39. "Salehi: Iran, Argentina adhere to agreement on AMIA case," Islamic Republic News Agency, February 12, 2013, http://www.irna.ir/en/News/80541859 /Politic/Salehi__Iran,_Argentina_adhere_to_agreement_on_AMIA_case.

40. "Una Provocación Chévere hacia Bush con Amenaza Diplomática . . . y Nuclear," *Página 12*, May 23, 2005.

41. See "Declaración Conjunta Venezuela-Irán," *El Nacional*, Caracas, March 15, 2005.

42. Kelly Hearn, "Iranian Pact with Venezuela Stokes Fears of Uranium Sales," *Washington Times*, March 13, 2006. See also Oscar Medina, "Ajedrez Nuclear," *El Universal*, March 19, 2006.

43. Associated Press, "Iran Presta Apoyo para Detectar Reservas de Uranio en Venezuela," Informe21.com, September 25, 2009.

44. Simon Romero, "Venezuela Says Iran Is Helping It Look for Uranium," *New York Times*, September 25, 2009.

45. Robert M. Morgenthau, "The Emerging Axis of Iran and Venezuela," *Wall Street Journal*, September 8, 2009, http://online.wsj.com/article/SB1000142 4052970203440104574400792835972018.html.

46. Roger Noriega, "Hugo Chávez's Criminal, Nuclear Network: A Grave and Growing Threat," American Enterprise Institute Online, October 14, 2009.

47. Romero, "Venezuela Says Iran Is Helping."

48. Douglas Farah, "Hezbollah in Latin America: Implications for U.S. Security," Testimony Before the House Committee on Homeland Security, July 7, 2011, 16.

49. Linda Robinson, "Terror Close to Home in Venezuela, a Volatile Leader Befriends Mideast, Colombia and Vuba," *U.S. News & World Report*, October 6, 2003; and Otto Reich and Ezequiel Vazquez, "How Ecuador's Immigration Policy Helps Al Qaeda," *Foreign Policy*, April 2, 2012.

50. Reich and Vazquez, "How Ecuador's Immigration Policy."

51. Dore Gold, *The Rise of a Nuclear Iran: How Tehran Defies the West* (Washington, DC: Regnery Publishing, 2009), 281.

52. Farah, "Hezbollah in Latin America," Testimony, 2.

53. "H.R. 4119 (112th): The Border Tunnel Prevention Act of 2012," http:// www.govtrack.us/congress/bills/112/hr4119/text.

54. Jesus J. Esquivel, "Mexican Drug Cartels and Islamic Radicals Working Together," July 14, 2008, http://mexidata.info/id1903.html.

55. Jon B. Perduc, *The War of All the People: The Nexus of Latin American Radicalism and Middle East Terrorism* (Washington, DC: Potomac Books, 2012), 186.

56. Testimony of Douglas Farah, 3.
57. Schoen and Rowan, *Threat Closer to Home*, 138.
58. Bill Roggio, "US designates two Hezbollah operatives in Venezuela as terrorists," *Long War Journal*, June 19, 2008, http://www.longwarjournal.org /archives/2008/06/us_designates_two_he.php.
59. "Treasury Targets Hizballah in Venezuela," U.S. Department of Treasury, June 18, 2008, http://www.treasury.gov/press-center/press-releases/Pages/hp1036 .aspx.
60. Schoen and Rowan, *Threat Closer to Home*, 126.
61. Roger Noriega, "Iran's Gambit in Latin America," *Commentary*, February 2012.
62. http:/groups.msn/AutonomiaIslamicaWayuu.
63. Karmon, *Iran and Its Proxy Hezbollah*.
64. Ely Karmon, "Hezbollah America Latina."
65. Karmon, *Iran and Its Proxy Hezbollah*, 22.
66. Ibid. 26–27.
67. Isaac Caro, "Conflicto y Pacificación en las relaciones entre las comunidades judías, árabes y musulmanas en Argentina y Chile," *Revista Encrucijada Americana*, 2, no. 1 (Fall–Winter 2008): 42–46.
68. "Amia: Su verdadera cara—Comunicado de Fearab Argentina," Prensa Islámica, December 21, 2010, http://www.prensaislamica.com/nota5985.html.
69. "Cruces entre el secretario de la FEARAB y el PRO," El Mensajerodiario .com, October 6, 2010, http://www.elmensajerodiario.com.ar/contenidos/ cruces-secretario-fearab-pro_1327.html.
70. Caro, "Conflicto y Pacificación," 50–51.
71. Perdue, *War of All the People*, 195.
72. "Venezuela's Chávez denies Iran-Syria weapons connection," AFP, December 23, 2008, http://www.google.com/hostednews/afp/article/ALeqM5jS Wad0K6HzuMtwp7IhR0AnHtoXyg.
73. Bill Gertz, "Iran Boosts Qods Shock Troops in Venezuela," *Washington Times*, April 21, 2010.
74. Ernest Fraenkel, *The Dual State: A Contribution to the Theory of Dictatorship* (New York: Octagon Books, 1969).
75. Farah, "Into the Abyss."
76. Ibid., 12.
77. Gold, *Rise of a Nuclear Iran*, 294–95.
78. Michael Ledeen, *The Iranian Time Bomb: The Mullah Zealots' Quest for Destruction* (New York: St. Martin's Press, 2007), 248–57.
79. General Fraser said these words on May 6, 2011, at the JW Marriott Hotel in Miami, during the Sixth Annual Latin American Conference, organized by the University of Miami-based Center for Hemispheric Policy.

Luis Fleischman, "Taking Iran's Missiles in Venezuela Seriously," *The Americas Report*, May 26, 2011, http://www.theamericasreport.com/2011/05/26/taking-irans-missiles-in-venezuela-seriously/.

80. Stephen Johnson, "Ahmadinejad in the Americas: What Is Iran Up To?," Center for Strategic & International Studies, January 3, 2012, http://csis.org/publication/ahmadinejad-americas-what-iran. The Congressional Research Service account is quoted in Noriega, "Iran's Gambit."

7. THE ROLES OF CHINA AND RUSSIA

1. Ministry of Foreign Affairs of the People's Republic of China, "China's Policy Paper on Latin America and the Caribbearn," www.chinaview.com, May 11, 2008, section 2, http://www.fmprc.gov.cn/eng/zxxx/t521025.htm.

2. Edward Friedman, "China's Challenge, Latin America's Opportunities," Center for Hemispheric Policy: Challenges to Security in the Hemisphere Task Force, December 1, 2009.

3. Andrew Erickson and Lyle J. Goldstein, "China Studies the Rise of Great Powers," in *China Goes to Sea: Maritime Transformation in Comparative Historical Perspective*, ed. Andrew S. Erickson, Lyle J. Goldstein, and Carnes Lord (Annapolis, MD: Naval Institute Press, 2009), 401–25.

4. Ibid.

5. Ibid.

6. Dan Blumenthal, "Testimony Before the Senate Foreign Relations Committee Subcommittee on Asia Hearing on Maritime Territorial Disputes in East Asia," July 2009, 1.

7. Ibid., 2.

8. Under the law of the sea an exclusive economic zone is a sea zone over which a state has special rights over the exploration and use of its marine resources. It stretches from the seaward edge of the state's territorial sea out to two hundred nautical miles from its coast.

9. Ibid., 4.

10. Constantine Menges, *China: The Gathering Threat* (New York: Nelson Current, 2005), 295–96.

11. Ibid., 379.

12. Ibid., 399; and Friedman, "China's Challenge," 2.

13. "China Hits Back at US over Taiwan Weapons Sale," BBC News, January 30, 2010, http://news.bbc.co.uk/2/hi/8488765.stm.

14. Lowell Dittmer, "China's Global Rise," *American Quarterly* 6, no. 1 (2012): 65.

15. Jaime Daremblum, "While Washington Sleeps," *Weekly Standard* 15, no. 18 (January 25, 2010), http://m.weeklystandard.com/articles/while-washington-sleeps.

16. Ibid.

17. Xinhua News Agency, "Chinese VP Predicts Bright Future for China-Venezuela Ties," China.org.cn, February 18, 2009, http://www.china.org.cn /international/2009-02/18/content_17299172.htm.
18. Maria Josefina Arce, "Continuar Profundizando las Relaciones entre Cuba y China," Radio Habana (2012), http://www.radiohc.cu/especiales/comentarios /10328-continuar-en-el-2012-profundizando-las-relaciones-entre-cuba-y -china.html.
19. Susan Kaufman Purcell, "Latin America in 2010: Right, Left, or the Center?," *Sun Sentinel*, December 20, 2009.
20. Lucas Kintto, "Comercio Ecuador: En Busca del Oriente Perdido," Inter-Press Services, November 24, 2007.
21. Jaime Daremblum, "The Chines Dragon Sweeps through Latin America," PJ Media, May 13, 2011, http://pjmedia.com/blog/the-chinese-dragon-sweeps -through-latin-america/.
22. Janie Hulse, "China's Expansion into and U.S. Withdrawal from Argentina's Telecommunications and Space Industries and the Implications for U.S. National Security" (Carlisle, PA: Strategic Studies Institute, September 2007), 2.
23. Ibid., 21.
24. Menges, *China*, 396.
25. Ibid., 397.
26. Ibid.
27. The Rodman Naval Station, http://www.angelfire.com/cantina/que_pasa /Rodman.html.
28. "Advance Questions for Lieutenant General John F. Kelly, USMC Nominee for Commander, United States Southern Command," Armed Services Committee, U.S. Senate, July 20, 2012, 5, http://www.armed-services.senate.gov /statemnt/2012/07%20July/Kelly%2007-19-12.pdf.
29. Menges, *China*, 397.
30. "U.S. Fears Chinese Companies Are Breaking Iran Sanctions," BBC News, October 18, 2010.
31. Leslie Hook, "U.S. Acts against Chinese Oil Trader," CNN, January 18, 2012, http://edition.cnn.com/2012/01/13/business/us-china-iran-oil/index .html.
32. Con Coughlin, "Turkey and China Helping Iran Evade UN Sanctions," *The Telegraph*, February 19, 2012.
33. Elizabeth Economy, "Time for a Strategic Reset," *Americas Quarterly* 6, no. 1 (2012): 55.
34. Menges, *China*, 310.
35. Edward Friedman, "China: A Threat to or Threatened by Democracy?," *Dissent* 56, no. 1 (Winter 2009): 7–12.

36. Ibid.
37. Quoted in ibid. See also Menges, *China*, 368.
38. José de Córdoba, "China-Oil Deal Gives Chávez a Leg Up," *Wall Street Journal*, November 9, 2011.
39. "Putin: Soviet Collapse a 'Genuine Tragedy,'" Associated Press, April 25, 2005.
40. Robert Kagan, *The Return of History and the End of Dreams* (New York: Alfred A. Knopf, 2008), 18–19.
41. Jim Nichol, "Russia-Georgia Conflict in South Ossetia: Context and Implications for U.S.Interests," Congressional Research Service Report for Congress (Washington, DC: Congressional Research Service, September 2008), 27–28.
42. Kagan, *Return of History*, 19.
43. Sebastian Alison and Henry Meyer, "Russia Offers Venezuela's Chávez Weapons, Nuclear Cooperation," Bloomberg News, September 25, 2008.
44. Ibid.
45. Juan Forero, "Venezuela acquires 1,800 antiaircraft missiles from Russia," *Washington Post*, December 11, 2010, http://www.washingtonpost.com/wp-dyn/content/article/2010/12/11/AR2010121102586.html.
46. Vanessa Neumann, "Hugo Chávez's Military Buildup and Iranian Ties," *The Weekly Standard*, October 19, 2010.
47. Sistema Económico Latinoamericano y del Caribe, "Las Relaciones económicas entre la Federación de Rusia y America Latina y el Caribe: Situatión actual y perspectivas" (Caracas: SELA, 2009), 46.
48. Ibid.
49. Timothy Bancroft-Hinchey, "Russia Boosts Relations with Latin America," *Pravda*, April 4, 2010, http://english.pravda.ru/world/americas/05-04-2010/112853-russia_latin_america-0/.
50. Stephen Blank, "Russia and Latin America: Geo-Political Games in the U.S.'s Neighborhood," *Russie.NEI.Visions* 38 (2009): 9.
51. Ibid., 11–16.
52. Neumann, "Hugo Chávez's Military Buildup." See also James Brooke, "Kremlin to Viktor Bout: Game Not Over," Voice of America, April 25, 2012, http://blogs.voanews.com/russia-watch/2012/04/25/kremlin-to-viktor-bout-game-not-over/.
53. "Viktor Bout sentenced to 25 years in prison," Associated Press, April 5, 2012, http://www.guardian.co.uk/world/2012/apr/05/viktor-bout-sentenced-25-years-prison.
54. Stephen Blank, "Russia and Latin America: Motives and Consequences," Center for Hemispheric Policy, University of Miami, April 13, 2010, 10.
55. Ibid., 11–13.

56. Cynthia Watson, "China's Arms Sales to Latin America: Another Arrow in the Quiver," *Intelligence Quarterly*, 2010.

57. Menges, *China*, 394.

58. Kagan, *Return of History*, 32.

59. Phil Stewart, "Venezuela No Military Threat—U.S. Defense Secretary," Reuters, April 13, 2010.

8. REGIONAL AND U.S. REACTIONS TO THE BOLIVARIAN REVOLUTION

1. Heraldo Muñoz, "Towards a Regime for Advancing Democracy in the Americas," in *The Future of Inter-American Affairs*, ed. Jorge Dominguez (New York: Routledge, 2000), 296.

2. Anita Isaacs, "International Assistance for Democracy: A Cautionary Tale," in ibid, 267–69.

3. Simon Romero, "Ecuador's Police Chief Steps Down after an Uprising by Striking Officers," *New York Times*, October 2, 2010.

4. Inter-American Commission on Human Rights Report, "Democracy and Human Rights in Venezuela," December 30, 2009, http://cidh.org/pdf%20 files/VENEZUELA%202009%20ENG.pdf.

5. Jaime Daremblum, "How to Save the OAS," *Real Clear World*, March 24, 2010.

6. Amnesty International, "Venezuela's break with regional human rights court 'an affront to victims,'" September 13, 2012, http://www.amnesty.org/en /news/venezuela-s-break-regional-human-rights-court-affront-victims-2012 -09-12.

7. Maria Anastasia O'Grady, "Ortega Squeezes, the OAS Is Silent," *Wall Street Journal*, July 20, 2010.

8. Article 20 of the OAS Democratic Charter states that in the event of an unconstitutional alteration of the constitutional regime "that seriously impairs the democratic order in a member state, any member state or the Secretary General may request the immediate convocation of the Permanent Council to undertake a collective assessment of the situation and to take such decisions as it deems appropriate." Depending on each situation, the Permanent Council may undertake the necessary diplomatic initiatives, including good offices, to foster the restoration of democracy. If such diplomatic initiatives prove unsuccessful, or if the urgency of the situation so warrants, the Permanent Council shall immediately convene a special session of the General Assembly. The General Assembly will adopt the decisions it deems appropriate, including the undertaking of diplomatic initiatives, in accordance with the Charter of the Organization, international law, and the provisions of this Democratic Charter. The necessary diplomatic initiatives, including good offices, to foster

the restoration of democracy will continue during the process. See Organization of American States, "Inter-American Democratic Charter," September 11, 2001, http://www.oas.org/OASpage/eng/Documents/Democractic_Charter.htm.

9. Roberto Alvarez, "OAS-Insulza Merits New Terms," *Miami Herald*, March 8, 2010.
10. Ibid.
11. Jorge Castañeda, "Where Do We Go from Here?," in Castañeda and Morales, *Leftovers*, 231.
12. Ibid., 235.
13. Ibid.
14. "Cristina felicitó a Chávez: 'Tu victoria también es la nuestra,'" *La Nacion*, October 8, 2012, http://www.lanacion.com.ar/1515396-cristina-felicito-a-Chávez-tu-victoria-tambien-es-la-nuestra (translation mine).
15. Martín Granovsky, "El voto de América latina junto a los venezolanos," Página/12, October 9, 2012, http://www.pagina12.com.ar/diario/elmundo/4-205204-2012-10-09.html (translation mine).
16. Ibid.
17. Ibid.
18. Ibid.
19. "Rousseff teme al boicot del Chávismo en Venezuela," Infobae América, January 2, 2013, http://america.infobae.com/notas/64121-Rousseff-teme-boicot-del-Chávismo-en-Venezuela; and Darío Pignotti, "Dilma quiere blindar el legado chavista," *Pagina/12*, January 6, 2013, http://www.pagina12.com.ar/diario/elmundo/4-211293-2013-01-06.html.
20. Pignotti, "Dilma quiere blindar" (translation mine).
21. See details in Fleischman, "Meaning and Implications."
22. Interview with Dan Fisk, senior director for the Western Hemisphere at the National Security Council during the Bush administration, October 29, 2010, Washington, D.C.
23. "Drugs and Democracy: Toward a Paradigm Shift," report presented by former president of Brazil Fernando Henrique Cardoso, former president of Colombia César Gaviria, and former president of Mexico Ernesto Zedillo, Latin Commission on Drugs and Democracy, February 2009, www.drogasedemocracia.org/Arquivos/declaracao_ingles_site.pdf.
24. Luis Andres Henao, "Latin America Rejects Old U.S. Approach in Drugs War," Reuters, January 29, 2010, http://www.reuters.com/article/2010/01/29/us-drugs-latinamerica-idUSTRE60S4MD20100129.
25. "Unasur acuerda crear mecanismo contra el crimen," *El Nacional*, May 5, 2012.

26. "The Merida Initiative and Central America," Brookings Institute, May 26, 2009, http://www.brookings.edu/events/2009/0526_merida_initiative.aspx.
27. Arturo Valenzuela, "U.S. Foreign Policy in the Obama Era," Remarks, Latin American Studies Association, Toronto, Canada, October 9, 2010.
28. Henry Raymont, *Troubled Neighbors: The Story of U.S.-Latin American Relations from FDR to the Present* (New York: Westview Press, 2005), 259–62.
29. Interview with Ambassador Otto Reich, Washington, D.C. November 4, 2010.
30. Interview with Dan Fisk, Washington, D.C., October 29, 2010, and November 1, 2010.
31. Interview with Ambassador Roger Noriega, Washington, D.C., November 22, 2010.
32. Ibid.
33. Interview with Fisk, October 29, 2010.
34. "Southern Command Chief Says There Is No Iranian Military Presence in Venezuela," *El Universal*, April 27, 2010.
35. "Advance Questions For Lieutenant General John F. Kelly."
36. Ibid., 29.
37. Ibid., 31–32.
38. Ibid., 32.
39. Ibid., 16.
40. Ibid., 24–25.
41. Interview with Reich, ibid.
42. Interview with Noriega, ibid.
43. Patrick Markey, "U.S. says Chávez creating haven for drug trade," Reuters, January 19, 2008, http://www.reuters.com/article/2008/01/19/us-venezuela-drugs-idUSN1936894520080119.
44. "Chávez permite narcotráfico en Venezuela segúne exembajador de Estados Unidos," *El Universal*, January 20, 2008.
45. "Venezuela, US consider renewing anti-drug cooperation despite rocky relations," Associated Press, July 17, 2008, http://www.startribune.com/templates/Print_This_Story?sid=25592234.
46. Ibid.
47. Lucia Newman, "Guatemala: A Narco State?," *Al Jazeera*, August 14, 2011, http://blogs.aljazeera.net/americas/2011/08/14/guatemala-narco-state.
48. They are the words of Kevin Casas-Zamora, a scholar at the Brookings Institution and former vice president of Costa Rica, in "The Merida Initiative."
49. "Central America and the Merida Initiative," Thomas A. Shannon, assistant secretary for Western Hemisphere, statement before the House Committee on Foreign Affairs Subcommittee on the Western Hemisphere, May 8, 2008.
50. Ibid.

51. Interview with Fisk, ibid.
52. Andrés Oppenheimer, "La Estrategia de Obama," *El Nuevo Herald*, October 4, 2009.
53. Peter Nicholas, "Obama defends greeting Hugo Chávez," *Los Angeles Times*, April 20, 2009, http://www.latimes.com/la-fg-obama-americas20-2009apr 20,0,1717554.story.
54. Remarks by President Barack Obama at the Summit of the Americas Opening Ceremony, Hyatt Regency, Port of Spain, April 17, 2009, http://www.whitehouse.gov/the-press-office/remarks-president-summit-americas -opening-ceremony.
55. Valenzuela, "U.S. Foreign Policy."
56. Abraham Lowenthal, "Obama and the Americas," *Foreign Affairs* 89, no. 4 (July/August 2010): 114.
57. Ibid.
58. Oppenheimer, "La Estrategia de Obama."
59. Quinn and Daniel, "U.S. Sanctions Venezuelan Oil Giant."

9. HALTING THE ADVANCE OF THE BOLIVARIAN REVOLUTION AND ITS ALLIES

1. Interview with Fisk.
2. Victor Salmeron, "Venezuela Is the OPEC Member State with the Worst Economic Performance," *El Universal*, September 2, 2010.
3. Antonio Maria Delgado, "Oposicion Venezolana Rechaza Amenaza de Jefe Militar," *El Nuevo Herald*, November 9, 2010.
4. Nelson Bocaranda Sardi, "Runrunes," *El Universal*, April 12, 2012.
5. Gerardo Blyde, "Comando autogolpe," *El Universal*, April 27, 2012, http://www.eluniversal.com/opinion/120427/comando-autogolpe.
6. Anibal Romero, "Presentation," Seventh Annual Latin American Conference, Center for Hemispheric Policy, University of Miami, May 2012.
7. María Teresa Romero, "Venezuela 2012: Escenarios Politico-Electorales," Seventh Annual Latin American Conference, Center for Hemispheric Policy, University of Miami, May 2012.
8. Ibid.
9. Interview with Gen. Carlos Peñaloza, Miami, Florida, May 11, 2012.
10. "El Chávismo arrasa en las regionales," EFE, December 17, 2012, http://eltiem polatino.com/news/2012/dec/17/el-Chávismo-arrasa-en-las-regionales/.
11. Hanna Fenichel Pitkin, as quoted in Ernesto Laclau, *On Populist Reason* (London: Verso, 2005), 159.
12. Dan Hellinger, "Caracas Connect: Chávez Misses January 10 Inauguration— the aftermath," Center for Democracy in the Americas, February 8, 2013, http://www.democracyinamericas.org/blog-post/caracas-connect-Chávez -misses-january-10-inauguration-the-aftermath/.

13. "Maduro dice que la evolución de Chávez ha pasado 'de estable a favorable,'" *El País*, December 13, 2012, http://internacional.elpais.com/internacional /2012/12/13/actualidad/1355422527_760073.html.

14. Luis Velazquez Alvaray, interview, "Historias Secretas de un Juez parte II, Completa," YoSOiTV, May 9, 2012, http://www.youtube.com/watch?v=jYL _774sNdY.

15. Florida representatives Connie Mack (R) and Ron Klein (D) introduced one of the proposals to designate Venezuela as a sponsor of terrorism in October 2009, based on Venezuela's connections to the FARC, Hezbollah, and Iran. See William Gibson, "Does Venezuela Sponsor Terrorism?," SunSentinel .com, October 28, 2009, http://weblogs.sun-sentinel.com/news/politics/dc blog/2009/10/does_venezuela_sponsor_terrori.html.

16. Reuters, "Chávez Backs Ecuador in Attacking U.S. Drug War," *New York Times*, December 21, 2006, http://www.nytimes.com/2006/12/21/world/ americas/21venez.html?_r=0.

17. Susan Kaufman Purcell, "Resetting Brazil-U.S. Relationships," *Política Externa* 20 (June/July/August 2010): 2.

18. "Mideast Peace Process Futile while the U.S. in Charge, Lula Says," Fox News Latino, December 20, 2010, http://latino.foxnews.com/latino/politics/ 2010/12/20/mideast-peace-process-futile-charge-lula-says/.

19. Kaufman Purcell, "Resetting Brazil-U.S. Relationships," 5.

20. "Bases en Colombia: Uribe evitó una condena en la cumbre de Unasur," Clarin.com, August 28, 2009.

21. Kaufman Purcell, "Resetting Brazil-U.S. Relationships," 9.

22. Ibid., 10–11.

23. Albert Fishlow, "Has President Dilma Succesfully Followed On?," Center for Hemispheric Policy, December 15, 2011, 11.

24. "Rousseff dice a Obama que alianzas con EEUU deben ser 'entre iguales,'" *El Nuevo Herald*, April 14, 2012.

25. Verónica Psetizki, "Mujica asumió la presidencia de Uruguay," BBC Mundo, March 1, 2010, http://www.bbc.co.uk/mundo/america_latina/2010/03/100 301_1323_mujica_uruguay_gtg.shtml.

26. Christopher Sabatini, "Rethinking Latin America," *Foreign Affairs*, March/ April 2012, 8–13.

27. "NATO partnership with India, Brazil is worth exploring: Pentagon," *The Economic Times*, March 2, 2012, http://articles.economictimes.india times.com/2012-03-02/news/31116815_1_nato-partnership-nato-summit -admiral-james-stavridis.

28. Lindsay Green-Barber, "After Correa's Pardon, Ecuador Should Forgive but Must Not Forget," *Americas Quarterly*, 2012, http://www.americasquarterly .org/taxonomy/term/603.

29. Ruben Perina, an official in the OAS Department for Democratic and Political Affairs raised this idea and was quoted in Larry Diamond, *The Spirit of Democracy: The Struggle to Build Free Societies throughout the World* (New York: Time Books/Henry Holt, 2008), 333–34.
30. Immanuel Kant, "Eternal Peace," in *The Philosophy of Kant: Immanuel Kant's Moral and Political Writings*, ed. Carl Friederich (New York: Modern Library, 1949), 430–76.
31. Paul Drake, "From the Good Men to Good Neighbors: 1912–1932," in *Exporting Democracy: The United States and Latin America*, ed. Abraham Lowenthal (Baltimore, MD: John Hopkins University Press, 1991), 13.
32. Guillermo O'Donnell, "Human Development, Human Rights, and Democracy," in *The Quality of Democracy*, ed. Guillermo O'Donnell, Jorge Vargas Cullel, and Osvaldo M. Iazzeta (Notre Dame, IN: University of Notre Dame Press, 2004), 9–92.
33. Ibid., 33.
34. Ibid. See also Paulo Sérgio Pinheiro, "The Rule of Law and the Underprivileged in Latin America," in Mendez et al., *(Un)Rule of Law*, 34.
35. Pinheiro, "Rule of Law," 1–15.
36. Ibid., 2.
37. Joe Foweraker and Roman Krznaric, "The Uneven Perfomance of Third Wave Democracies: Electoral Politics and the Imperfect Rule of Law in Latin America," in *Latin American Democratic Transformations: Institutions, Actors, and Processes*, ed. William C. Smith (Sussex, UK: John Wiley, 2009), 53–78.
38. Charles Tilly, *Democracy* (New York: Cambridge University Press, 2007).
39. Programa de las Naciones Unidas para el Desarrollo, Secretaria General de la Organizacion de los Estados Americanos (OEA), *Nuestra Democracia* (Tlalpan, Mexico: Fondo de Cultura Económica, 2010), 137–38.
40. Ibid.
41. Kevin Casas-Zamora, "Caminar entre Riscos: Sobre la Democracia y sus Desafíos en America Latina," *La Democracia en América Latina* 2 (Miami: Interamerican Institute for Democracy, February 2010): 17–18.
42. Manuel Alcántara, "Partidos con programas versus conducciones generalizadas," Programa de las Naciones Unidas para el Desarrollo, Secretaria General de la OEA, *Nuestra Democracia*.
43. Ibid., 109.
44. Ibid., 136.
45. The World Bank, "Brazil Overview" (Washington, DC: World Bank, 2012), http://www.worldbank.org/en/country/brazil/overview.
46. Daniel Brinks, "De la pobreza legal a la participacion en el sistema legal: Instauracion del estado de derecho en Latinoamerica," *Nuestra Democracia*, 133.

47. Wendy Hunter, "Brazil: The PT in Power," in Levitsky and Roberts, *Resurgence of the Latin American Left,* 316.
48. U.S. General Accounting Office, *Foreign Assistance: U.S. Democracy Programs in Six Latin American Countries Have Yielded Modest Results* (Washington, DC: U.S. General Accounting Office, March 2003), http://www.gao.gov /new.items/d03358.pdf.
49. Interview with Ambassador Paul Trivelli, Miami, Florida, May 14, 2012.
50. Ibid.
51. Ibid.
52. Ibid.
53. Fernando Cepeda Ulloa, "Introduction," in *Latin America and the Multinational Drug Trade,* ed. Elizabeth Joyce and Carlos Malamud (New York: St Martin's, 1998), 15–16.
54. "Colombia Sees 'Window' to Push Trade Deal," Reuters, 2008.
55. Interview with Trivelli.

SELECTED BIBLIOGRAPHY

Arendt, Hannah. *On Revolution*. London: Penguin Books, 1988.

Barrett, Patrick, Daniel Chávez, and Cesar Rodrigez-Garavito. *The New Latin American Left: Utopia Reborn*. Amsterdam: Pluto Press, 2008.

Bolivar, Simón. "An American's Conviction." In Lynch, *Latin American Revolutions, 1808–1826*, 308–20.

Brinks, Daniel. Programa de las Naciones Unidas para el Desarrollo, Secretaria General de la Organizacion de los Estados Americanos. *Nuestra Democracia*. Tlalpan, Mexico: Fondo de Cultura Económica, 2010.

Bruhn, Kathleen. "The Evolution of the American Left." In Castañeda and Morales, *Leftovers*.

Buxton, Julia. "Venezuela: The Political Evolution of Bolivarianism." In Lievesley and Ludlam, *Reclaiming Latin America*, 57–74.

Casas-Zamora, Kevin. "Caminar entre Riscos: Sobre la Democracia y sus Desafíos en America Latina." *La Democracia en América Latina* 2 (February 2010): 11–34.

Castañeda, Jorge. "Not Ready for Prime Time: Why Including Emerging Powers at the Helm Would Hurt Global Governance." *Foreign Affairs*, September/October 2010, 109–23.

———. "Where Do We Go from Here?" In Castañeda and Morales, *Leftovers*, 231–43.

Castañeda, Jorge, and Marco Morales, eds. *Leftovers: Tales of the Latin American Left*. New York: Routledge, 2008.

Close, David. "Nicaragua: The Return of Daniel Ortega." In Lievesley and Ludlam, *Reclaiming Latin America*, 109–22.

Coppedge, Michael. "Venezuela: The Rise and Fall of Patriarchy." In Dominguez and Lowenthal, *Constructing Democratic Governance*, 3–19.

Corrales, Javier, and Michael Penfold-Becerra. "Venezuela: Crowding Out of the Opposition." *Journal of Democracy* 16, no. 2 (2007): 99–112.

251

Dandler, Jorge. "Indigenous People and the Rule of Law in Latin America: Do They Have a Chance?" In Mendez, O'Donnell, and Pinheiro, *The (Un)Rule of Law.*

Daremblum, Jaime. "Democracy Is under Attack in Nicaragua." *Journal of the American Enterprise Institute*, February 2, 2009.

Diamond, Larry. *The Spirit of Democracy: The Struggle to Build Free Societies throughout the World.* New York: Time Books/Henry Holt, 2008.

Dominguez, Jorge. *The Future of Inter-American Affairs.* New York: Routledge, 2000.

Dominguez, Jorge, and Jeanne Kinney Giraldo. "Conclusion: Parties, Institutions, and Market Reform." In Dominguez and Lowenthal, *Constructing Democratic Governance.*

Dominguez, Jorge, and Abraham Lowenthal, eds. *Constructing Democratic Governance: South America in the 1990s.* Baltimore, MD: John Hopkins University Press, 1996.

Drake, Paul. "From the Good Men to Good Neighbors: 1912–1932." In *Exporting Democracy: The United States and Latin America,* edited by Abraham Lowenthal, 3–40. Baltimore, MD: John Hopkins University Press, 1991.

Fishlow, Albert. "Has President Dilma Succesfully Followed On?" Center for Hemispheric Policy, December 15, 2011.

Fisk, Dan. Personal interview, October 29, 2010 and November 1, 2010, Washington, D.C.

Fleischman, Luis. "State and Civil Society in Argentina." PhD diss., Michigan University Press, New School for Social Research, 1997.

Foweraker, Joe, and Roman Krznaric. "The Uneven Performance of Third Wave Democracies: Electoral Politics and the Imperfect Rule of Law in Latin America." In *Latin American Democratic Transformations: Institutions, Actors, and Processes,* edited by William C. Smith, 53–78. Sussex, UK: John Wiley, 2009.

Frank, Andre Gunder. *Latin America: Underdevelopment or Revolution: Essays on the Development of Underdevelopment and the Immediate Enemy.* New York: New York Monthly Review Press, 1969.

Friedman, Edward. "China: A Threat or Threatened by Democracy." *Dissent Magazine,* 2009.

Gamarra, Eduardo. "Bolivia: Managing Democracy in the 1990s." In Dominguez and Lowenthal, *Constructing Democratic Governance,* 72–98.

Green-Barber, Lindsay. "After Correa's Pardon, Ecuador Should Forgive but Must Not Forget." *Americas Quarterly,* 2012.

Hartlyn, Jonathan, Jennifer McCoy, and Thomas M. Mustillo. "Electoral Governance Matters: Explaining the Quality of Elections in Contemporary Latin America." *Comparative Political Studies* 41, no. 1 (January 2008): 73–98.

Helmke, Gretchen, and Steven Levitsky, eds. *Informal Institutions and Democracy: Lessons from Latin America.* Baltimore, MD: John Hopkins University Press, 2006.

Henrique Cardozo, Fernando. "More than Ideology: The Conflation of Populism with the Left in Latin America." *Harvard International Review,* Summer 2006.

Hunter, Wendy. "Brazil: The PT in Power." In Levitsky and Roberts, *The Resurgence of the Latin American Left,* 306–24.

International Institute of Strategic Studies. *The FARC Files: Venezuela, Ecuador, and the Secret Archives of "Raúl Reyes."* London: International Institute of Strategic Studies, 2011.

Isaacs, Anita. "Ecuador: Democracy Standing the Test of Time?" In Dominguez and Lowenthal, *Constructing Democratic Governance,* 42–57.

———. "International Assistance for Democracy: A Cautionary Tale." In Dominguez, *The Future of Inter-American Affairs,* 259–86.

Jarkin, Edmundo. "Sobre el Futuro Democratico en America Latina." In *La Democracia en America Latina.* The Democracy Papers No. 2, Interamerican Institute for Democracy, February 2010, 35–56.

Kant, Immanuel. "Eternal Peace." In *The Philosophy of Kant: Immanuel Kant's Moral and Political Writings,* edited by Carl Friederich, 430–76. New York: Modern Library, 1949.

Krauze, Enrique. *El Poder y el Delirio.* Barcelona: Tusquets Editores, 2008.

———. "Looking at Them: A Mexican Perspective on the Gap with the United States." In *Falling Behind: Explaining the Development Gap between Latin America and the United States,* edited by Francis Fukuyama, 48–71. New York: Oxford University Press, 2008.

Lander, Edgardo. "Venezuela, Populism, and the Left: Alternatives to Neo Liberalism." In Barrett, Chávez, and Rodriguez-Garavito, *The New Latin American Left,* 69–98.

Ledeen, Michael. *The Iranian Time Bomb: The Mullah Zealots' Quest for Destruction.* New York: St. Martin's Press, 2007.

Levitsky, Steven, and Kenneth Roberts. *The Resurgence of the Latin American Left.* Baltimore, MD: John Hopkins University Press, 2011.

Lievesley, Geraldine, and Steven Ludlam, eds. *Reclaiming Latin America: Experiments in Radical Social Democracy.* New York: Zed Books, 2009.

Linz, Juan. *Totalitarian and Authoritarian Regimes.* Boulder, CO: Lynne Rienner Publishers, 2000.

Luhmann, Niklas. *The Differentiation of Society.* Translated by Stephen Holmes and Charles Larmore. New York: Columbia University Press, 1982.

Lynch, John, ed. *Latin American Revolutions, 1808–1826: Old and New World Origins.* Norman: University of Oklahoma Press, 1994.

Mackinnon, María Moira, and Mario Alberto Petrone, eds. *Populismo y neopopulismo en América Latina: el problema de la Cenicienta.* Buenos Aires: Editorial Universitaria de Buenos Aires, 1998.

Madrid, Raúl. "Bolivia: Origins and Policies of Movimiento al Socialismo." In Levitsky and Roberts, *The Resurgence of the Latin American Left.*

Marcano, Cristina, and Barrera Tyszka, Alberto. *Hugo Chávez: Sin Uniforme.* Buenos Aires: Editorial Sudamericana, 2005.

Mayorga, Rene Antonio. "Bolivia's Democracy at the Crossroads." In *The Third Wave of Democratization in Latin America: Advances and Setbacks*, edited by Frances Hagopian and Scott Mainwaring, 149–78. New York: Cambridge University Press, 2005.

Mendez, Juan, Guillermo O'Donnell, and Paulo Sérgio Pinheiro, ed. *The (Un) Rule of Law: The Underprivileged in Latin America.* Notre Dame, IN: University of Notre Dame Press, 1999.

Menges, Constantine. *China: The Gathering Threat.* New York: Nelson Current, 2005.

———. *Venezuela: Overview of Politically Active Groups and Current Trends.* Washington, DC: Hudson Institute, 2002.

Muñoz, Heraldo. "Towards a Regime for Advancing Democracy in the Americas." In Dominguez, *The Future of Inter-American Affairs*, 287–300.

Natanson, José. *La Nueva Izquierda.* Buenos Aires: Editorial Sudamericana, 2008.

Noriega, Ambassador Roger. Personal interview, November 22, 2010, Washington, DC.

O'Donnell, Guillermo. "Delegative Democracy." *Journal of Democracy*, 1993, 59–60.

———. "Human Development, Human Rights, and Democracy." In *The Quality of Democracy*, edited by Guillermo O'Donnell, Jorge Vargas Cullel, and Osvaldo M. Iazzeta, 9–92. Notre Dame, IN: University of Notre Dame Press, 2004.

Peñaloza, Gen. Carlos. Personal interview, May 11, 2012, Miami, Florida.

Philip, George. *Democracy in Latin America: Surviving Conflict and Crisis.* Cambridge, UK: Polity Press, 2003.

Pinheiro, Paulo Sérgio. "The Rule of Law and the Underprivileged in Latin America." In Mendez, O'Donnell, and Pinheiro, *The (Un)Rule of Law*, 1–15.

Purcell, Susan Kaufman. "Resetting Brazil-U.S. Relationships." *Política Externa* 20 (June/July/August 2010): 2.

Rawls, John. *Political Liberalism.* New York: Columbia University Press, 1996.

Reich, Ambassador Otto. Personal interview, November 4, 2010, Washington, DC.

Romero, Anibal. "Presentation." Seventh Annual Latin American Conference. Miami, FL: Center for Hemispheric Policy, University of Miami, 2012.

Romero, Maria Teresa. "Venezuela 2012: Escenarios Politico-Electorales." Seventh Annual Latin American Conference. Miami, FL: Center for Hemispheric Policy, 2012.

Sabatini, Christopher. "Rethinking Latin America." *Foreign Affairs*, March/April 2012, 8–13.

Sanchez Urribarri, Raul. "Venezuela, Turning Further Left?" In Castañeda and Morales, *Leftovers*, 174–92.

Sidicaro, Ricardo. "Consideraciones Sociológicas Sobre las Relaciones entre el Peronismo y la Clase Obrera en la Argentina, 1943–1955." In Mackinnon and Petrone, *Populismo y Neo-Populismo en America Latina*, 153–72.

Tapia, Luis. "Bolivia: The Left and the Social Movements." In Barret, Chávez, and Rodriguez-Garavito, *The New Latin American Left*, 215–31.

Touraine, Alain. *What Is Democracy?* Translated by David Macey. Boulder, CO: Westview Press, 1997.

Trivelli, Ambassador Paul. Personal inteview, May 14, 2012, Miami, Florida.

Ulloa, Fernando Cepeda. "Introduction." In *Latin America and the Multinational Drug Trade*, edited by Elizabeth Joyce and Carlos Malamud, 3–20. New York: St Martin's Press, 1998.

U.S. General Accounting Office. *Foreign Assistance: U.S. Democracy Programs in Six Latin American Countries Have Yielded Modest Results*. Washington, DC: U.S. General Accounting Office, 2003.

Verbitsky, Horacio. *Robo para la Corona*. Buenos Aires: Ed. Planeta, 1991.

Weber, Max. *Economy and Society*. Berkeley: University of California Press, 1978.

Weffort, Francisco. "El Populismo en la Politica Brasilera." In Mackinnon and Petrone, *Populismo y Neo-Populismo en America Latina*, 135–52.

The World Bank. "Brazil Overview." Washington, DC: World Bank, 2012.

Zakaria, Fareed *The Future of Freedom: Illiberal Democracy at Home and Abroad*. New York: W. W. Norton, 2003.

INDEX

ABOUT THE AUTHOR

Luis Fleischman has worked as senior adviser for the Menges Hemispheric Security Project at the Center for Security Policy, where he serves as coeditor of *The Americas Report*. Fleischman's opinion pieces appear regularly in online publications such as *The Americas Forum, The Cutting Edge News,* and *Scholars for Peace in the Middle East*. Fleischman is a frequent guest on Spanish-language and English-language TV and radio programs on issues related to Latin America, the Middle East, and international affairs. He has been interviewed and quoted in a number of national publications, including *Forbes, Fox Business Network,* and *NewsMax*. His articles have appeared in *Americas Quarterly, The Journal of International Security Affairs,* the *Middle Atlantic Council of Latin American Affairs (MACLAS) Review,* and *inFOCUS Quarterly Journal*.

Fleischman has a PhD in sociology from the New School for Social Research in New York City, an MA from the New School as well, and a BA in political science and labor studies from Tel Aviv University. He is also an adjunct professor of sociology and political science at the Harriet L. Wilkes Honors College of Florida Atlantic University and the university's Lifelong Learning Society. He has taught courses on democracy and dictatorship, the Middle East, Latin America, political sociology, conservative and neoconservative thought, and the sociology of rogue states.